IMAGES
of America

CLARK REVISITED

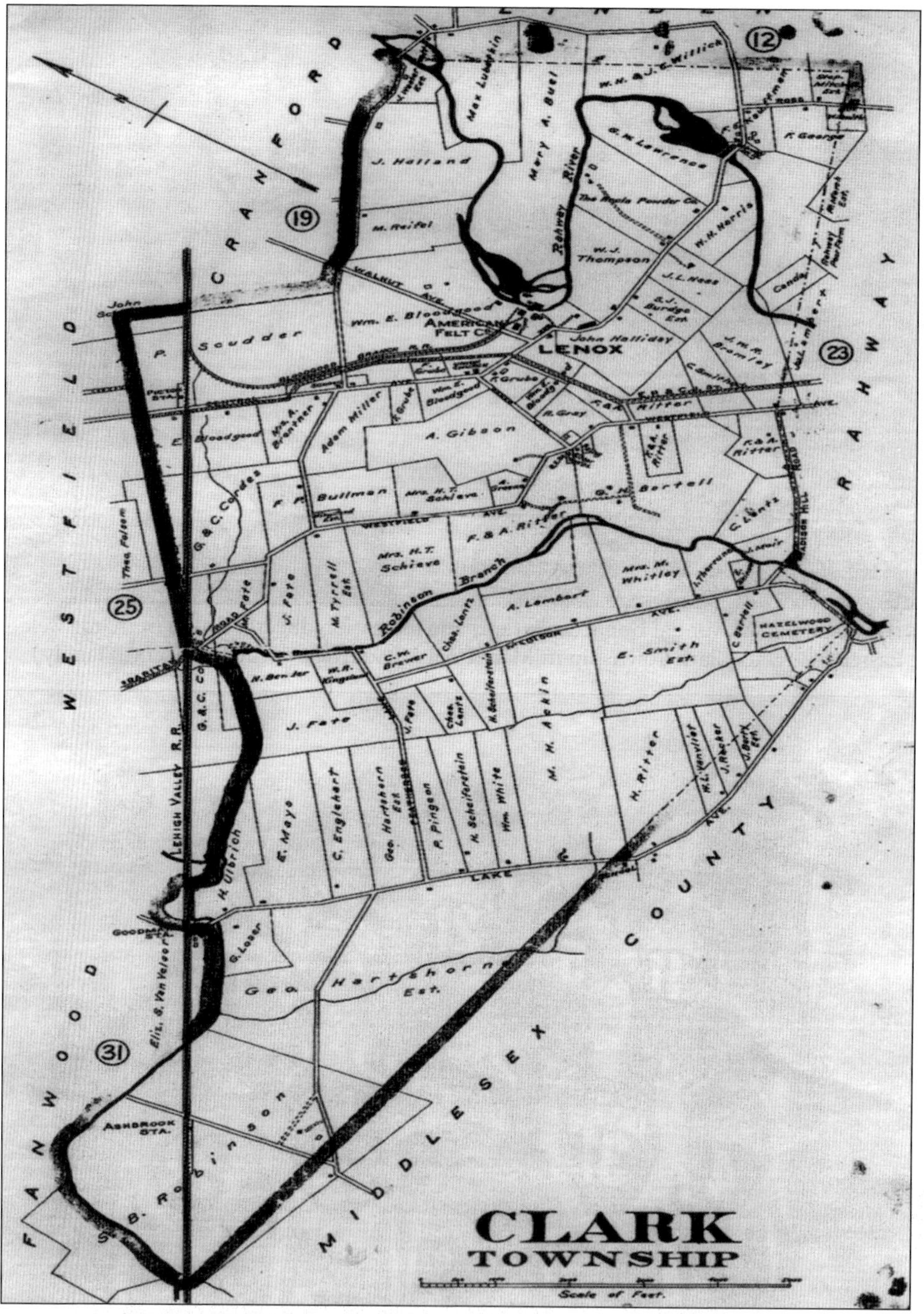

Township of Clark, 1906. Shown is a map of Clark Township dated 1906. (Courtesy of the Clark History Room.)

On the Cover: "Lover's Bridge," c. 1900. Albert Lambert sits on Clark Lovers Bridge, which crossed the Robinson's Branch. This bridge got its name because the area was a common place for young couples to visit and spend quality time together. This area is presently where the Garden State Parkway Bridge crosses the Clark Reservoir. (Courtesy of the Clark History Room.)

IMAGES
of America

CLARK REVISITED

Brian P. Toal

ARCADIA
PUBLISHING

ISBN 978-1-4671-3427-9

Published by Arcadia Publishing
Charleston, South Carolina

Printed in the United States of America

Library of Congress Control Number: 2015938221

For all general information, please contact Arcadia Publishing:
Telephone 843-853-2070
Fax 843-853-0044
E-mail sales@arcadiapublishing.com
For customer service and orders:
Toll-Free 1-888-313-2665

Visit us on the Internet at www.arcadiapublishing.com

To Diane Frank Metz and David Koch, who gave countless hours of their time and dedication to the project

Contents

ACKNOWLEDGMENTS

One cannot write this type of history book without the assistance of some very wonderful people. Thank you to my mother, Kathleen Toal; brother Kevin Toal; sister-in-law Lois Toal; John Metz; Henry and Florence Metz; Susan Frank Bruno; Carl and Mildred Frank; Kim Frank; Russel Frank; Amanda Frank Miller; Robert Miller; Kevin Koch; June Koch; Karen Koch; Kathy Koch; Linda Cohen; Frank and Terry Mazzarella; Edie Merkel; Steve Decana; Susan Perez; police chief Pedro Matos; Dr. Denis Connell; Laurie Sheldon; Richard Seng; Henry Meyer; Daniel Sexton; Gerard Ziobro Sr.; Jessica Malinchok from St. Agnes Church; Barbara Keller Gallagher; and Anglea Mondi Bove.

A special appreciation goes to the following for allowing their family and personal photographs to be used in this publication: Mayor Sal Bonaccorso, Victor Demarzo, Susan Alacchi, and Jenny Waterson Black for her generous contribution of family photographs, as well as Laurie Sheldon and the Clark Volunteer Emergency Squad, Clark fire chief Frank Cerasa, and the Clark History Room for its extensive collection.

A big thank you must be extended to longtime Clark resident and retired police captain William J. "Duff" Duffy for his contributions to the final chapter of this book. He has been researching Clark's fallen heroes for over 40 years and has graciously allowed his research material to be used in this book.

Many of the photographs featured in this book are from the King family collection, which was donated to the Clark History Room by the late Emma Taylor King. The King family's influence and generous contribution to the preservation of Clark's history is greatly appreciated.

INTRODUCTION

When people hear "Clark, New Jersey," they typically think of just another exit along the Garden State Parkway. Clark is located at exit 135 off the parkway. The area now designated as the Township of Clark was originally the hunting and fishing grounds of the local Lenni Lenape tribe. These early inhabitants of the area established their encampments and villages in the Watchung Mountains, utilizing nearby streams and waterways such as the Rahway River and the Robinson's Branch for fishing. Clark would remain the Lenapes' land until the arrival of early settlers in the 17th century.

The first official landowner in Clark was Dr. William Robinson, who emigrated from Scotland to New Jersey with his family. He purchased 700 acres to build his plantation home. Robinson was one of the first physicians in Clark. His home, officially named the Dr. William Robinson Plantation, was added to the National Register of Historic Places in 1974. It opened to the public as the Dr. William Robinson Plantation Museum in 1978. With the passage of time and the arrival of more European settlers, Clark Township was part of Rahway, New Jersey.

The land of present-day Clark became a crossroads of the American Revolution, with many skirmishes between American minutemen and British redcoats occurring in the town. As the 13 colonies separated from England and New Jersey received its statehood, Clark territory remained a part of Rahway until 1864. Rahway was a small village that was incorporated into a city in 1861, with Clark territory being designated Rahway's fifth ward.

The residents of Rahway's fifth ward became disgruntled with their leaders because they felt they were being improperly taxed and were not receiving their fair share of services. Declaring their independence during the height of the Civil War, Rahway's fifth ward became Clark Township. Clark was named in honor of local American patriot and signer of the Declaration of Independence Abraham Clark.

Prior to the outbreak of the Civil War, the southern section of the township became a settlement for the local Quakers who established a schoolhouse and meetinghouse known as the Locust Grove School. It was from this school that an Underground Railroad society was established, and several depots were operated from the late 1850s until the outbreak of the Civil War. Several Quaker homes along present-day Lake Avenue were also used as stopping stations for escaped slaves who made their way up north through Clark and Rahway to New York City and on to Canada by the Atlantic Ocean.

During the Civil War, the township remained steadfast behind President Lincoln, while the rest of New Jersey was against the conflict and the great loss of life. Clark saw the war at its doorstep with the death of the town's favorite family's son, James Bullman. Bullman, a prominent farmer who lived along present-day Raritan Road, lost his life at the Battle of Cold Harbor in Virginia on June 1, 1864. This tragic loss had a deep impact on the residents of Clark Township.

During the post–Civil War period of the 1870s and 1880s, the township remained mostly rural farmland, with agriculture as the center of industry and the main products being vegetables, corn, and strawberries. The Madison Hill Road area was famous for garden-fresh strawberries, when weather allowed. The township in the late 1800s was a green paradise that began to draw more attention from the newly arriving emigrants from Europe.

From the 1900s to the 1920s, Clark Township experienced a large influx of German and Italian immigrants. This new mixture of cultures would slowly begin to change the township forever by bringing in new cuts and styles not seen in this area, such as agricultural practices and education. It affected how the township was run and the way business was conducted. The larger farms would begin to be broken up into smaller tracts of land as the older farmers passed away or divided their property into smaller lots among their children. Farms were being sold to newly arriving immigrants, who were able to create their own American Dream. As the population grew, so did the need for food. Produce needs increased dramatically, and the demand for labor rose. The Clark farmers worked to meet the growing demand by bringing outside laborers to help them tend to their crops. The local farmers would harvest their crops and take them to the Elizabeth, New Jersey, farmer's market to be sold at auction.

With the end of World War I, the pace of life in the township began to slowly speed up. In the 1920s, prosperity swept across Clark and America, and the local residents enjoyed these booming times. Clark was known in the 1920s for being a red-light district. During the age of Prohibition, the farmers were approached by outside elements to aid them in conducting business in illegal whiskey, gambling, and prostitution. Though closely monitored by the local police and the FBI, local farmers could add to their income by illegally storing whiskey behind their hay in the barn, a common practice. A former could make up $100 a week for keeping a bootlegger's alcohol in his barn for a short period of time. The only drawback was the chance of being caught by the police or FBI, who were famous for making unannounced visits to the local farmers on the claim of a welfare check or livestock check. When Prohibition ended in early 1930s, so did Clark's red-light district days.

Clark's population remained steady until 1946, when the State of New Jersey announced plans to build a superhighway directly through the township. Originally to be called State Highway 4, it would later be renamed the Garden State Parkway. This highway, constructed from 1946 to 1950, would change Clark. The once-sleepy rural farm community over the course of the next 20 years would double in population and change from a farm community to a suburban township.

As the older residents and farmers passed away with the passage of time, their children chose not to continue farming the land. Farming is a 24-hour-a-day operation. They chose instead to pursue a 9-to-5 job or work in a factory with a health plan.

The farmers began to slowly sell their land off to developers, who would build homes on the land to meet the post–World War II baby boom and the returning GIs who needed to place a roof over their growing families.

The demand for housing superseded the need for farmland. This would change Clark Township forever from a farm town to a suburban community with commercial, industrial, and residential areas.

One

The King Family

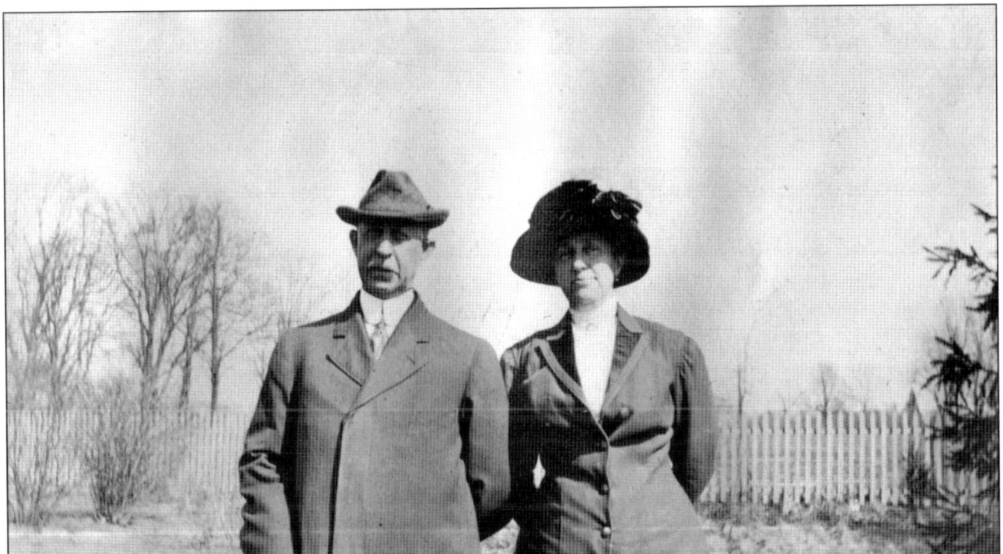

Mr. And Mrs. Benjamin King. Benjamin and Dora King were one of the most powerful couples of Clark, New Jersey. For well over 40 years, they helped advance culture, religion, education, and the overall well-being of the citizens of Clark, New Jersey. (Courtesy of the Clark History Room.)

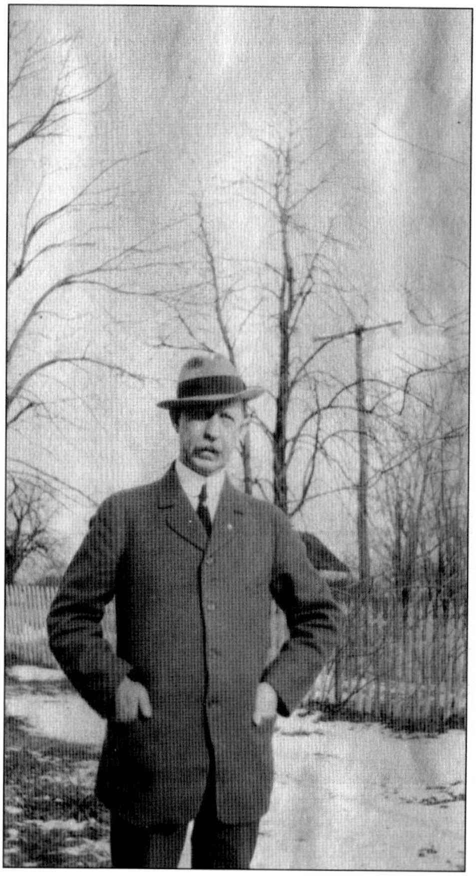

Benjamin King (1856–1929). Benjamin King was born in England, and in 1876, he came to the United States, where he met and married Dora Schumacher, the wealthy daughter of porcelain manufacturer Andreas Friedrich Christopher Schumacher. Benjamin began work as the superintendent of Essex Felt Mills, located in Clark, New Jersey. (Courtesy of the Clark History Room.)

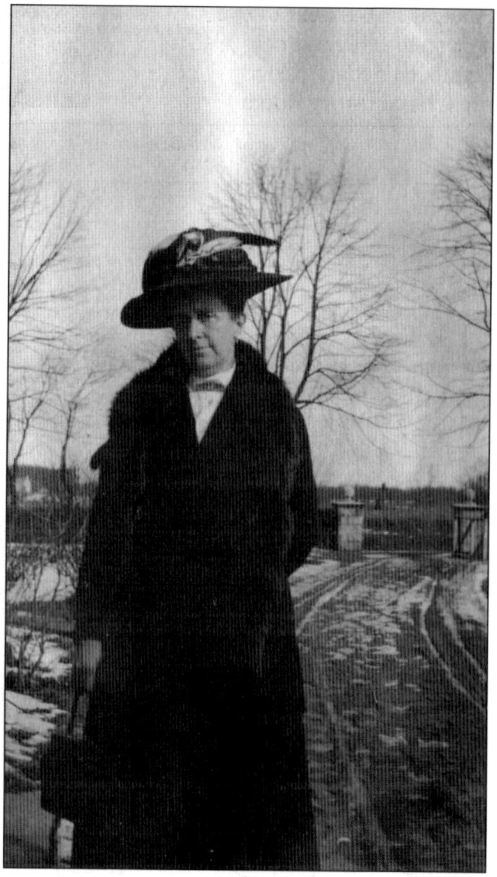

Dora L. King (1855–1928). Dora King was the devoted wife of Benjamin and mother of Emma Taylor King and Benjamin Schumacher King. Born into a wealthy German family, she instilled education, culture, and a moral compass into her family's lifestyle as well as the township of Clark. She was a community leader at the Bethlehem Chapel, where she was in charge of Sunday school programs. (Courtesy of the Clark History Room.)

A LEADER IN THE COMMUNITY. Benjamin King was a major in the New Jersey National Guard during the Spanish-American War. He was also a Union County freeholder, serving as its chairman. He served as the mayor of Clark Township and the superintendent of the largest business in Clark, Essex Felt Mills. (Courtesy of the King family collection of the Clark History Room.)

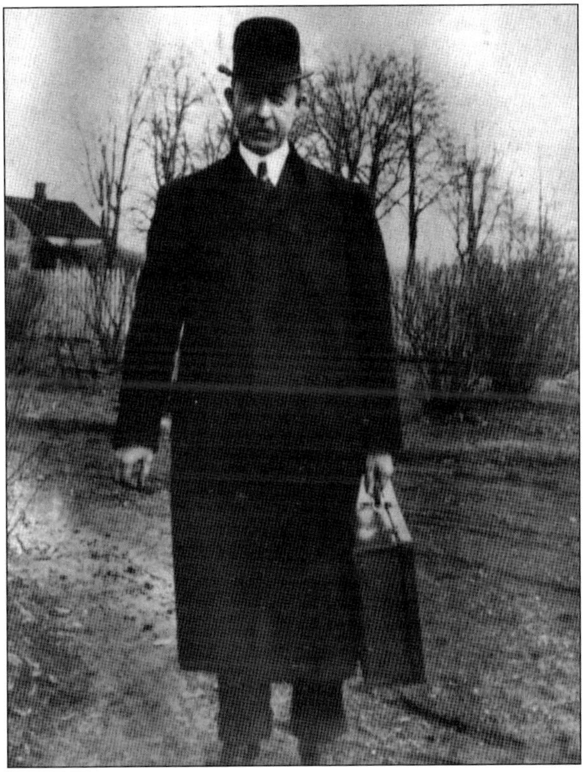

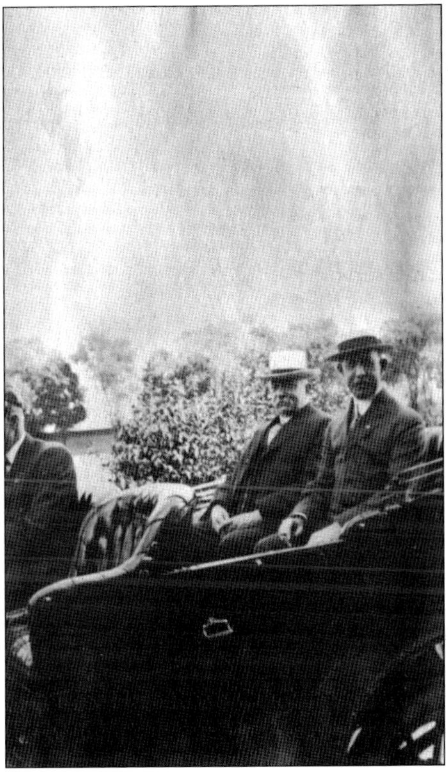

FREEHOLDER KING. Benjamin King was mayor of Clark from 1896 to 1899 and 1914 to 1923, when he was elected the Union County board of chosen freeholders. Serving as the board's chairman, through his position he was able to bring many civic projects and improvements to the citizens of Clark, New Jersey. Examples are the construction of the new bridge at Jackson Falls, located on Valley Road, and blacktop paving of Raritan Road and Westfield Avenue. Many improvements to Clark with county funding were directly credited to Benjamin King. (Courtesy of the Clark History Room.)

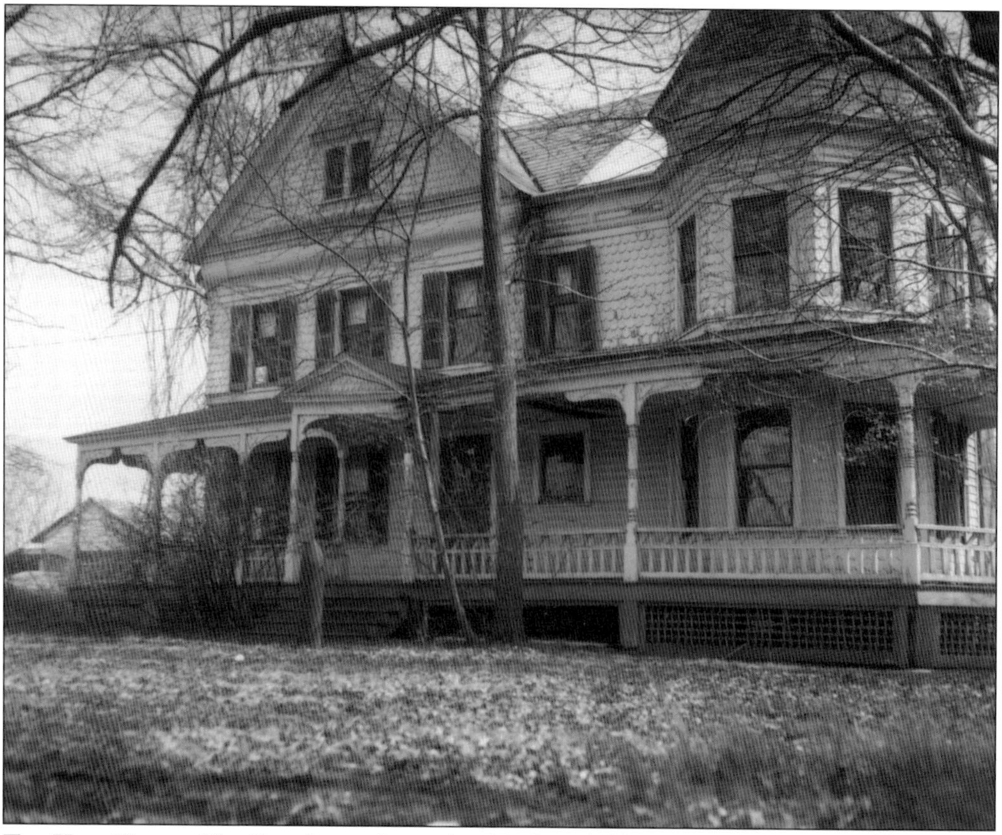

The King House. The King house, located at 211 Westfield Avenue, was the home of the most well-known family in Clark until 1978. (Courtesy of the Clark History Room.)

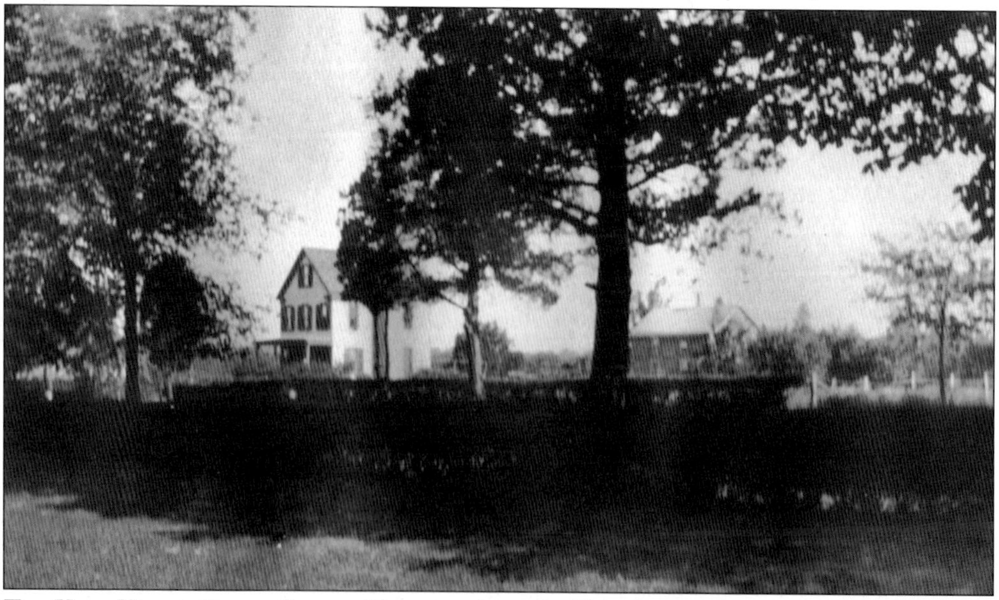

The King House, Front Porch. This view from the King house's front porch looks out onto Westfield Avenue North. (Courtesy of the Clark History Room.)

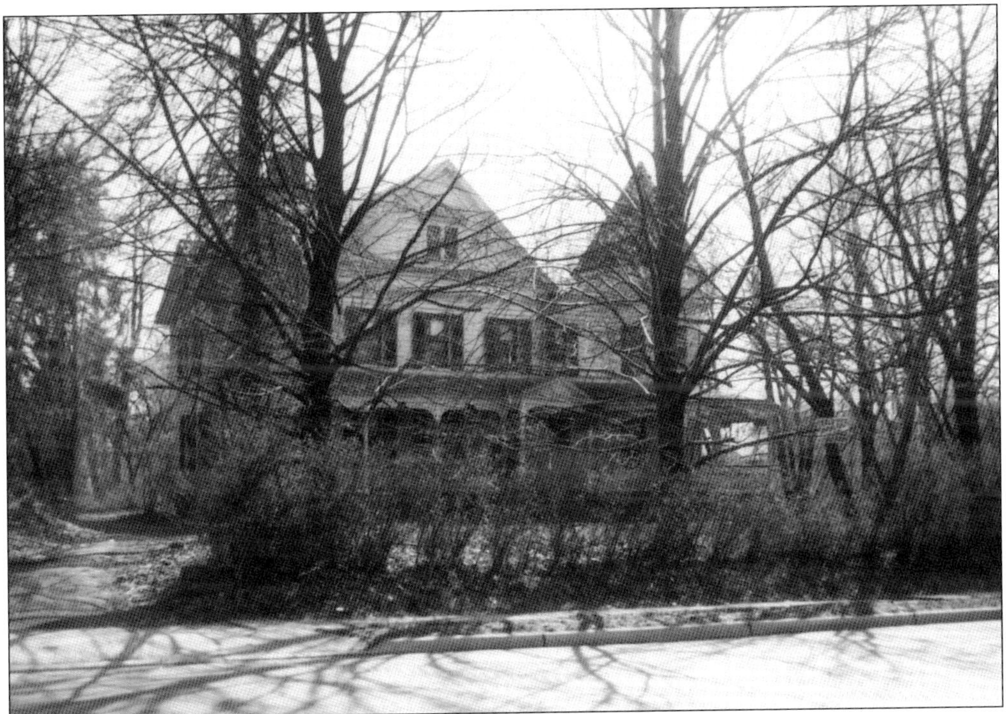

Building a Home. The King house was built in three phases, with the first being the construction of the main house in 1877. In 1888, additions were made to the home, and finally, in 1902, a new kitchen was built, as was a carriage house for guests. The photograph below was taken in 1978, shortly after the passing of owner Emma King. (Both, courtesy of the Clark History Room.)

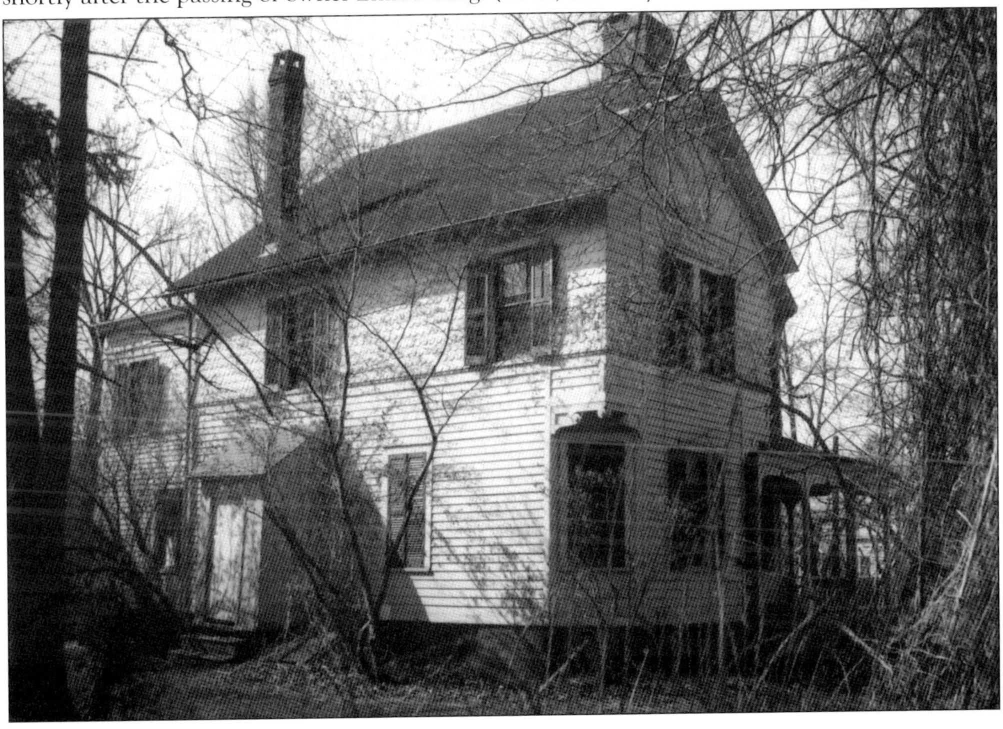

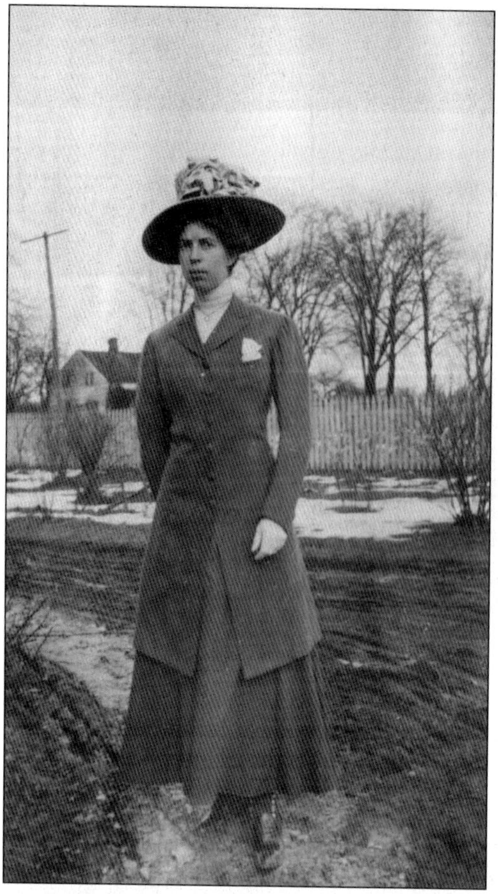

Emma Taylor King (1888–1978). The daughter of Benjamin and Dora King, Emma Taylor King lived her childhood years on Westfield Avenue, along with her brother, Benjamin Schumacher King. She also spent her final days there, passing away in 1978. In this 1906 photograph, Emma is shown walking along Westfield Avenue in front of her home. (Courtesy of the King family collection of the Clark History Room.)

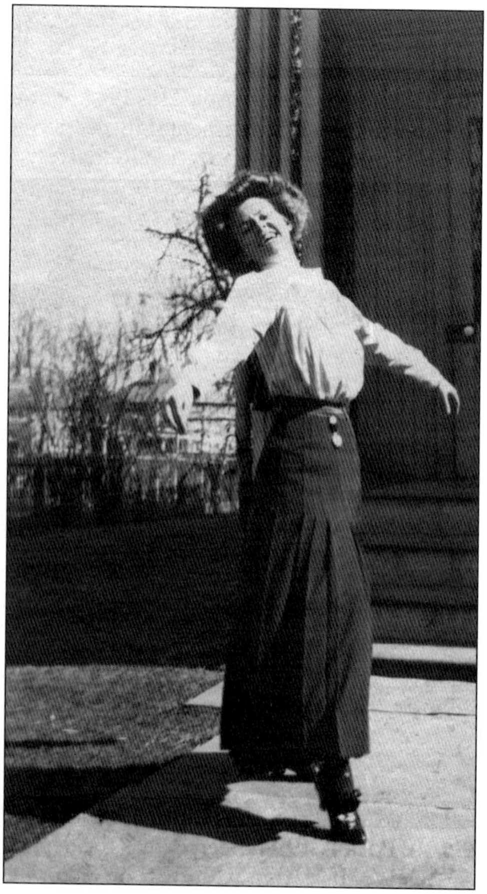

Rahway High School Dance, 1906. This image shows Annie Schumacher, first cousin of Emma Taylor King. (Courtesy of the Clark History Room.)

A Cruise Down Westfield Avenue. This 1906 photograph shows a young Benjamin King heading out for a motorcycle ride down Westfield Avenue. (Courtesy of the King family collection of the Clark History Room.)

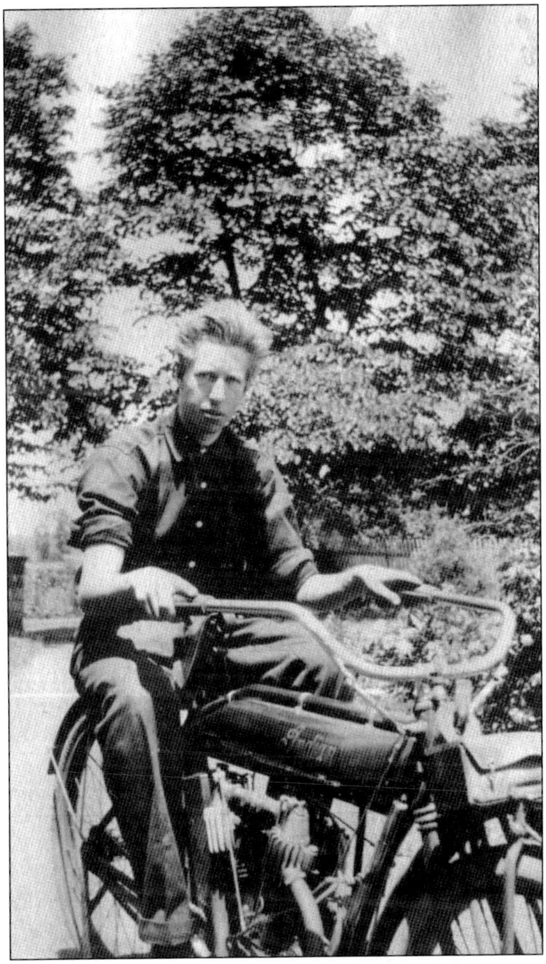

Benjamin Schumacher King (1890–1945). In this photograph, Benjamin S. King prepares for the annual Fourth of July bicycle race held in the nearby town of Rahway. (Courtesy of the Clark History Room.)

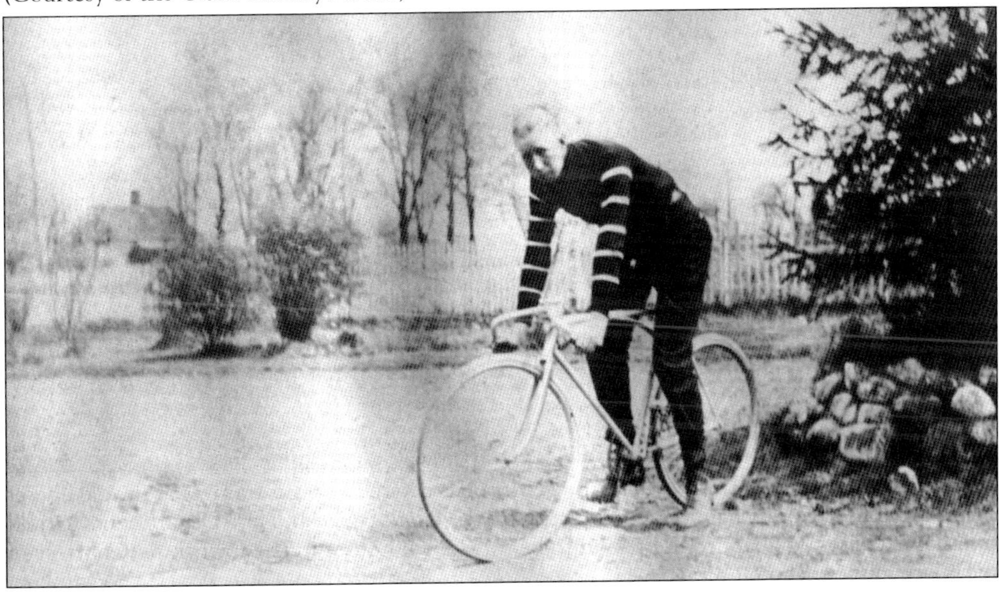

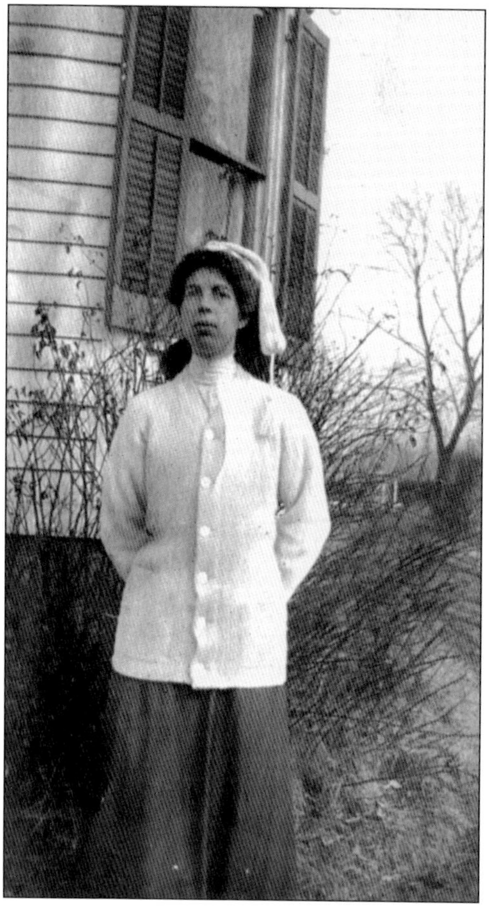

RAHWAY HIGH SCHOOL, CLASS OF 1906. Emma Taylor King is seen here preparing for school during her senior year at Rahway High School in 1906. (Courtesy of the Clark History Room.)

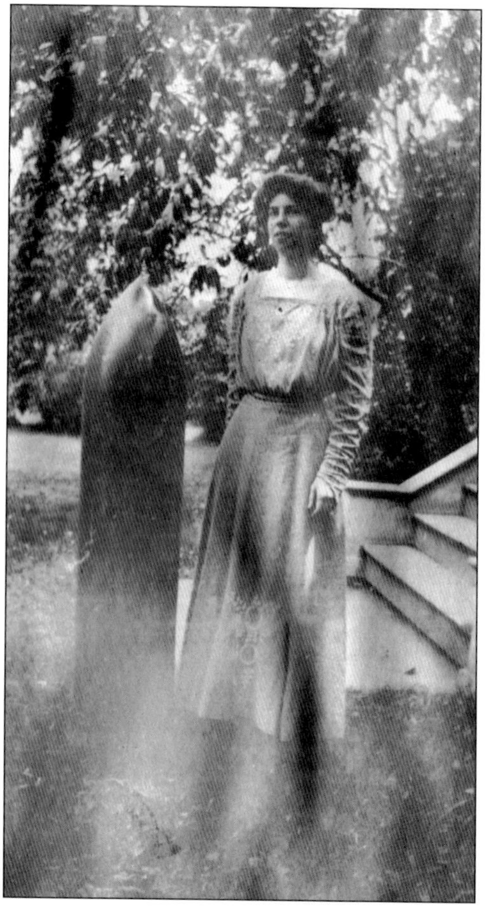

EMMA TAYLOR KING AND THE BOMB. In this rare photograph, Emma King is seen standing next to her father's Spanish-American War souvenir, a live artillery shell from the USS *Brooklyn*, which was a US armored cruiser under the direction of Commodore W.S. Schley. The ship served as a blockade ship during the battle of Santiago, Cuba. After hostilities, Commodore Schley had the live artillery shell sent to Mayor King's home as a lawn ornament. (Courtesy of the Clark History Room.)

Emma King Rides a Motorcycle. It was unheard of in its day for a woman to drive and operate a motorcycle. Emma was a leader in local women's affairs and would go on to become deeply involved in women's suffrage efforts in the 1920s. (Courtesy of the Clark History Room.)

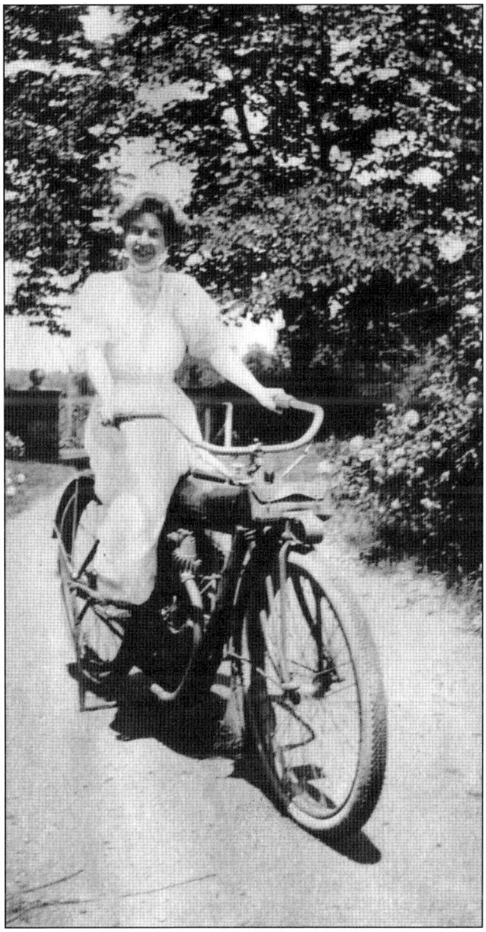

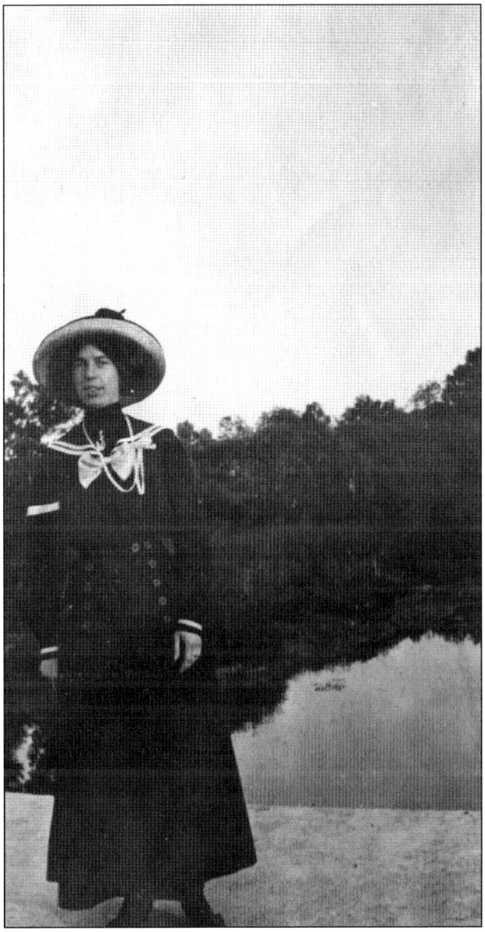

Emma at the Rezzy. This image shows Emma King posing next to the Robinson's Branch at the "Clark Rezzy" (also known as the Clark Reservoir) during the fall of 1906. (Courtesy of the Clark History Room.)

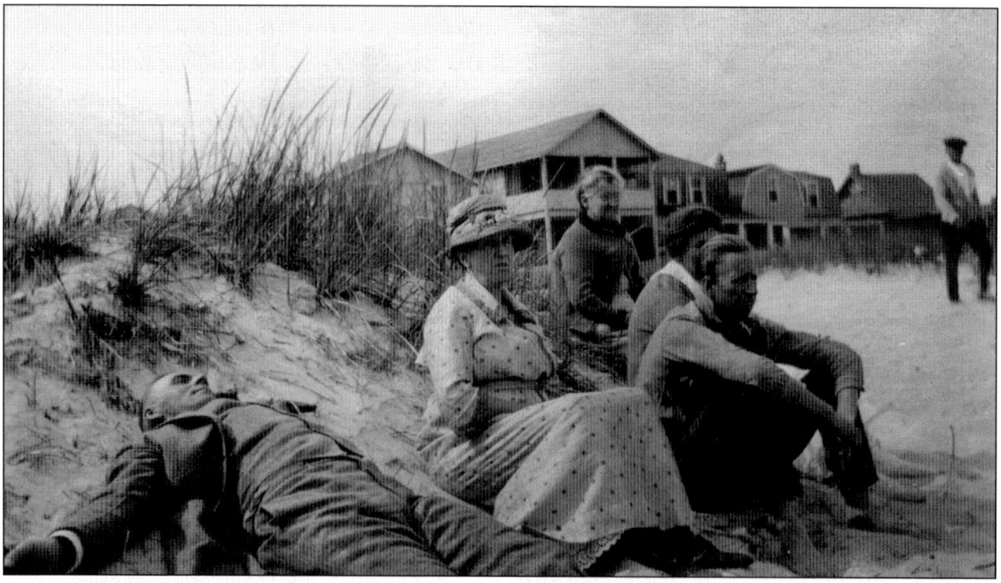

Boyton Beach, New Jersey. The resort town of Boyton Beach, New Jersey, was the summer vacation getaway for the King family. Seen in this 1906 photograph are Dora King (second from left), Benny King (seated next to Dora), and members of the Schumacher family. (Courtesy of the Clark History Room.)

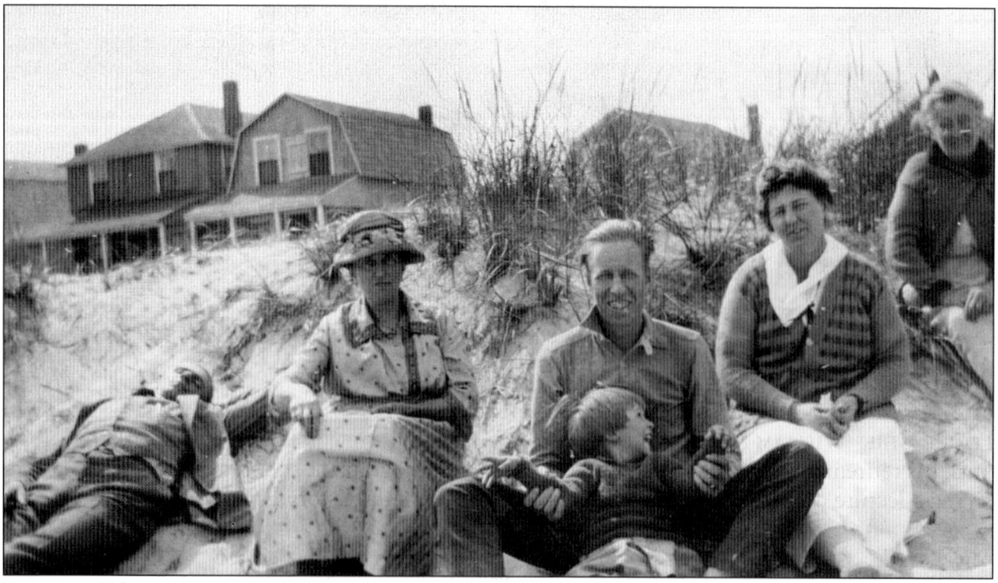

Summer Vacation, 1906. The family enjoys the ocean breeze and warmth during their summer vacation in 1906 at their vacation house in Boyton Beach, New Jersey. Pictured are Dora King (second from left) and son Benny King (third from left) with other Schumacher family members. (Courtesy of the Clark History Room.)

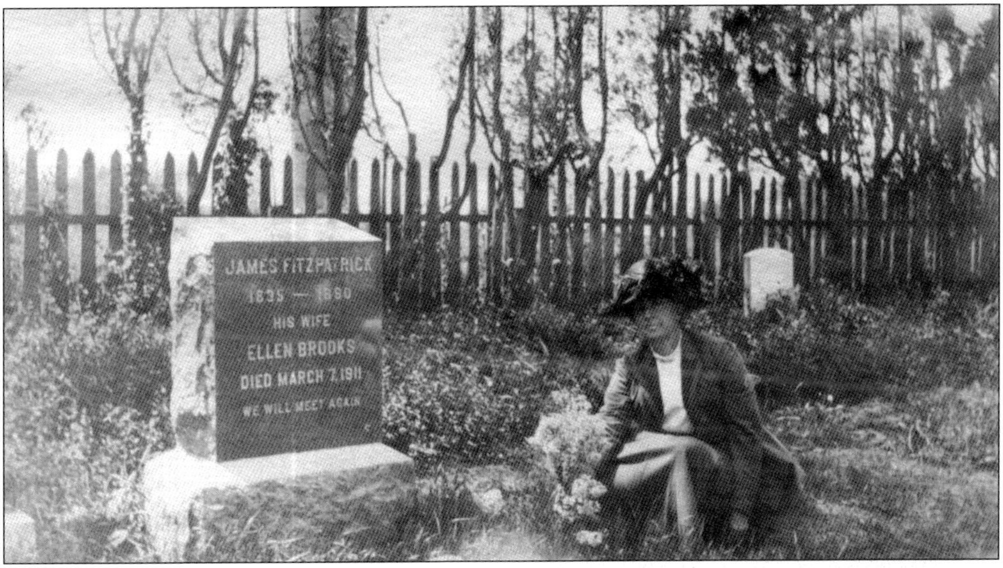

Paying Respects. Dora King shows her family the value of respecting those who have come before by reflecting at the gravesite of a family friend in 1912. (Courtesy of the Clark History Room.)

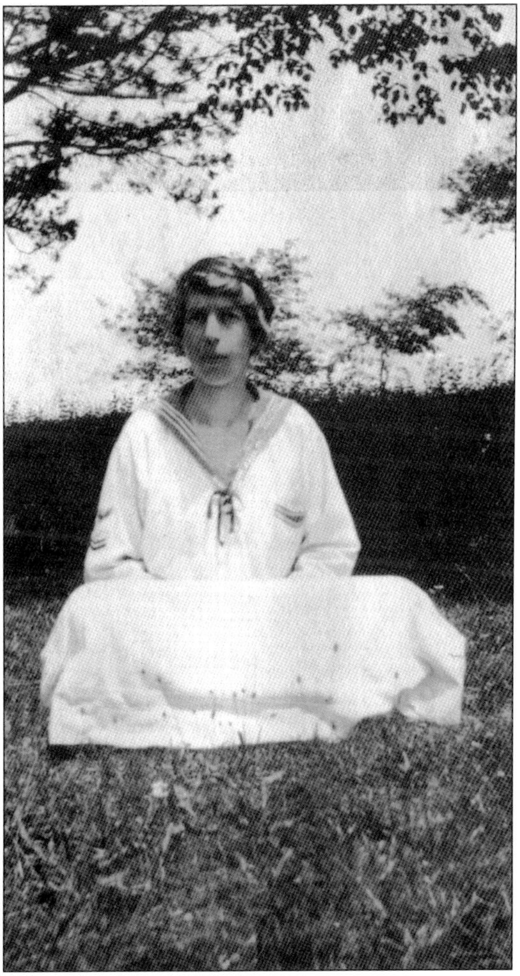

Leisure on Westfield Avenue. Emma Taylor King sits in the fields along Westfield Avenue in 1906. (Courtesy of the Clark History Room.)

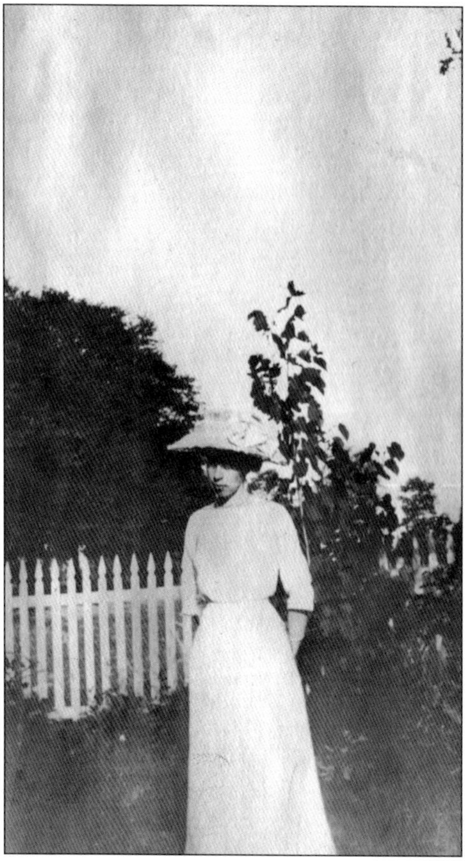

EASTER ON WESTFIELD AVENUE, 1906. Emma Taylor King takes a stroll in her Easter bonnet in front of her home on Westfield Avenue. (Courtesy of the Clark History Room.)

KROWICKI GORNY MEMORIAL HOME. When Emma King passed away in 1978, she left all of her money and her estate to the Township of Clark. The township, unable to fund repairs to the home at the time, sold the property at a public auction, and it was converted into the present-day Krowicki Gorny Memorial Home in 1981. (Courtesy of the Clark History Room.)

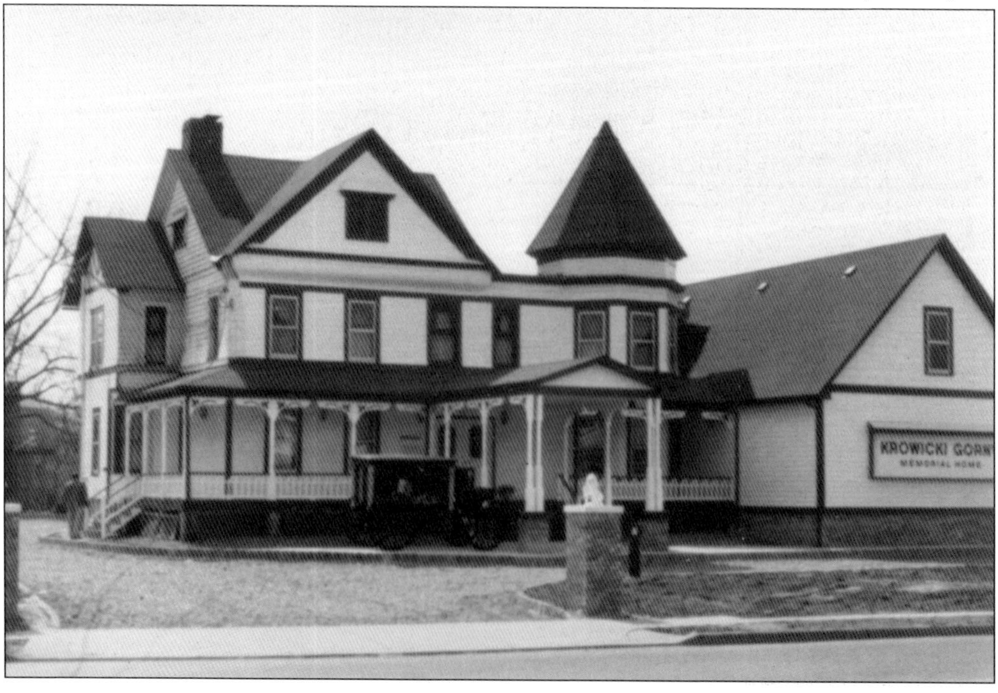

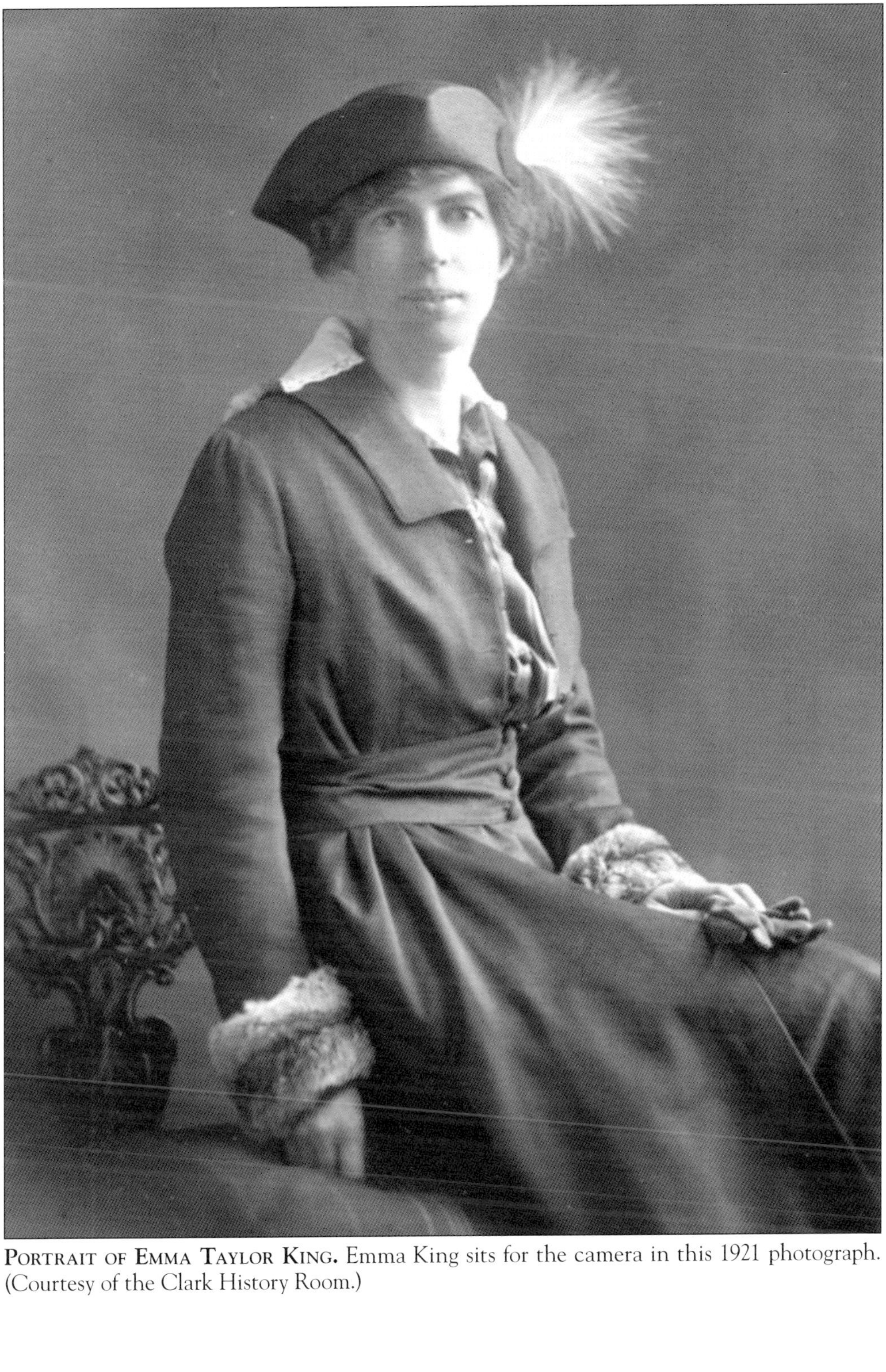

Portrait of Emma Taylor King. Emma King sits for the camera in this 1921 photograph. (Courtesy of the Clark History Room.)

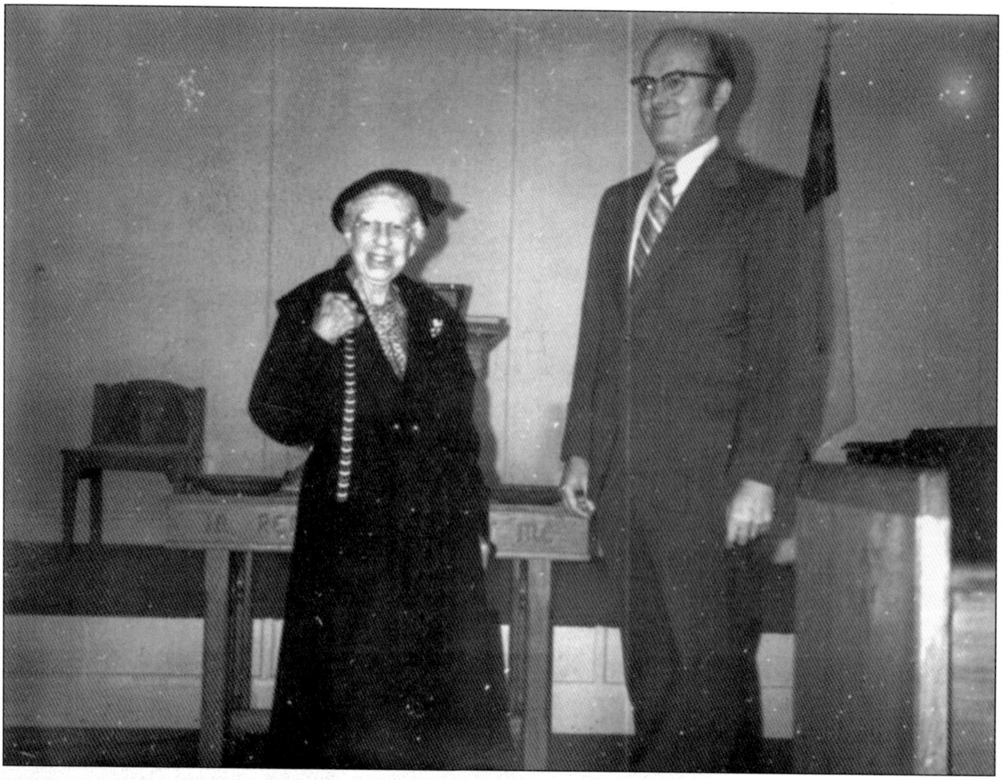

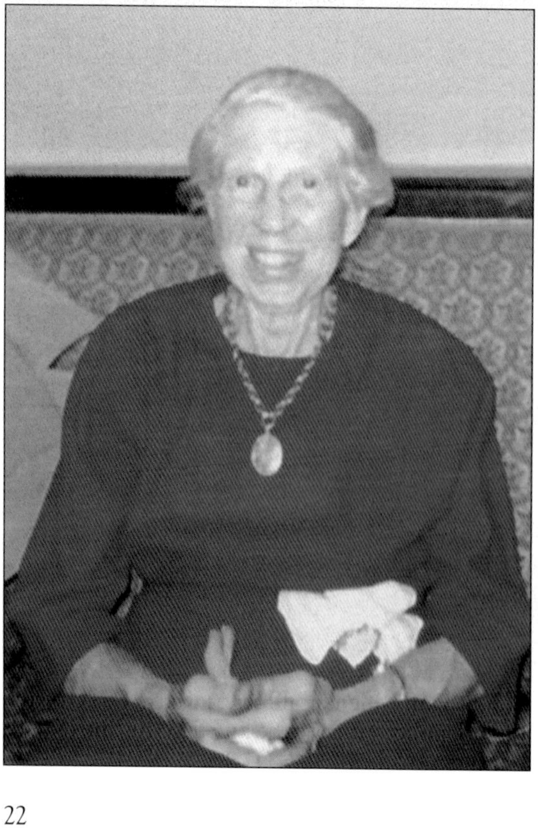

Emma Taylor King, Citizen of the Year, 1970. Emma Taylor King is shown here receiving the citizen of the year award in 1970. She was honored for her many years of dedicated services to the citizens of Clark. (Courtesy of the Clark History Room.)

Emma Taylor King. Emma Taylor King is shown in this last photograph before her death in August 1978. (Courtesy of the Clark History Room.)

Two

MAYOR BONACCORSO

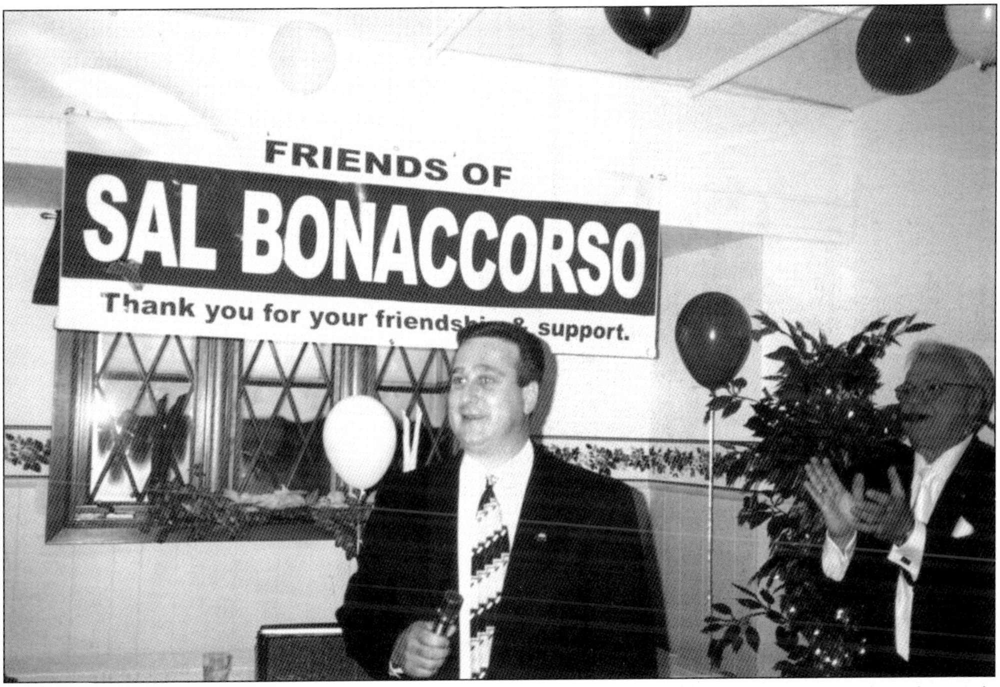

SALVATORE F. BONACCORSO. Salvatore F. "Sal" Bonaccorso (born December 2, 1960) is the 40th mayor of Clark, New Jersey. Bonaccorso, a Republican, is the longest-serving mayor in the history of the town. He was first elected to a four-year term in 2000; was reelected in 2004, 2008, and 2012; and will be finishing his 16th year in office in 2016. (Courtesy of the Bonaccorso family.)

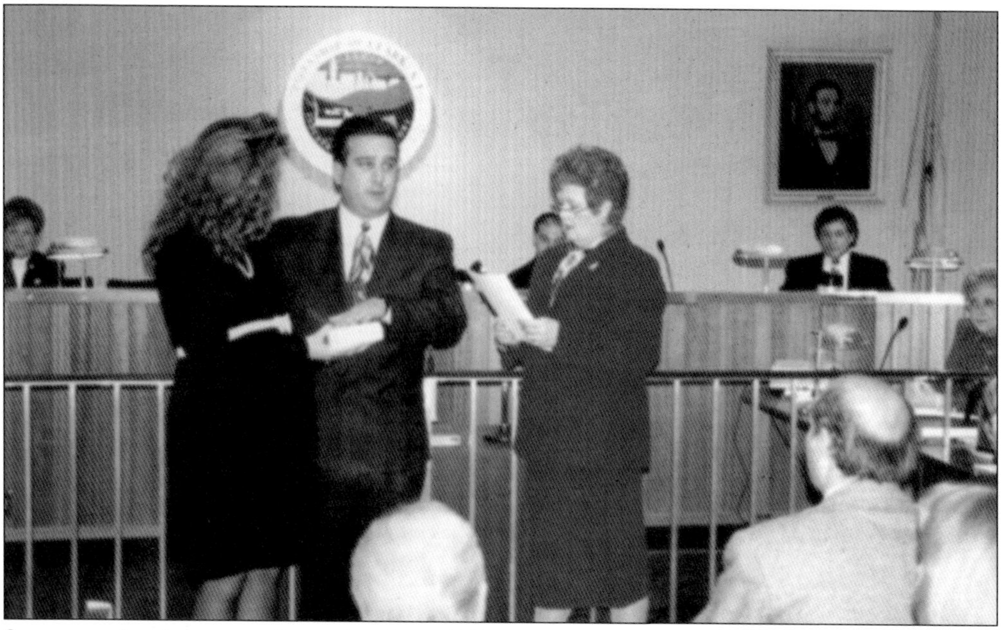

Swearing-In Ceremony. Council-at-large Sal Bonaccorso is sworn into his first elected office on January 1, 1997, after receiving the most votes in the township's 1996 election. Bonaccorso served one term on the township council, ending his run in 2000. (Courtesy of the Bonaccorso family.)

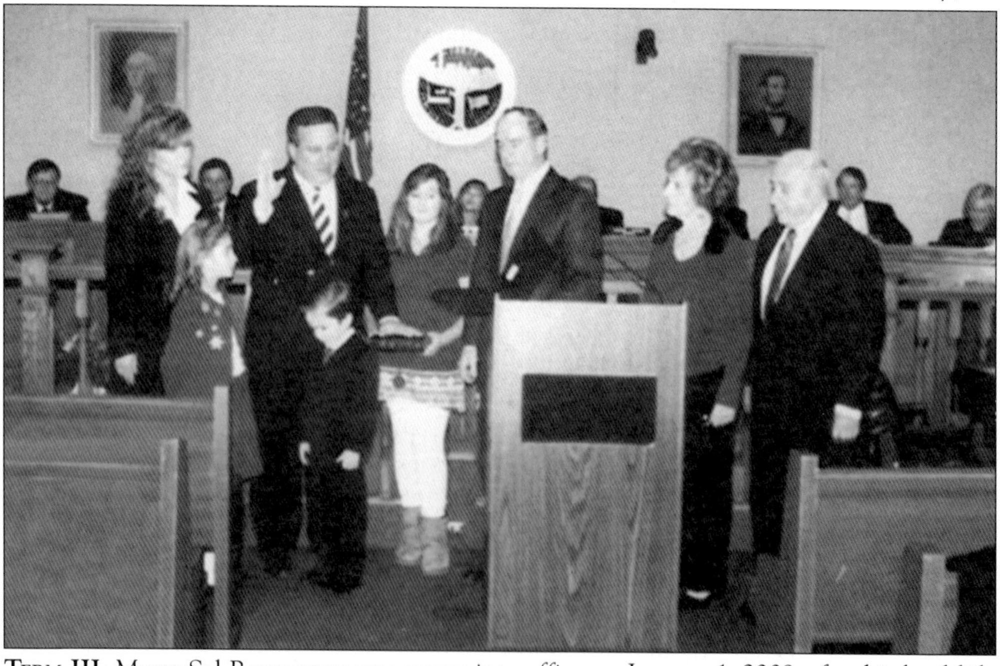

Term III. Mayor Sal Bonaccorso was sworn into office on January 1, 2009, after his landslide reelection in November 2008. He is the first mayor in the history of Clark to be elected to a third four-year term. Pictured from left to right are Geraldine Bonaccorso, daughter Kelly Bonaccorso, Mayor Sal Bonaccorso, son Joseph Bonaccorso III, eldest daughter Christine Bonaccorso, New Jersey governor Donald DiFrancesco, mother of the mayor Anna Bonaccorso, and father of the mayor Joseph Bonaccorso Sr. (Courtesy of the Bonaccorso family.)

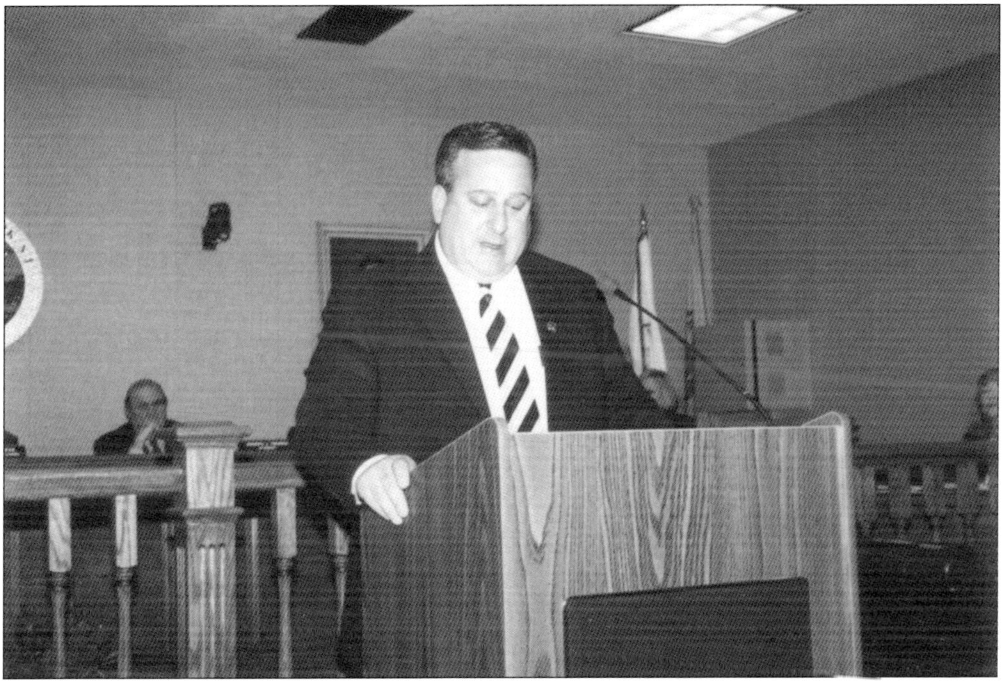

State of the Township. During Mayor Bonaccorso's eighth state of the township address on January 1, 2009, he highlights the progress Clark made in 2008. (Courtesy of the Bonaccorso family.)

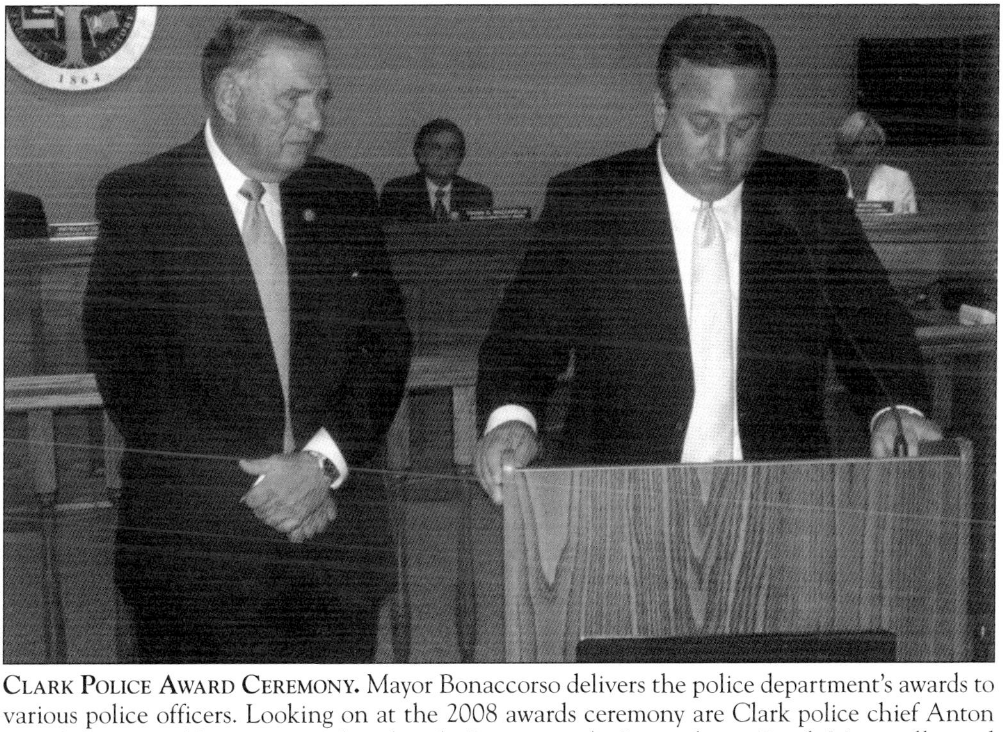

Clark Police Award Ceremony. Mayor Bonaccorso delivers the police department's awards to various police officers. Looking on at the 2008 awards ceremony are Clark police chief Anton "Sandy" Danco (the man standing beside Bonaccorso), Councilman Frank Mazzarella, and Councilwoman Shelia Whitting. (Courtesy of the Bonaccorso family.)

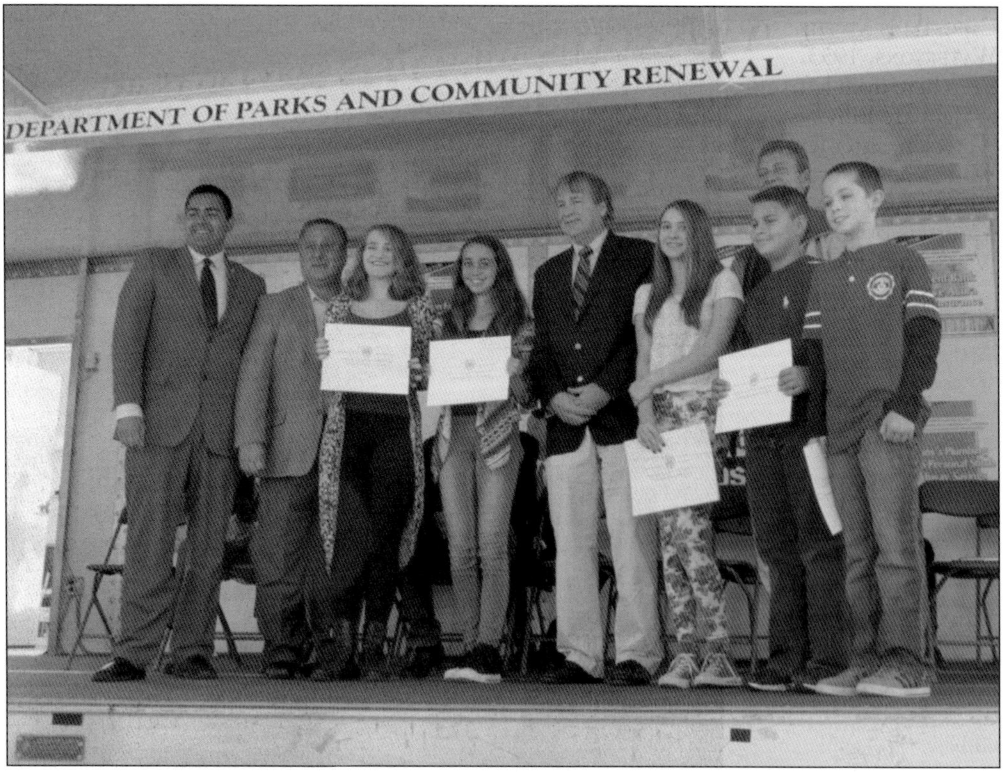

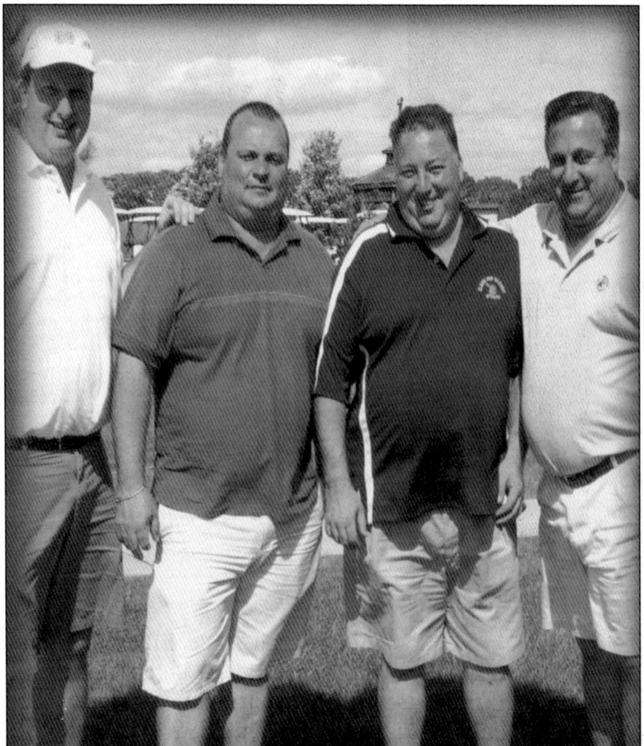

CLARK UNICO ANNUAL COLUMBUS DAY ITALIAN AMERICAN FEAST. Since the beginning of the Bonaccorso administration in 2001, the township and Clark UNICO, under the direction of Mayor Bonaccorso, recreation director Ralph Bernardo, and UNICO president Henry Vanniano, have held a Columbus Day essay contest for the Clark children. (Courtesy of the Bonaccorso family.)

CLARK POP WARNER GOLF OUTING, 2006. The Clark Pop Warner Golf Outing is an annual event to raise funds for the purchase of equipment and uniforms for the children and programs. (Courtesy of the Bonaccorso family.)

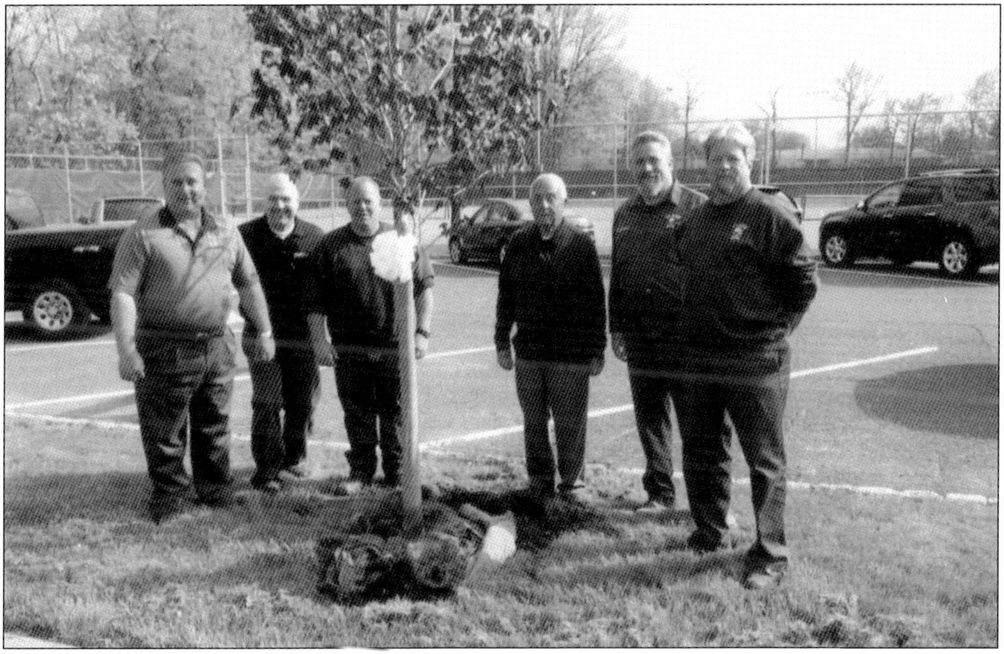

Earth Day, 2014. Mayor Sal Bonaccorso welcomes Earth Day 2014 with a new township tree sponsored by local business ProCare Rehabilitation. Helping with the planting are, from left to right, Mayor Bonaccorso, unidentified, Scott McCabe, public works director Joe Bonaccorso, and public works employees Adam Lambert and Eric Johnson. (Courtesy of the Bonaccorso family.)

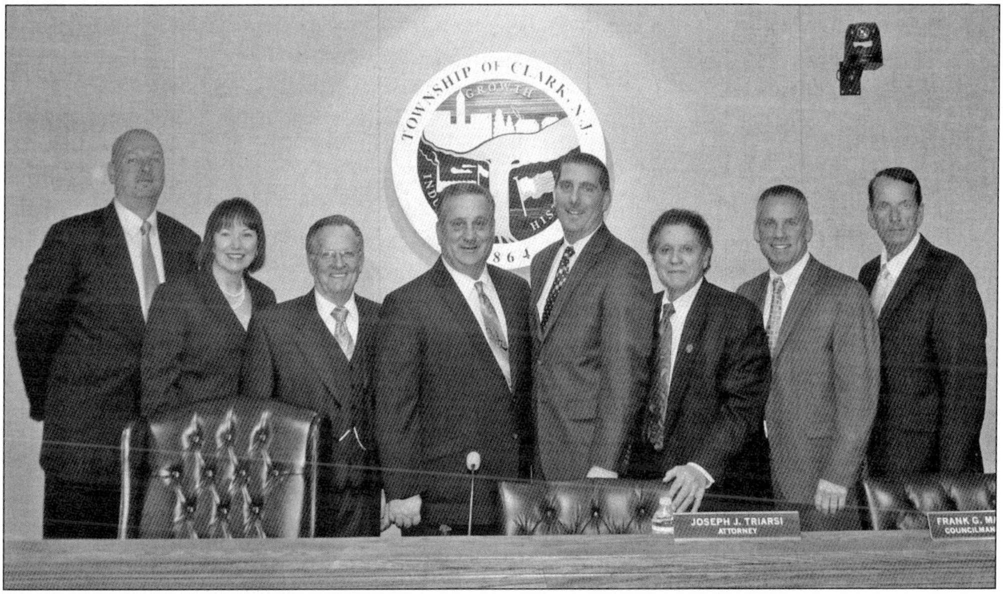

Clark Mayor and Council 2015. Shown in this photograph are Mayor Bonaccorso and the 2015 council members in the municipal chambers. From left to right are Third Ward councilman Steven Hund, Councilwoman at Large Angel Albanese, Councilman at Large Alvin Barr, Clark mayor Sal Bonaccorso, Council Pres. William Smith, First Ward councilman Frank Mazzarella, Second Ward councilman Patrick O'Connor, and Fourth Ward councilman Brian Toal. (Courtesy of the Bonaccorso family.)

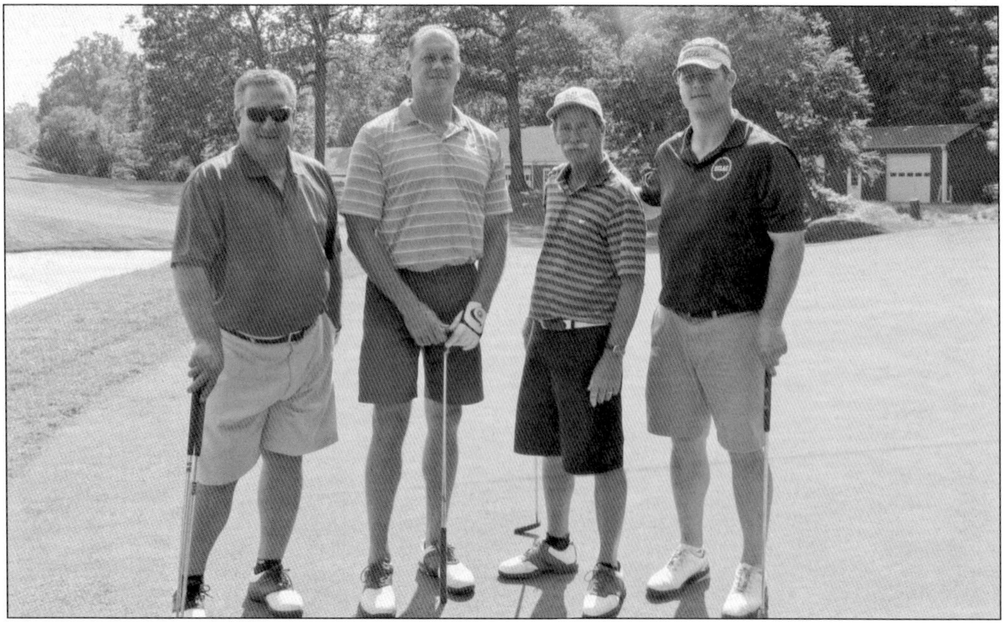

2015 Clark Mayor's Golf Outing. This annually held event at Echo Lake Country Club in Westfield, New Jersey, is a fundraiser to help support local organizations and youth. Shown in the photograph are, from left to right, Mayor Bonaccorso, John Ehling, Paul DiGiano, John Shutte. (Courtesy of the Bonaccorso family.)

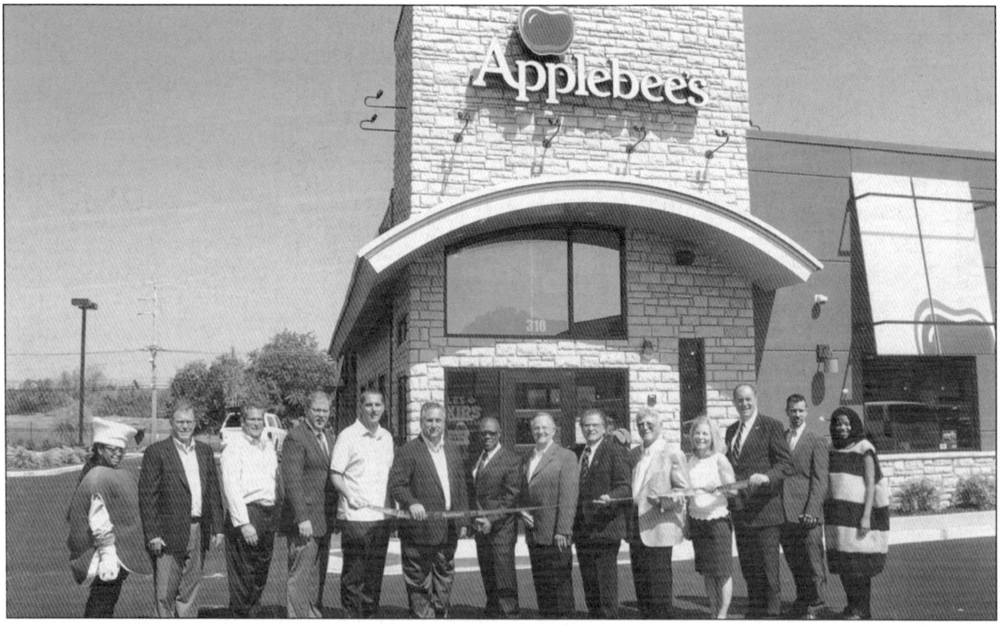

Clark Applebee's Grand Opening Ceremony. Union County freeholder vice chairman Bruce H. Bergen and Union County sheriff Joseph Cryan joined Clark mayor Sal Bonaccorso, Clark council president Bill Smith, Councilman Alvin Barr, Councilman Frank Mazzarella, business administrator John Laerra, township clerk Edie Merke, and Applebee's director of operations Kevin Coughlin, vice president of operations David DiBartolo, and area director Brian Orgodnick at the Clark Applebee's Grand Opening Ceremony on July 20, 2015. (Photograph by Jim Lowney/County of Union.)

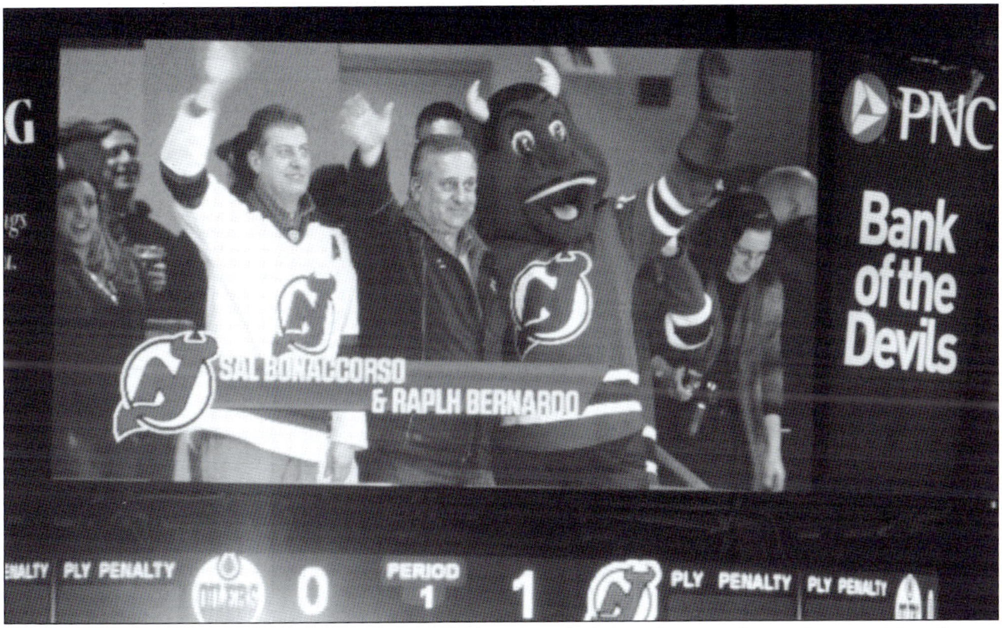

New Jersey Devils. In February 2015, Clark Township was honored as a feature New Jersey community by the New Jersey Devils hockey team at the Prudential Center in Newark, New Jersey. Seen on the jumbo screen are recreation director Ralph Bernardo (left), Mayor Bonaccorso, and the New Jersey Devil. (Courtesy of the Bonaccorso family.)

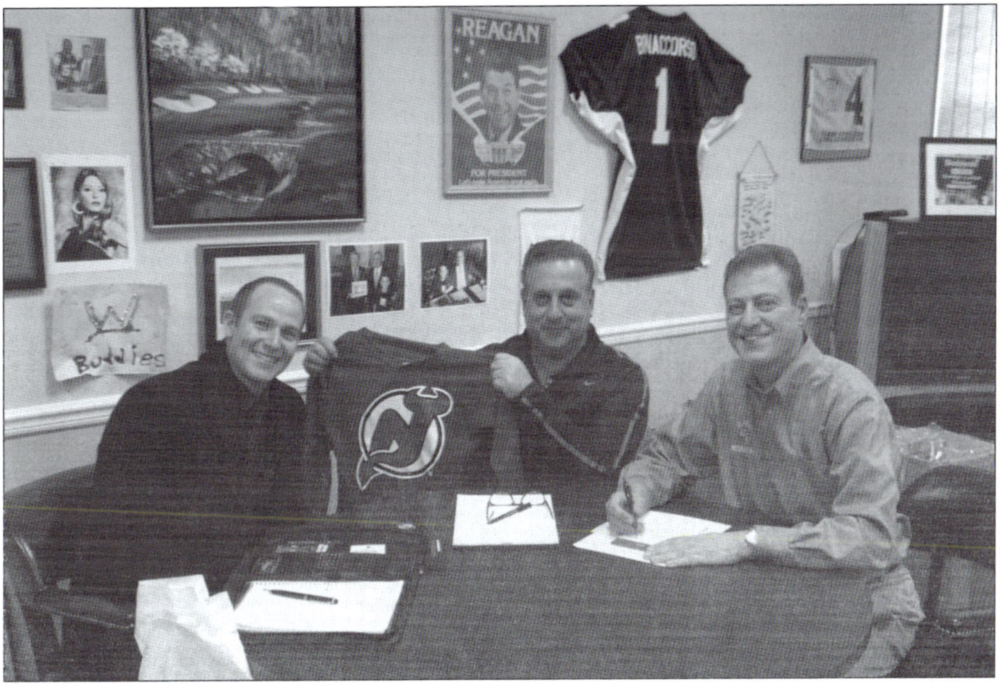

Showing New Jersey Devil Pride. Shown here is the planning for "Our Town" night at the Prudential Center that honored the township of Clark in February 2015. Pictured from left to right are Criss Rugers of the New Jersey Devils, Mayor Bonaccorso, and recreation director Ralph Bernardo. (Courtesy of the Bonaccorso family.)

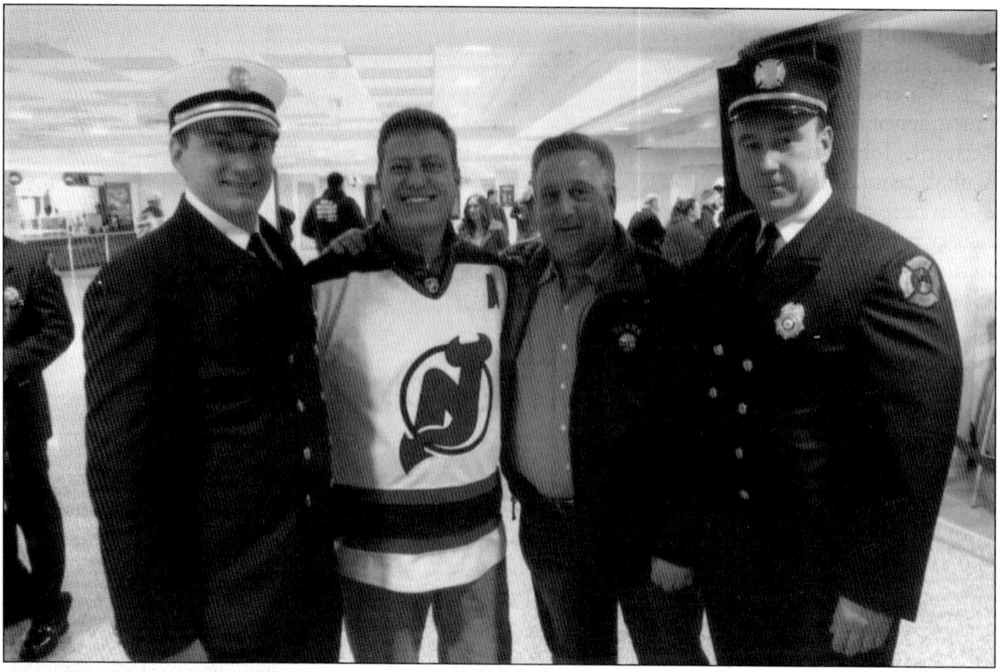

Our Town. Showing their support for Clark, New Jersey, and the New Jersey Devils are representatives of the New Jersey Firemen's Association, Ralph Bernardo, and Mayor Bonaccorso (in the jersey) in February 2015. (Courtesy of the Bonaccorso family.)

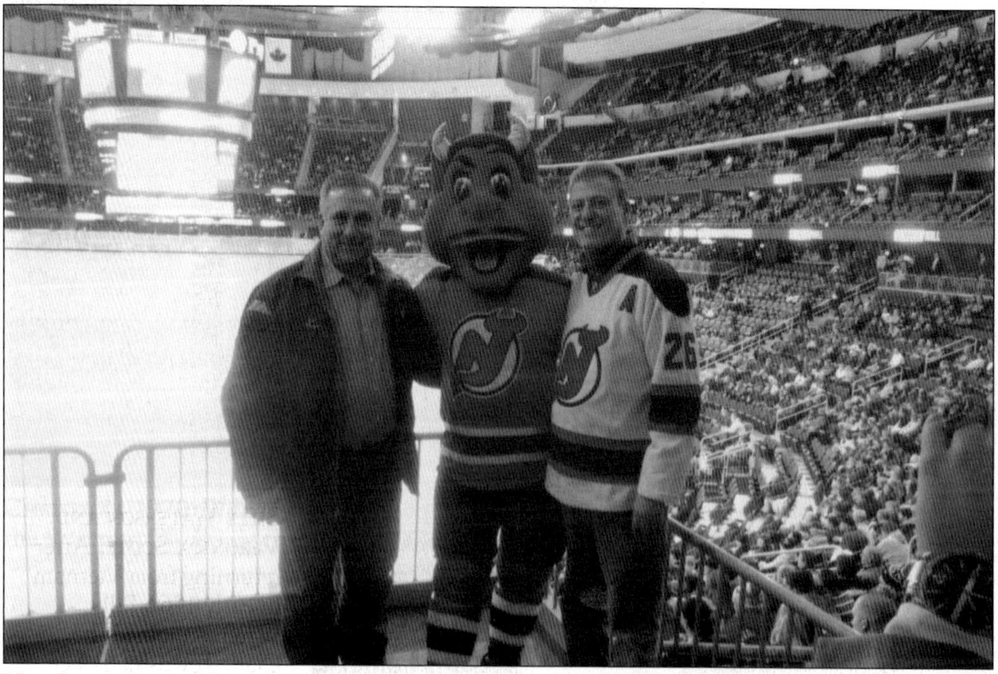

New Jersey Devil Mascot. The New Jersey Devil mascot takes Mayor Bonaccorso and recreation director Ralph Bernardo under his wing as he helps honor Clark, New Jersey, during the "Our Town" celebration held in February 2015 at the Prudential Center in Newark, New Jersey. (Courtesy of the Bonaccorso family.)

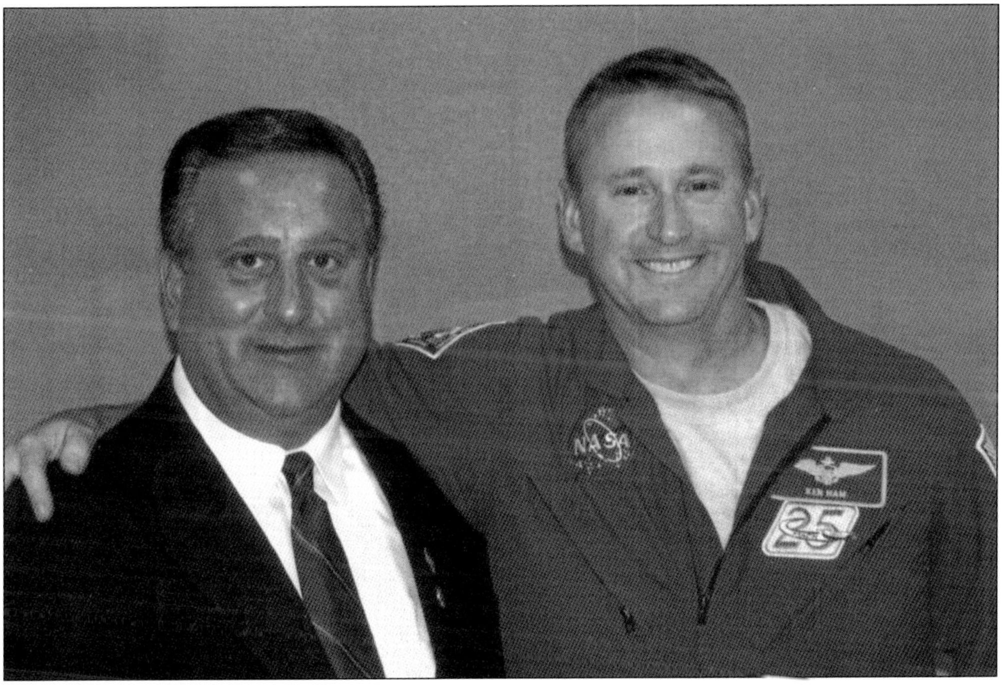

Mayor and Clark Astronaut Ken Ham. Mayor Bonaccorso welcomes home Arthur L. Johnson High School class of 1983 alumnus and NASA shuttle pilot Kenneth Ham. (Courtesy of the Bonaccorso family.)

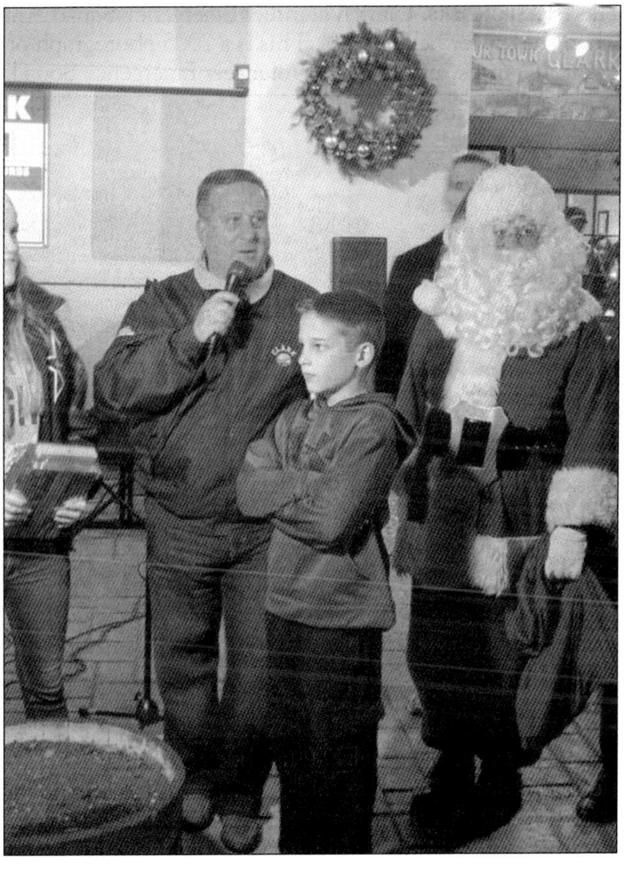

Season's Greetings, 2014. Under the terms of office, Mayor Bonaccorso has conducted many community holiday programs, from breakfast with Santa for the Clark children to the holiday lighting to Chanukah celebrations. Pictured from left to right are Courtney O'Connor, Mayor Bonaccorso, Joseph Bonaccorso, and Santa Claus. (Courtesy of the Bonaccorso family.)

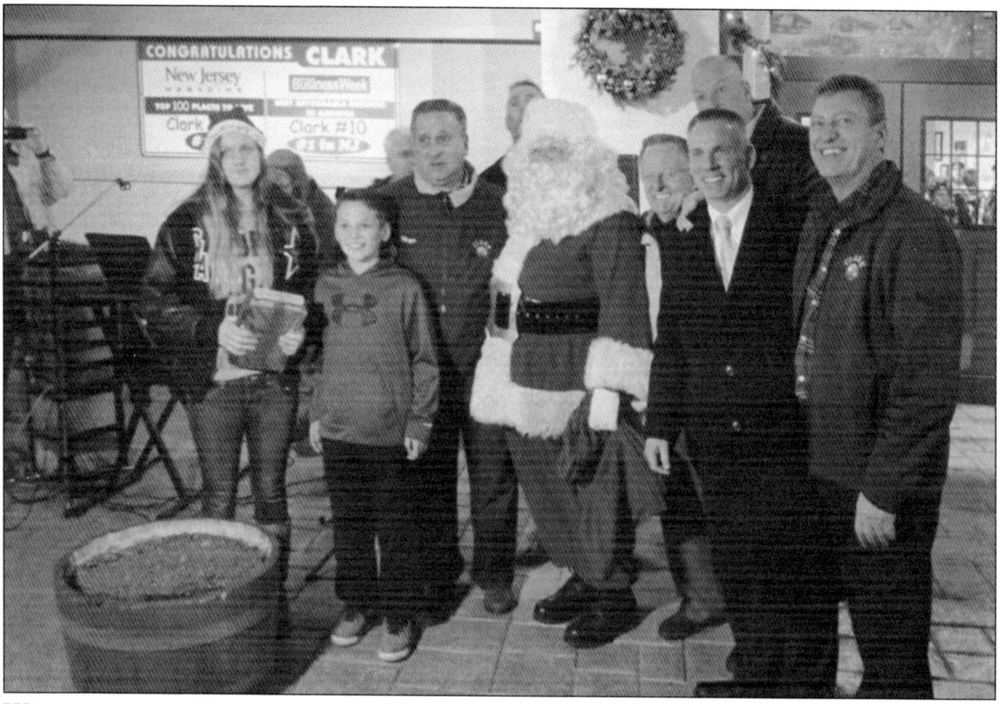

Welcoming the Holidays, 2014. The annual tree lighting, held on the first Sunday after Thanksgiving, has become a tradition in Clark. Seen here are, from left to right, Courtney O'Connor, Joseph Bonaccorso, Mayor Bonaccorso, Santa, Councilman Alvil Bar, Councilman Steven Hund, Councilman Pat O'Connor, and recreation director Ralph Bernardo. (Courtesy of the Bonaccorso family.)

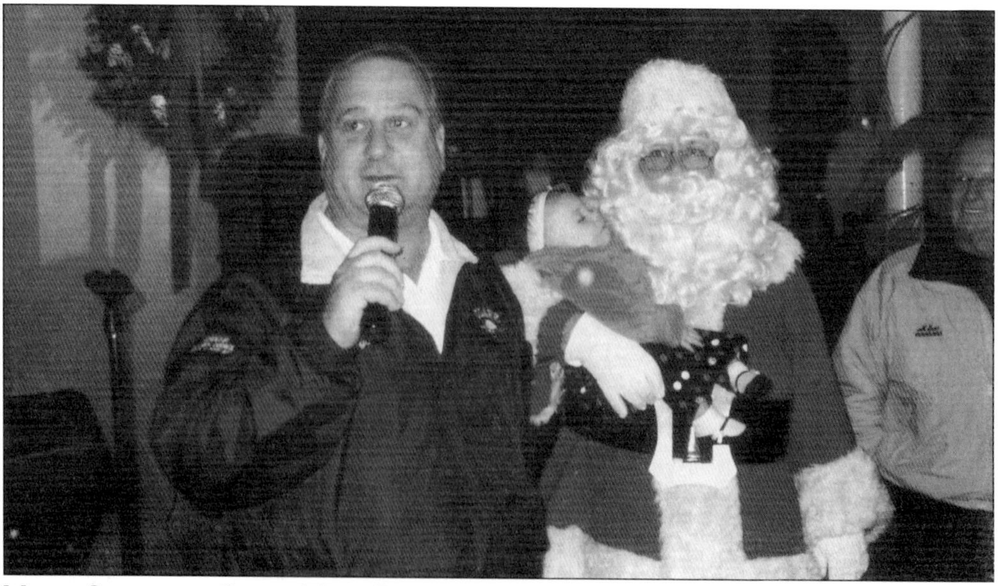

Merry Christmas, Clark. Mayor Bonaccorso speaks to the residents who have come out for the annual holiday tree and menorah lighting, which is held every year on the first Sunday after Thanksgiving in Clark to kick off the holiday season. Pictured here are Mayor Bonaccorso and Santa Claus. (Courtesy of the Bonaccorso family.)

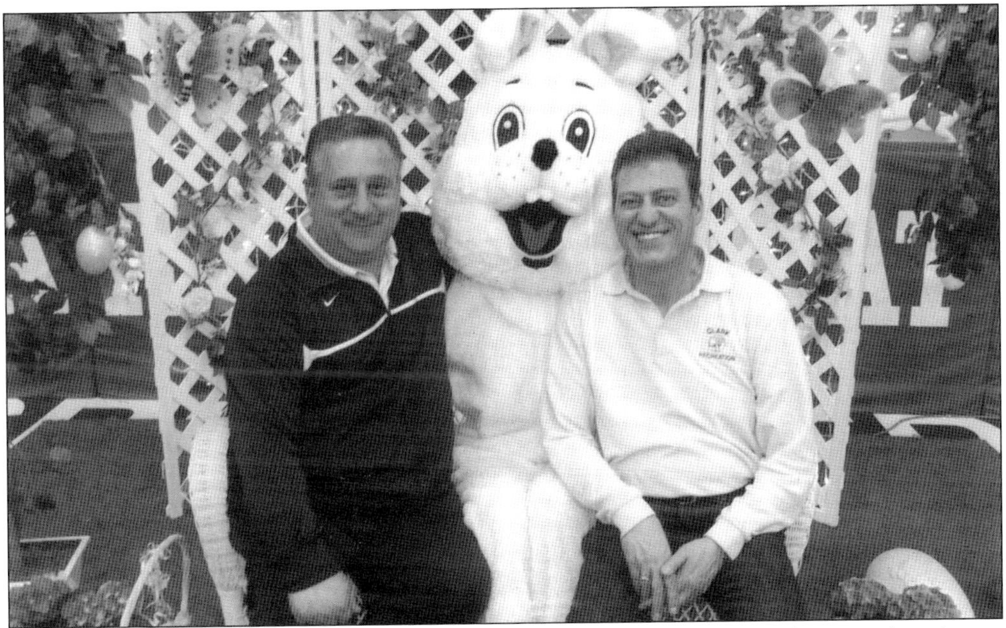

Easter in Clark. Mayor Sal Bonaccorso (left) and recreation director Ralph Bernardo welcome the Easter Bunny to Clark Township in March 2013. (Courtesy of the Bonaccorso family.)

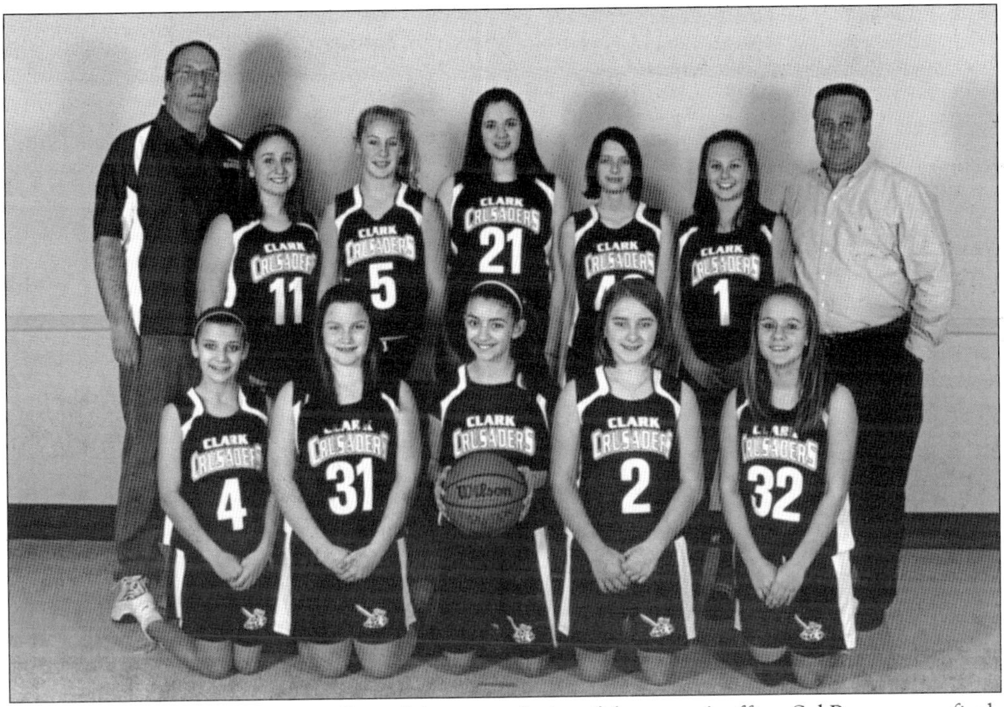

Girls' Traveling Basketball. One of the many duties of the mayor's office, Sal Bonaccorso finds the time to coach his oldest daughter's girls' basketball team. Seen in this 2012 photograph are, from left to right, (first row) Lauren Beek, Kate Doherty, Mia Ehling, Janet Vill, and Jess Zambrano; (second row) coach John Doherty, Christiana Bonaccorso, Samantha Cimbolici, Natalie Stanzione, Lauren Margel, Emily Bailey, and Mayor Bonaccorso. (Courtesy of the Bonaccorso family.)

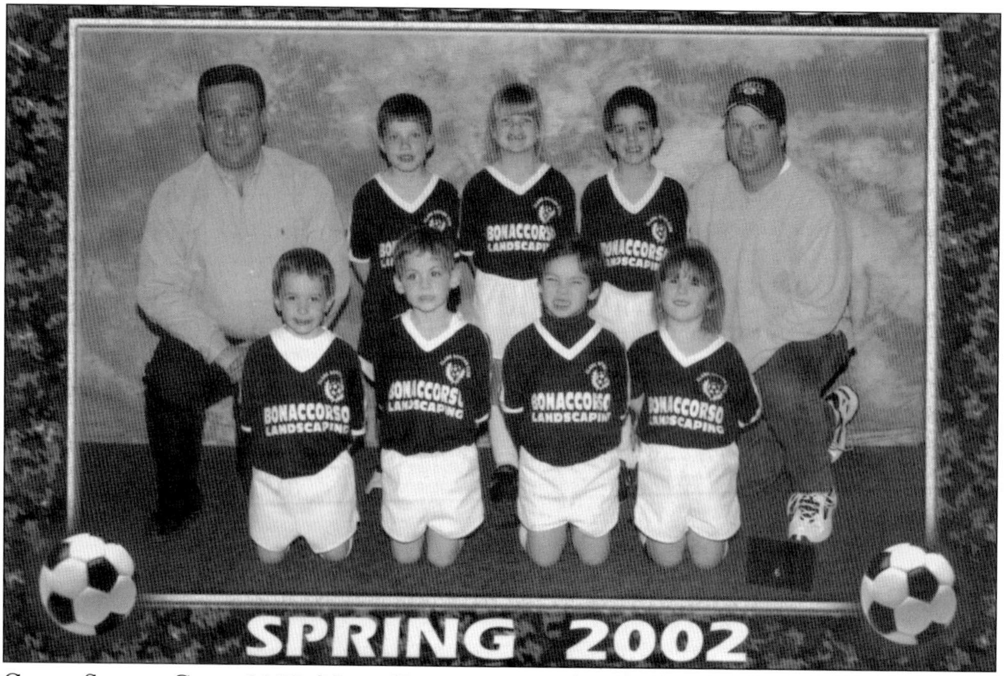

CLARK SOCCER CLUB, 2002. Mayor Bonaccorso coaches the boys' midget team of 2002. The boys are four years old and in the instructional league, which teaches the basics of the game. (Courtesy of the Bonaccorso family.)

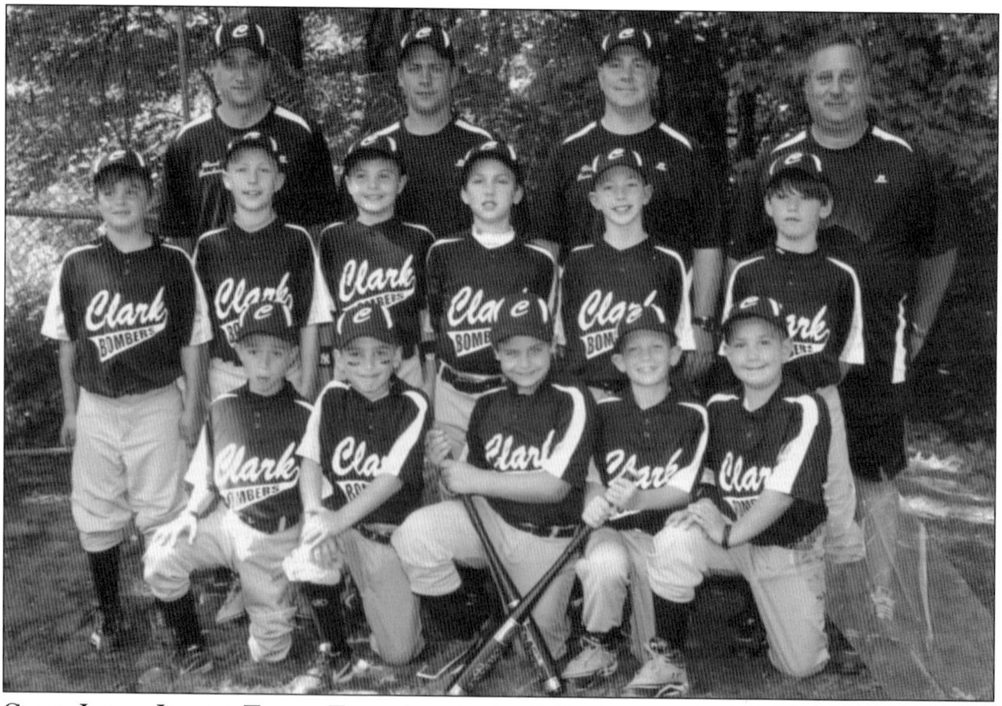

CLARK LITTLE LEAGUE TRAVEL TEAM. Seen in this 2013 photograph, this team of nine-year-olds spent the summer going to competitions in and around Central New Jersey under the direction of Coach Bonaccorso. (Courtesy of the Bonaccorso family.)

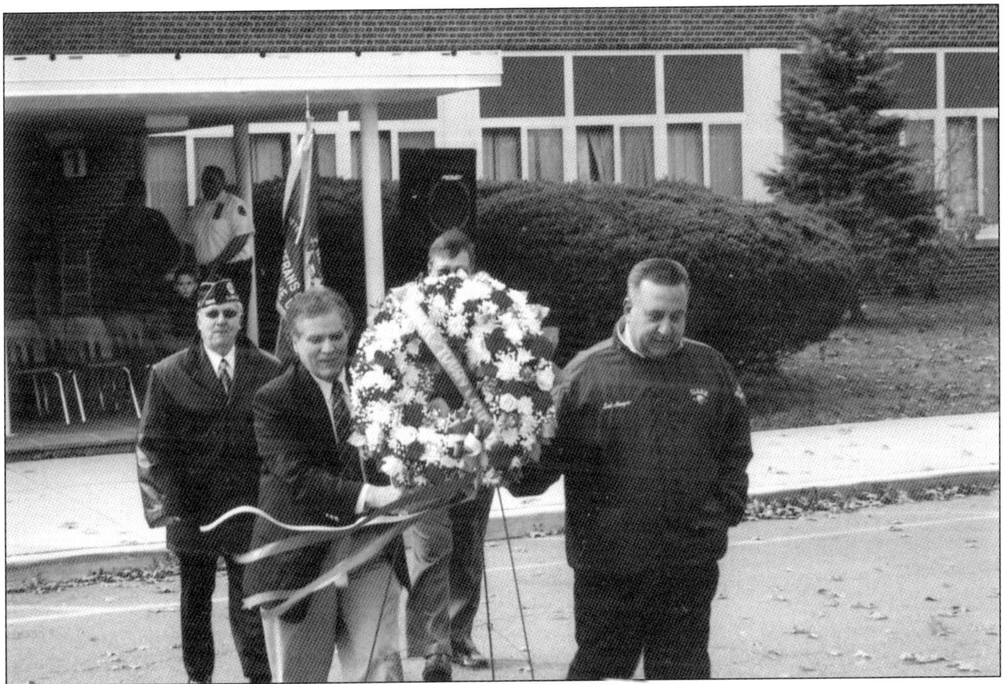

Veterans Day, 2010. Placing a memorial wreath in November 2010 are, from left to right, Councilman Alvin Barr, Councilman Frank Mazzarella, Councilman Richard Kaznowski, and Mayor Bonaccorso. (Courtesy of the Bonaccorso family.)

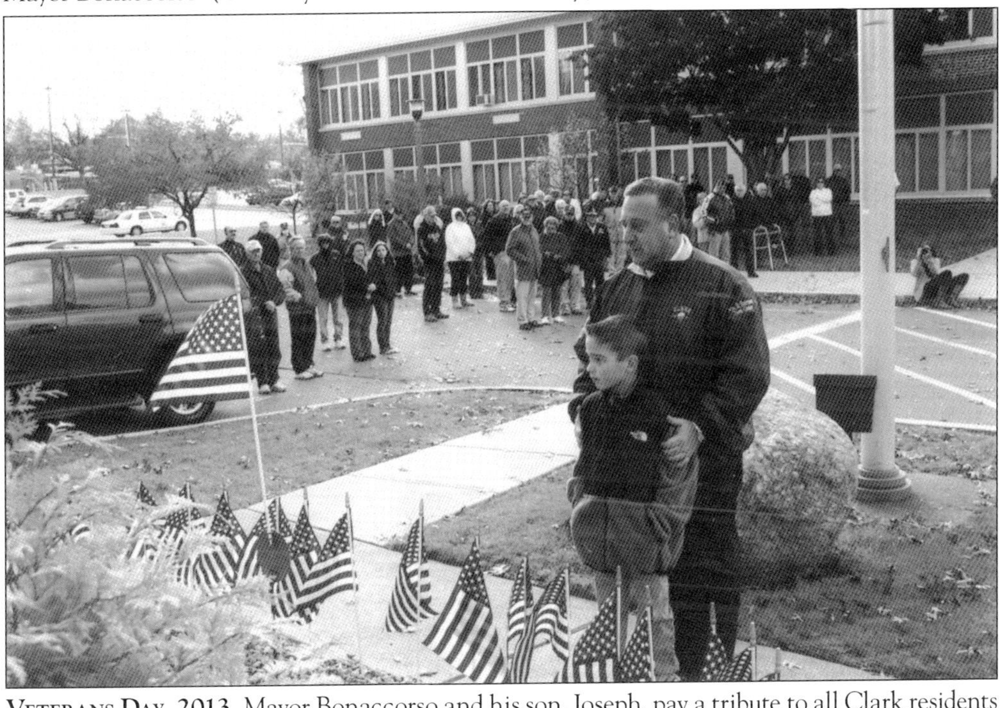

Veterans Day, 2013. Mayor Bonaccorso and his son, Joseph, pay a tribute to all Clark residents who have served. This photograph was taken in front of the high school at Clark Memorial Honor Roll. (Courtesy of the Bonaccorso family.)

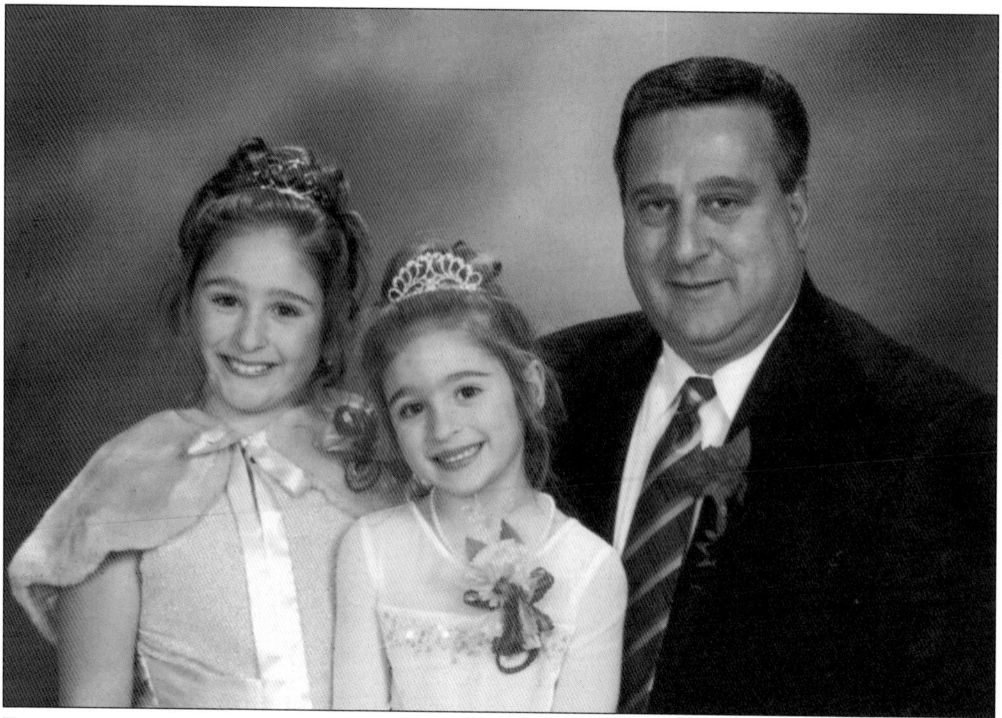

Fathers' Day Dance, 2003. The Clark Girl Scouts host their annual Father's Day dance. Pictured at the event are Mayor Bonaccorso and daughters Christina (left) and Kelly Bonaccorso. (Courtesy of the Bonaccorso family.)

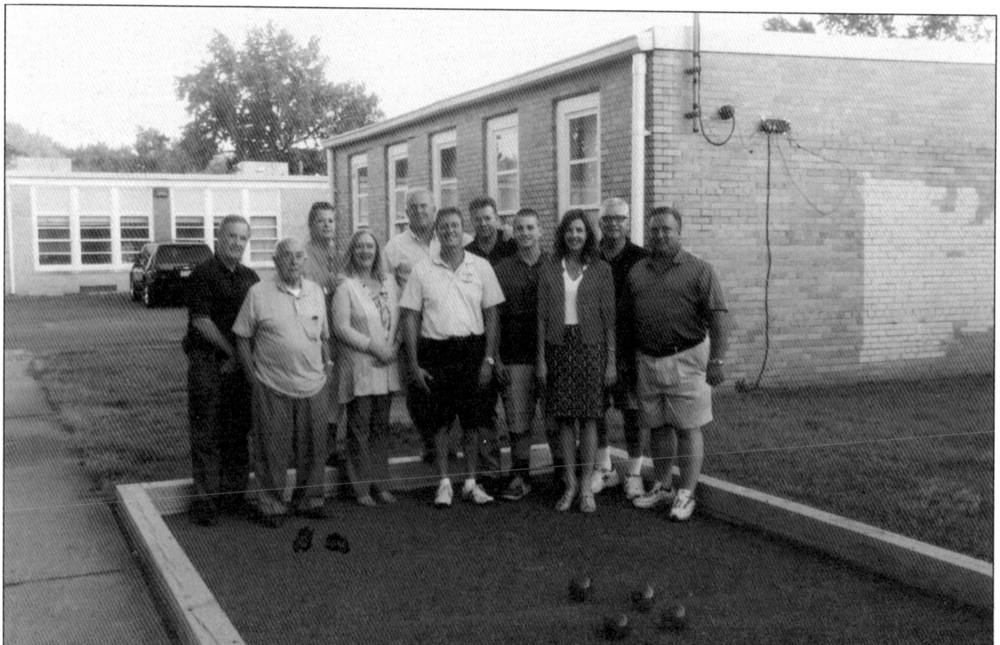

Clark Bocce Court Dedication. In 2014, the township opened its first bocce court for residents to enjoy located at the rear of the Brewer Municipal Complex on Westfield Avenue. (Courtesy of the Bonaccorso family.)

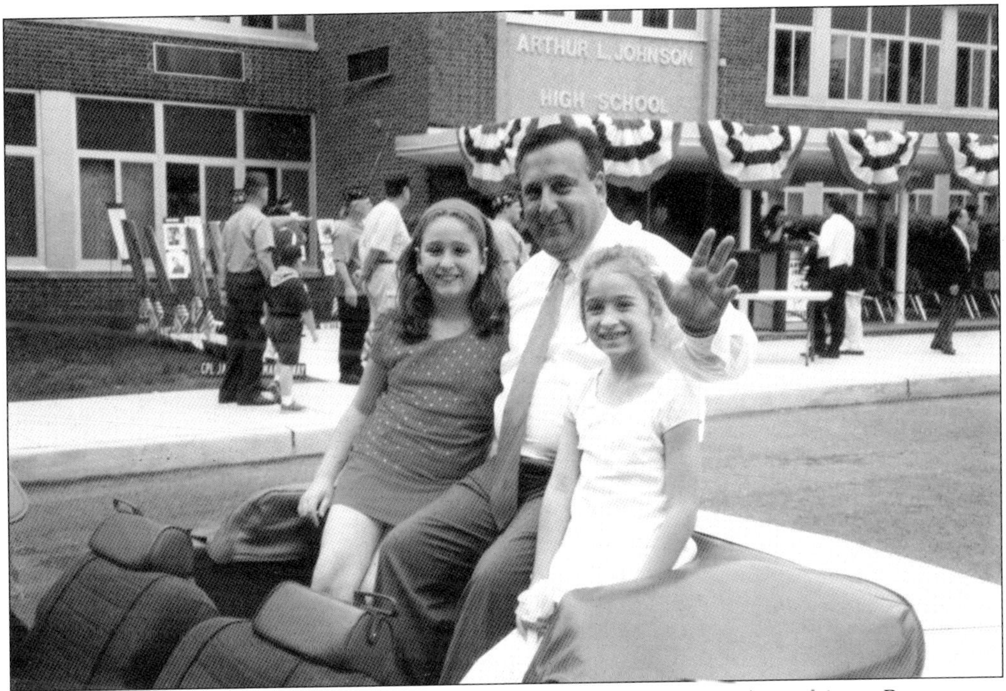

Clark's First Memorial Day Parade 2002. Seen in this photograph are Mayor Bonaccorso and his daughters riding in a 1976 Cadillac Eldorado Convertible. From left to right are Christine Bonaccorso, Mayor Bonaccorso, and Kelly Bonaccorso. (Courtesy of the Bonaccorso family.)

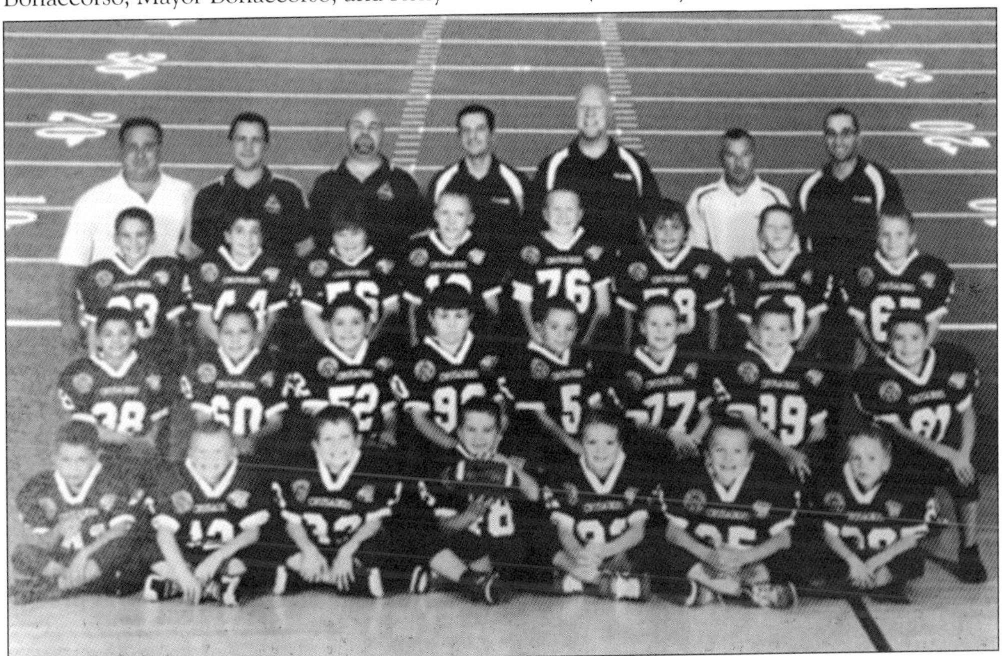

Clark Pop Warner, 2011. Shown in this 2011 photograph is the Clark Pop Warner football team. Some of those included in this photograph are Mayor Bonaccorso, Andy Trocyznski, Ralph Talarico, Anthony Campiglia, Joe Carney, Chris Nudo, Dino Bendvanga, and members of the Little Crusaders football team. (Courtesy of the Bonaccorso family.)

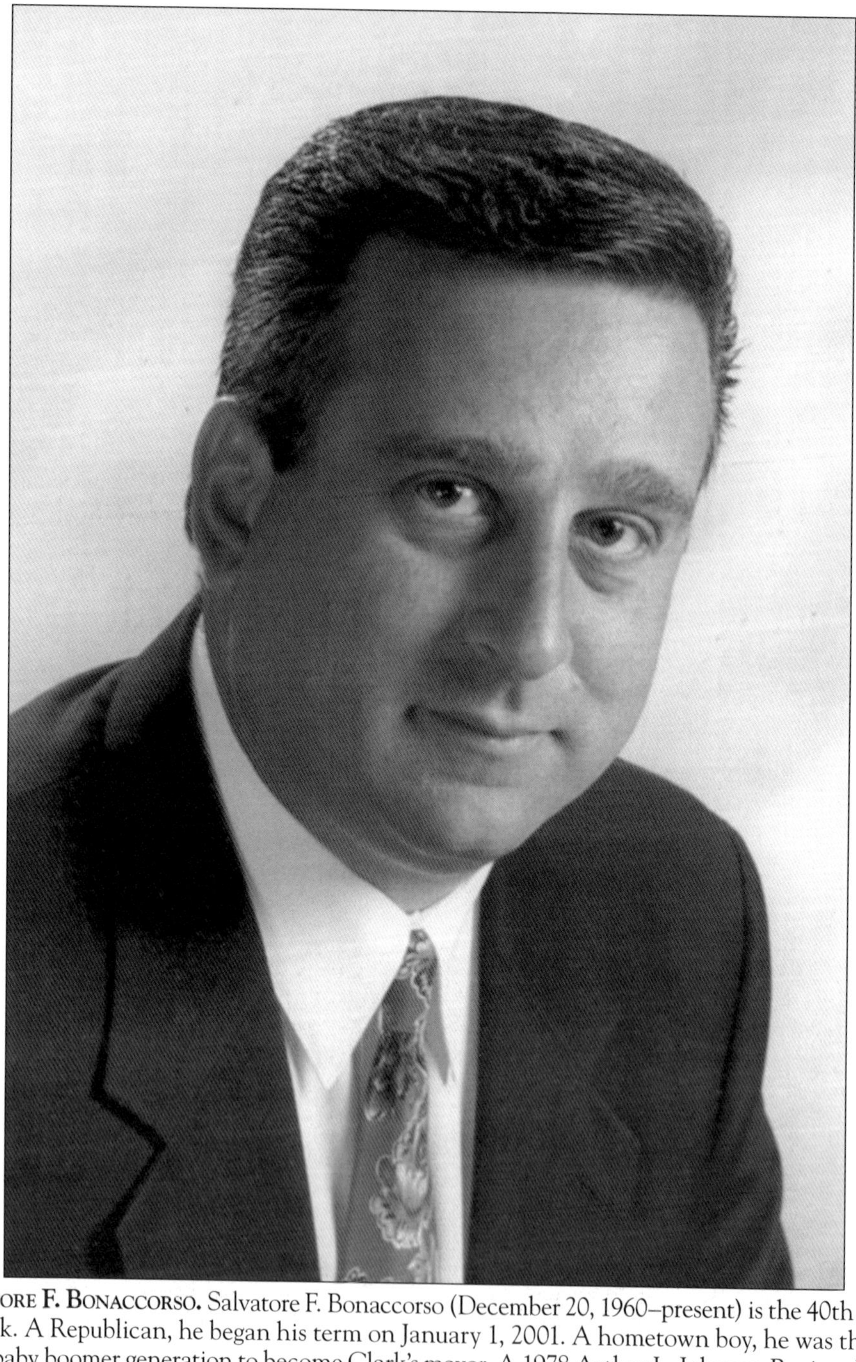

Salvatore F. Bonaccorso. Salvatore F. Bonaccorso (December 20, 1960–present) is the 40th mayor of Clark. A Republican, he began his term on January 1, 2001. A hometown boy, he was the first of the baby boomer generation to become Clark's mayor. A 1978 Arthur L. Johnson Regional High School graduate, he is the president of Bonaccorso Landscaping, a third-generation family-owned business. Mayor Bonaccorso has been an advocate of cleaning up Clark's image and revitalizing the senior center and recreation department. He established the town's first senior-citizen fitness in 2003 and has been instrumental in many progressive programs. He resides in Clark with his wife Geraldine, his two daughters, Christine and Kelly, and his son, Joseph. He is the longest-serving elected mayor in the township's history. (Courtesy of the Bonaccorso family.)

Three

THE POLICE DEPARTMENT

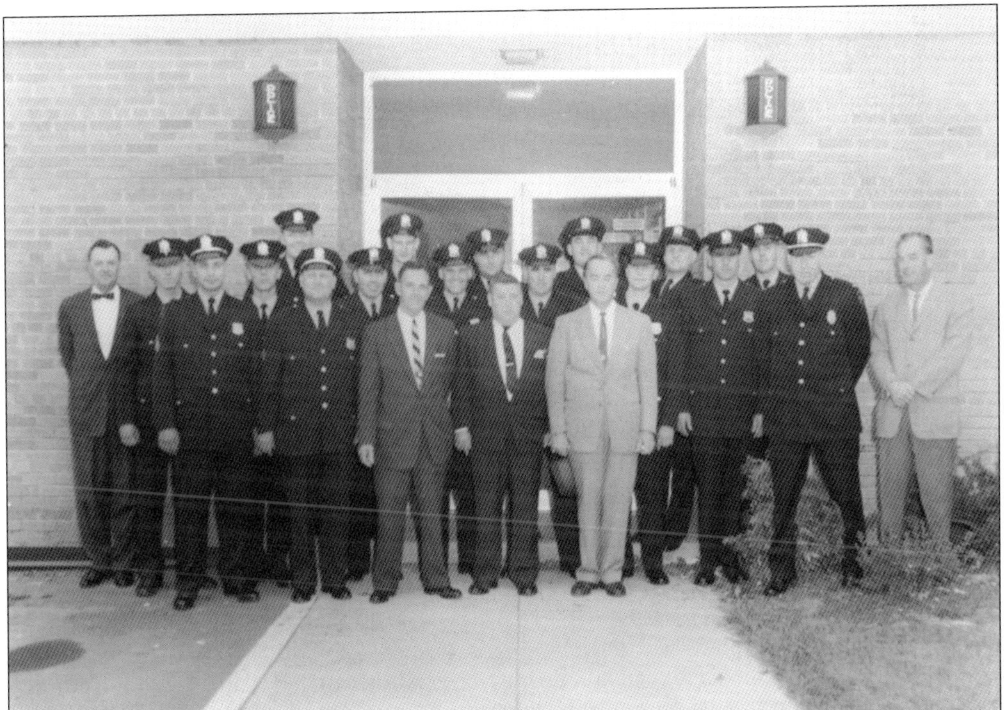

CLARK POLICE DEPARTMENT, 1960. Members of the Clark Police Department stand in front of the side entrance to the police headquarters, located at 315 Westfield Avenue. Mayor John O'Connor is seen to the far right. (Courtesy of the Clark History Room.)

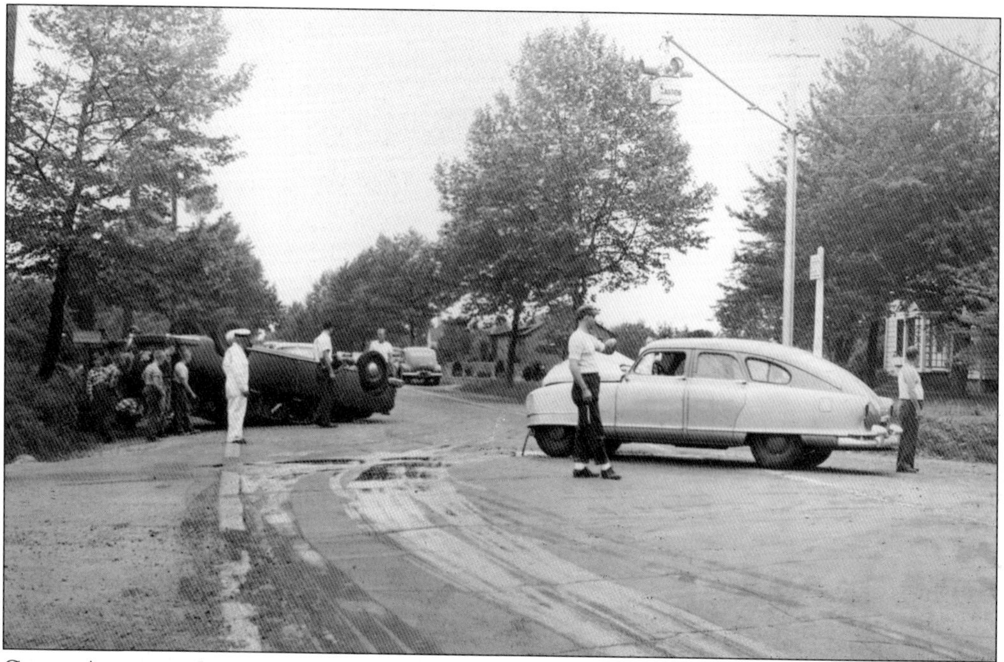

CLARK ACCIDENT SCENE, 1954. Members of the police department respond to a motor vehicle accident at the intersection of Westfield Avenue and Raritan Road. (Courtesy of the Clark History Room.)

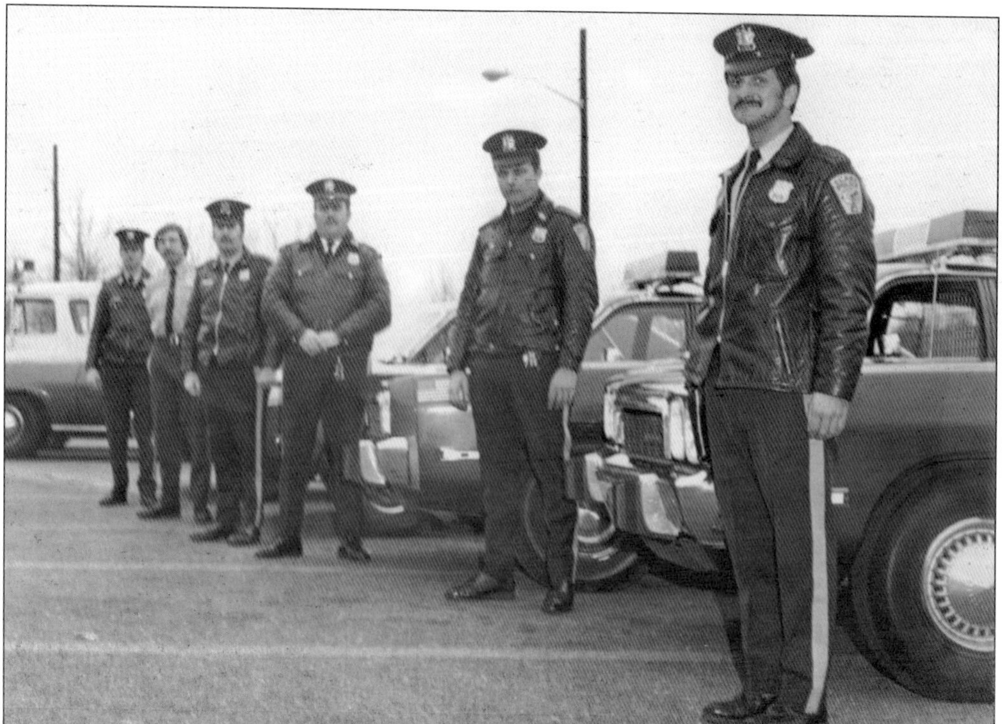

CLARK POLICE, 1974. Pictured from left to right are Herb Johnson, Al Williams, Guy Everest, Art Wesley, Bill Brozick, and Vic Demarzo. (Courtesy of Victor DeMarzo.)

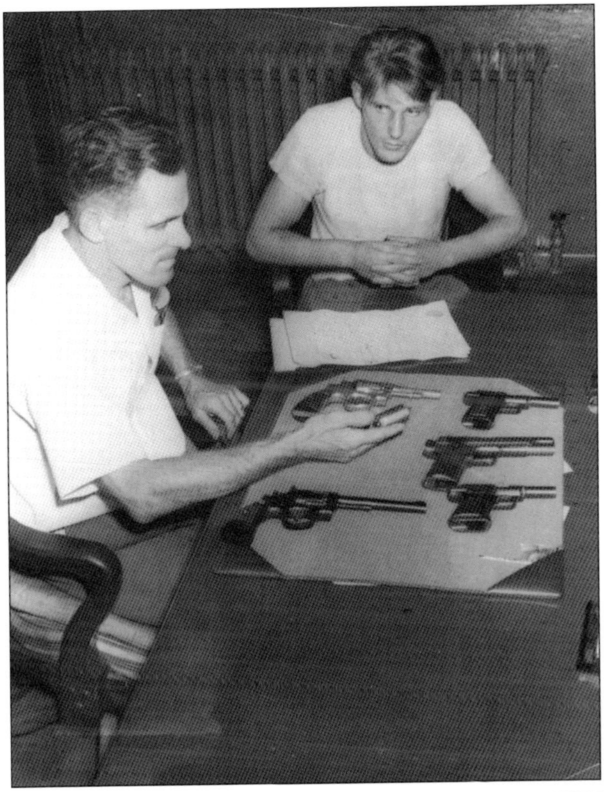

Department Inspection. Chief William Muth conducts a regular inspection of the police department handguns in 1956. (Courtesy of the Clark History Room.)

Clark Police Car, 1942. Clark police officer Charles Fullager stands next to the department's brand new 1942 Plymouth Sedan. (Courtesy of the Clark History Room.)

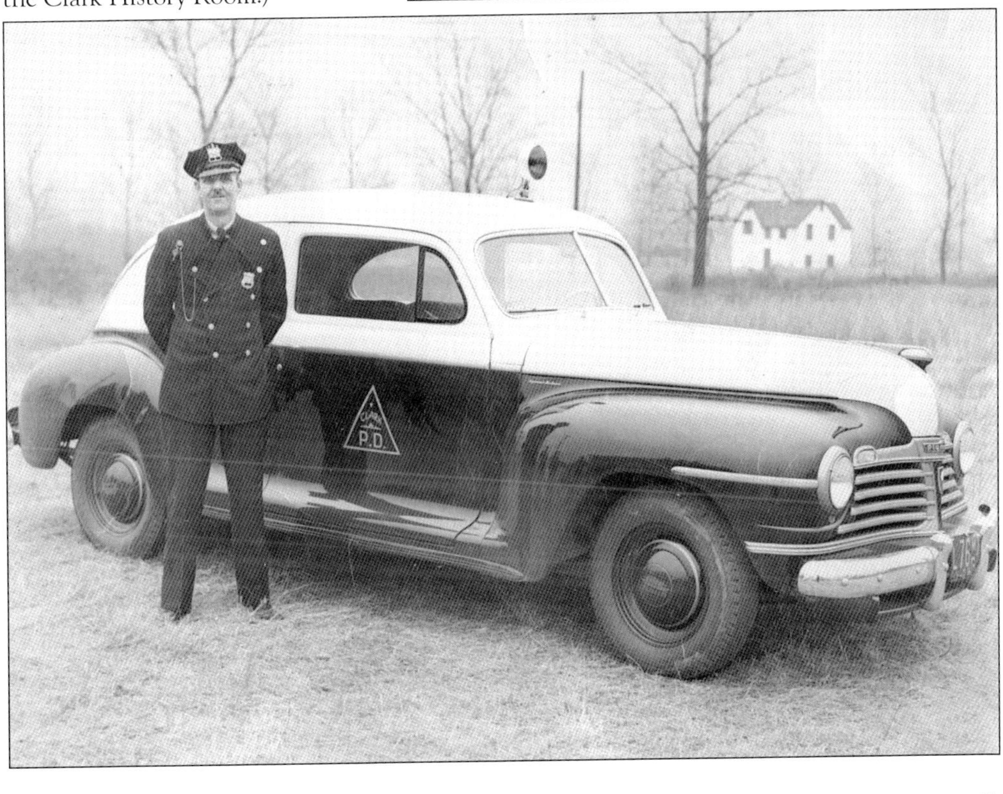

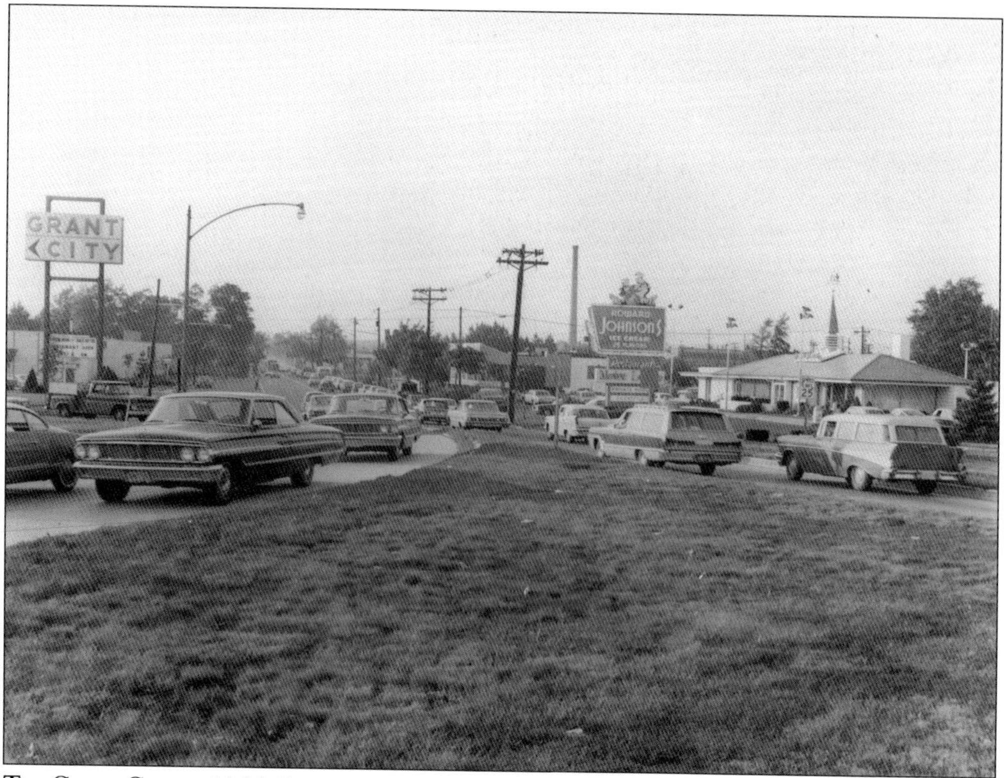

The Clark Circle, 1966. Since its inception in 1950, the Clark Parkway Circle, at exit 135 of the Garden State Parkway, has always been a high point of activity for the Clark Police Department. (Courtesy of the Clark History Room.)

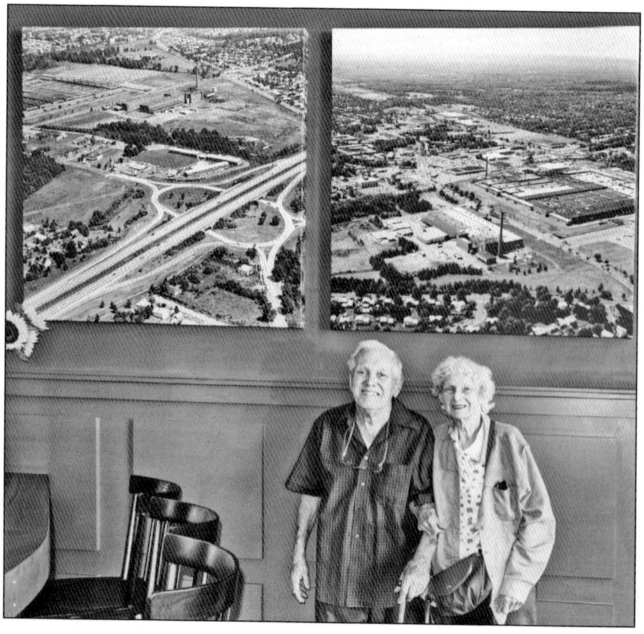

Working from the Air. Clark aerial photographer Carl S. Frank, a longtime resident and professional photographer, began taking aerial photographs of Clark, New Jersey, in 1952 and would continue until the year 2000. His photographs were giving to the police department to assist them in developing new safety measures for the growing township. Seen in this July 7, 2015, photograph are Carl Frank and his wife, Mildred Frank, at the dedication and grand opening of Whole Foods Clark. Three of Carl Frank's aerial photographs are on permanent display in the new store. (Courtesy of Diane Frank Metz.)

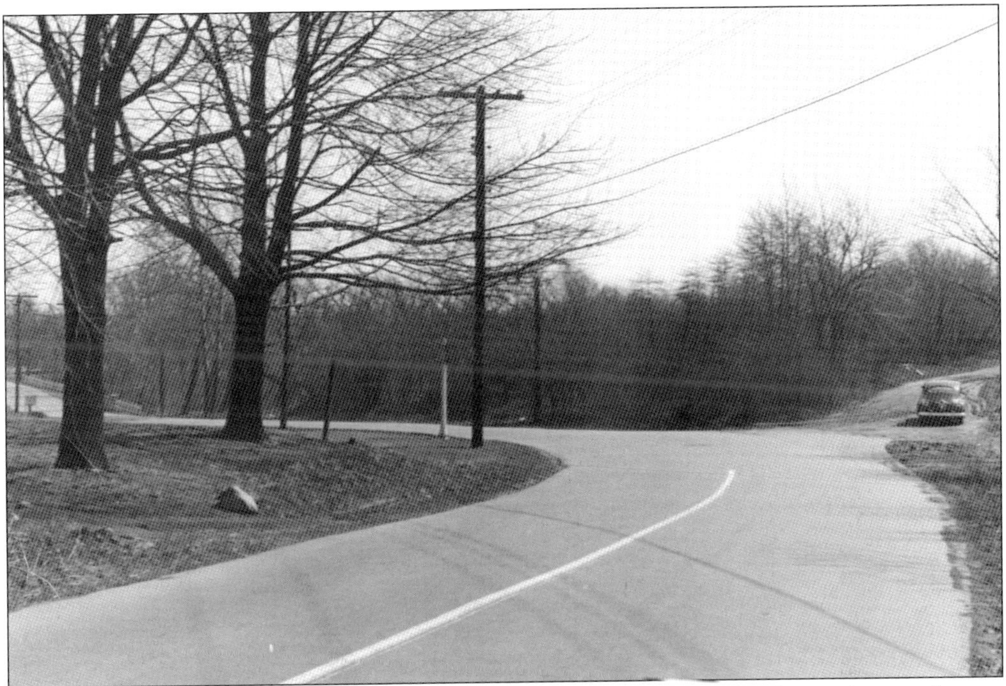

Madison Hill Road Curve. With the advancement of the automobile, this roadway and curve became a center of Clark police activity though much of the 1950s until the 1970s, with a large volume of motor vehicle accidents. (Courtesy of the Clark History Room.)

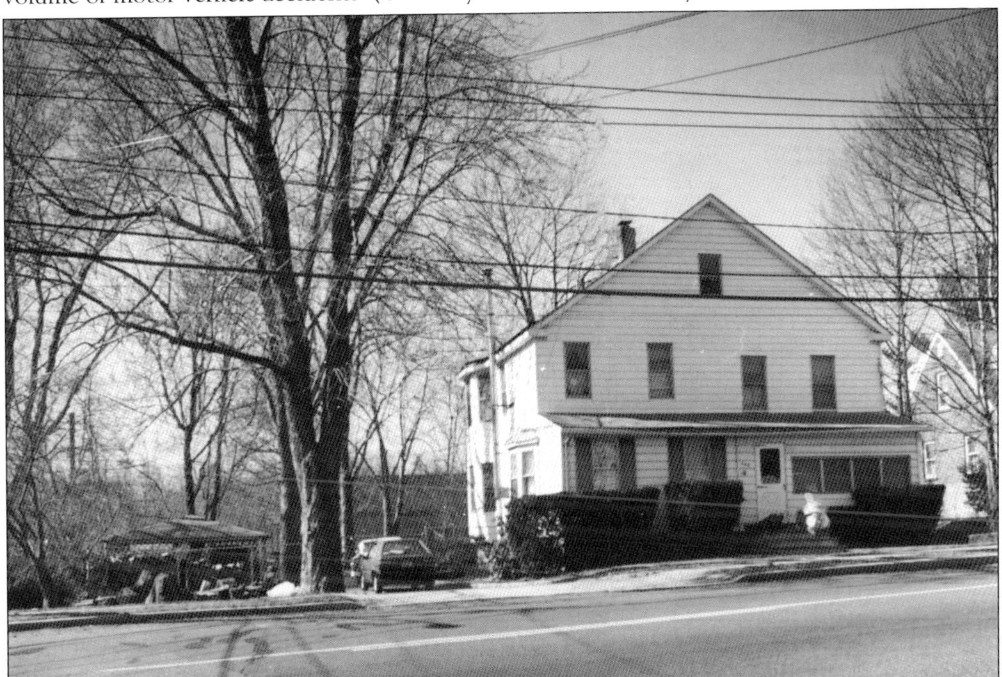

Madison Hill Road Curve and House. Through much of the 1970s, this roadway curve and the house located at Madison Hill Road were the scene of many fatal accidents and community tragedies that became a major concern for Clark Police. (Courtesy of the Clark History Room.)

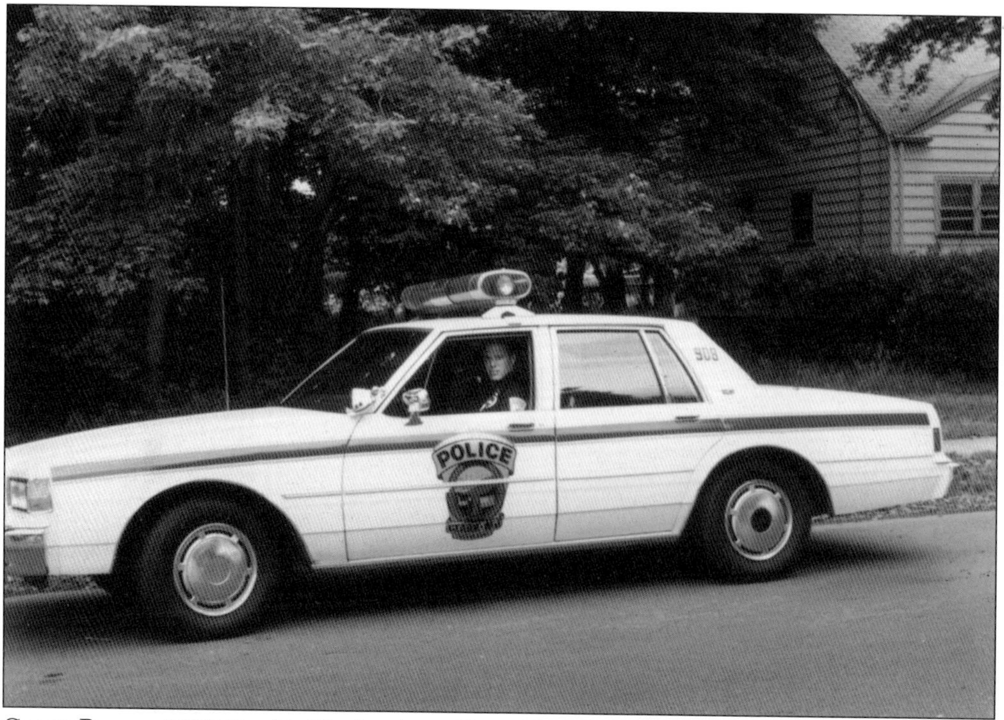

Clark Police, 1990. Rookie Clark police officer Alan Sherb sits in a brand new 1990 Chevrolet Caprice in this July 1990 photograph. (Courtesy of the Clark History Room.)

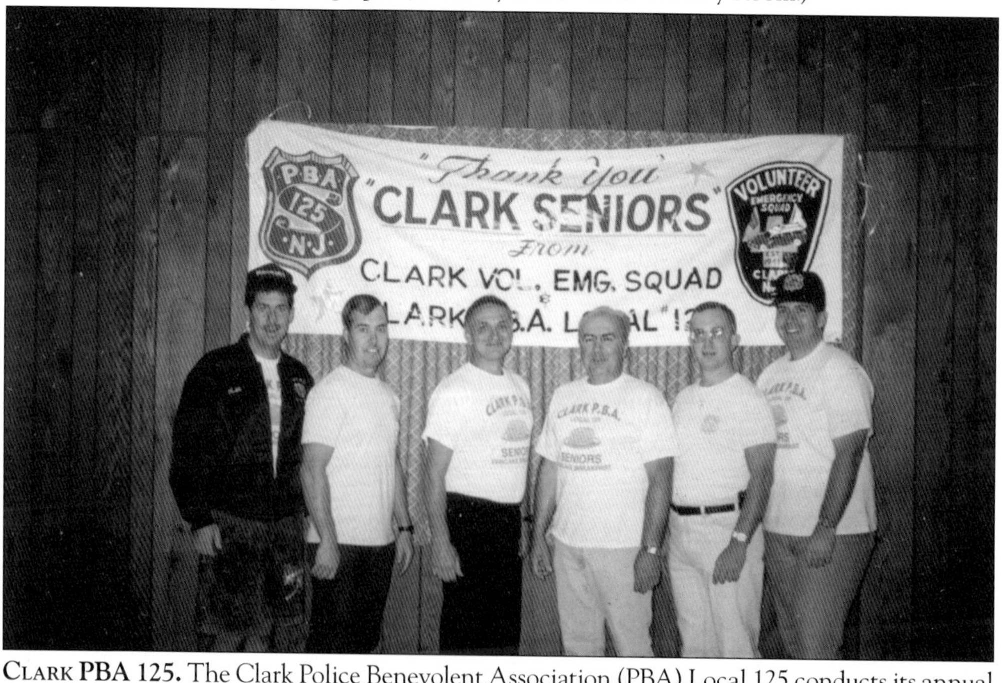

Clark PBA 125. The Clark Police Benevolent Association (PBA) Local 125 conducts its annual pancake breakfast at the Volunteer Emergency Squad House as a way to reach out to Clark seniors. Pictured from left to right are police officers Keith Dunn, Walt Merfert, Sgt. Vic DeMarzo, Bob Bob Romano, Walter Lelanko and Dennis Reilly. (Courtesy of Victor DeMarzo.)

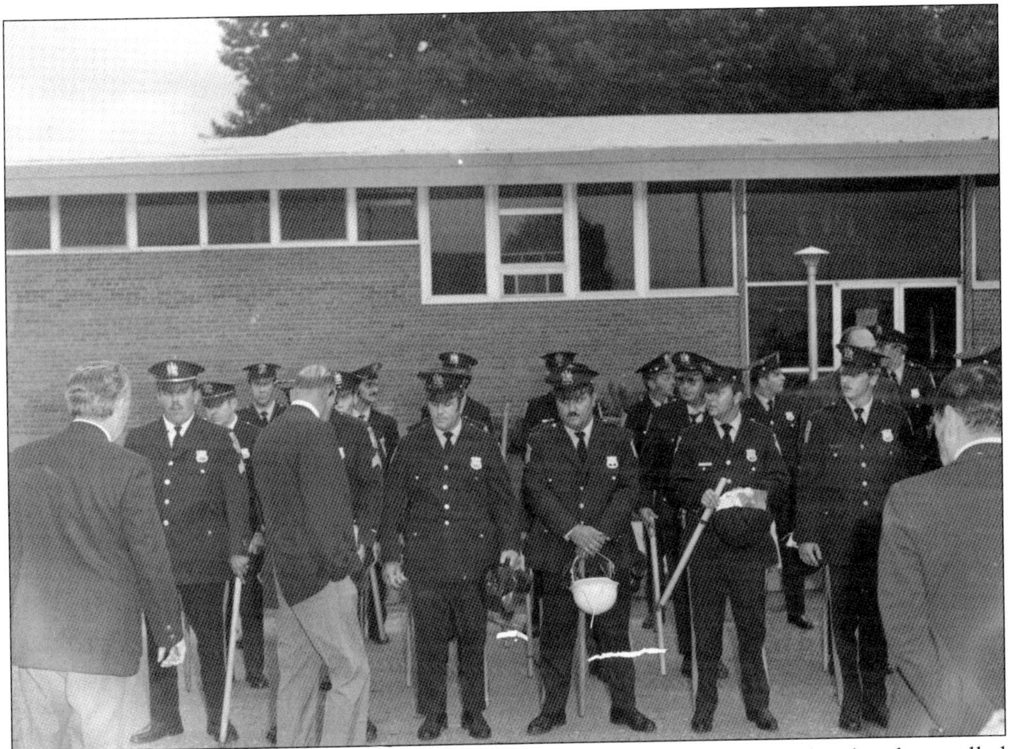

Roll Call and Inspection. This 1964 photograph shows members of the Clark police force called to order to have a departmental inspection with police captain John Waterson, who conducts a troop and equipment inspection. (Courtesy of Victor DeMarzo.)

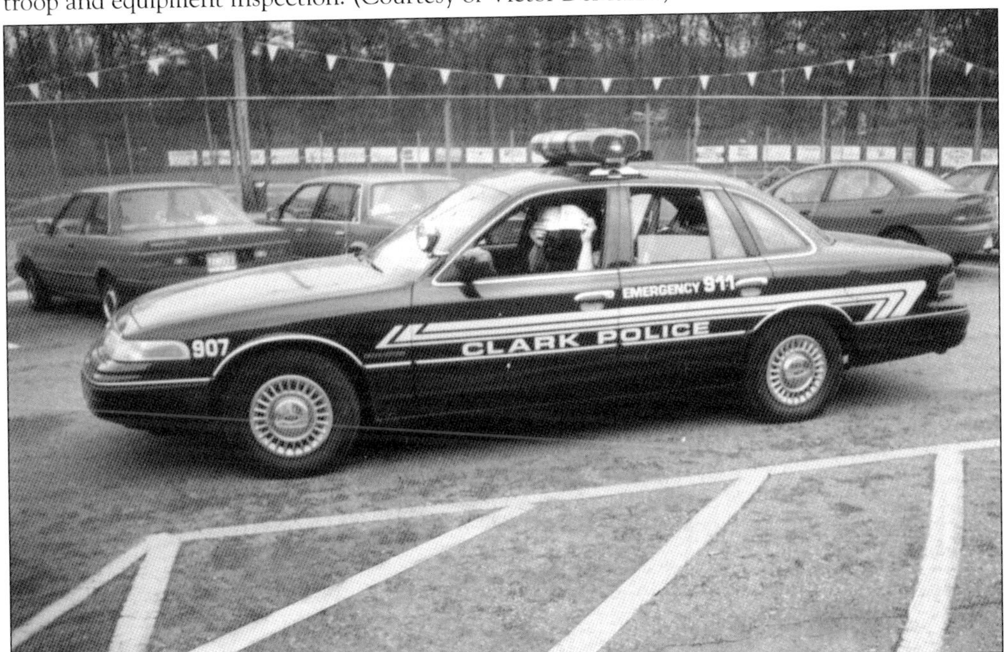

Clark Police, 1994. Seen here is the department's new 1994 Ford Police Inceptor in a new color scheme for the 1990s. (Courtesy of Victor DeMarzo.)

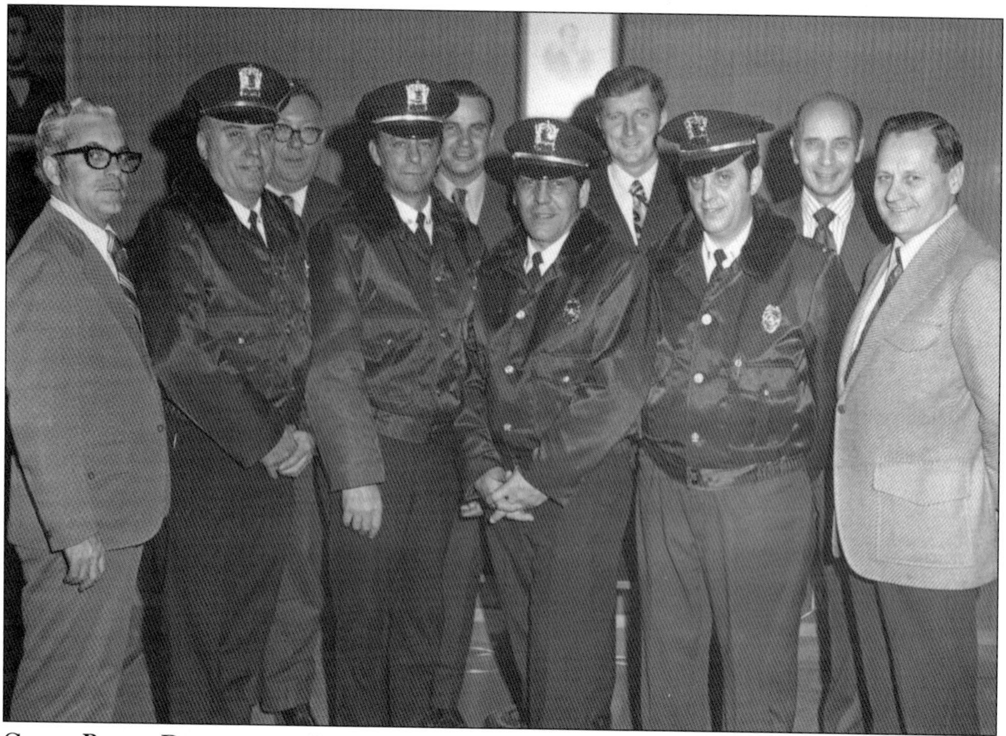

Clark Police Department Special Traffic Bureau. In 1976, the Clark Police Department added a specially trained part-time police officer to its ranks. These officers were used to fill in areas where regular police officers were not available, including at local sporting events, parades, and community celebration events. From left to right are (first row) Councilman Manuel Dios; special police officers Harry Mathis, Gordon Lechner, Joseph Antunci, unidentified, and Mayor Bernard Yarusavage; (second row) public safety director Robert Taylor, two unidentified, and police chief Anthony Smar. (Courtesy of the Clark History Room.)

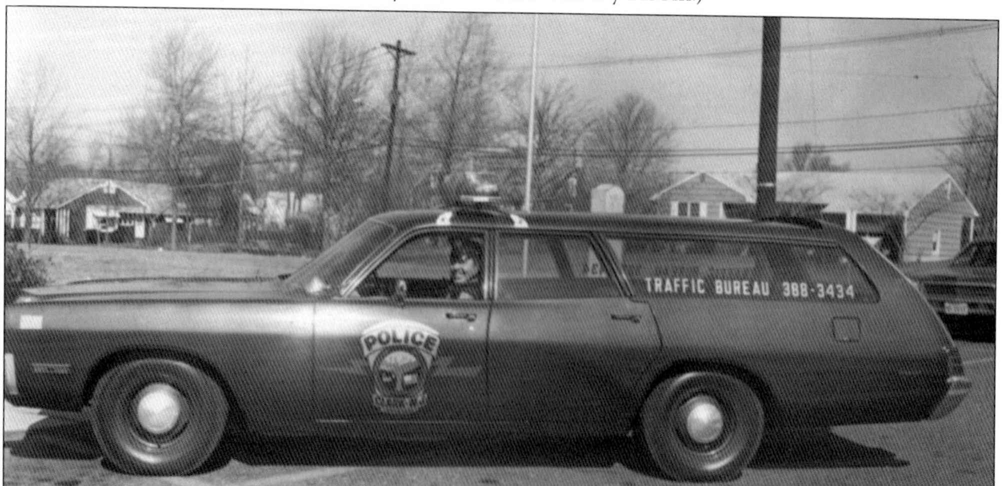

Clark Traffic Bureau. During the 1960s and 1970s, Clark Township Police Department Traffic Bureau was led by one of the department's more popular officers, Roy George, who handled all the traffic and safety issues. (Courtesy of the Clark History Room.)

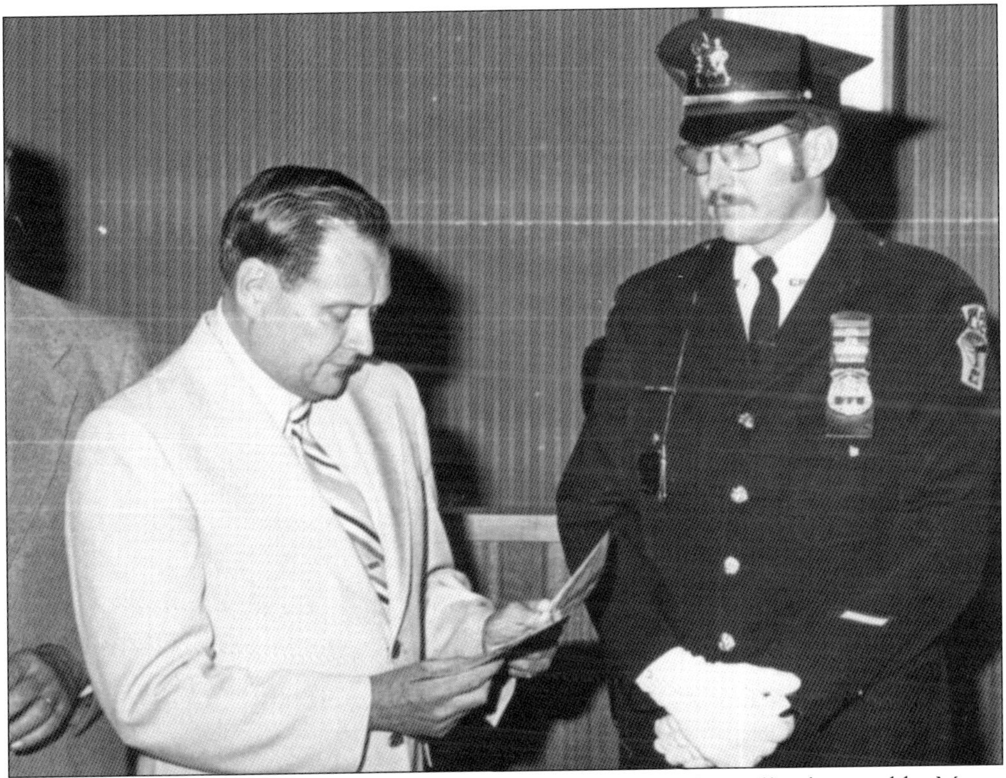

Saving Lives. On January 17, 1977, Clark police officer Denis Connell is honored by Mayor Bernard G. Yarusavage and the township council with a medal of honor. He saved the lives of three residents in a house fire in December 1976 on Haliday Street. The fire claimed two lives in the community tragedy. (Courtesy of the Clark History Room.)

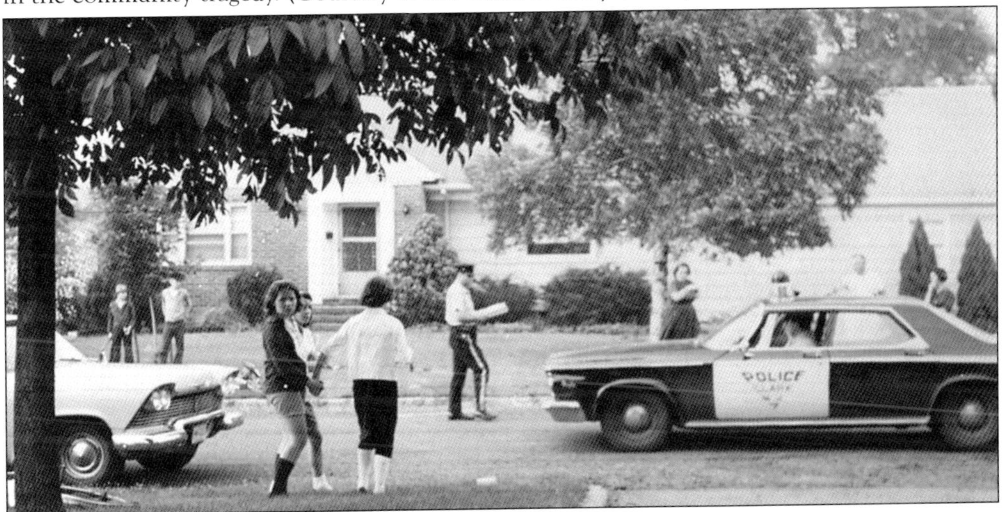

Responding to Aid a Clark Child Trapped Under Her Parents' Vehicle. Clark police officer Robert Hartong Sr. responds to aid the five-year-old girl, Susan Frank Bruno, while riding her tricycle on Wendell Place. When her father's vehicle's brakes failed, the vehicle rolled back and trapped the young girl underneath it. Police and rescue squad member were ablel to save the girl's life. The photograph was taken June 8, 1964. (Courtesy of Kim Frank.)

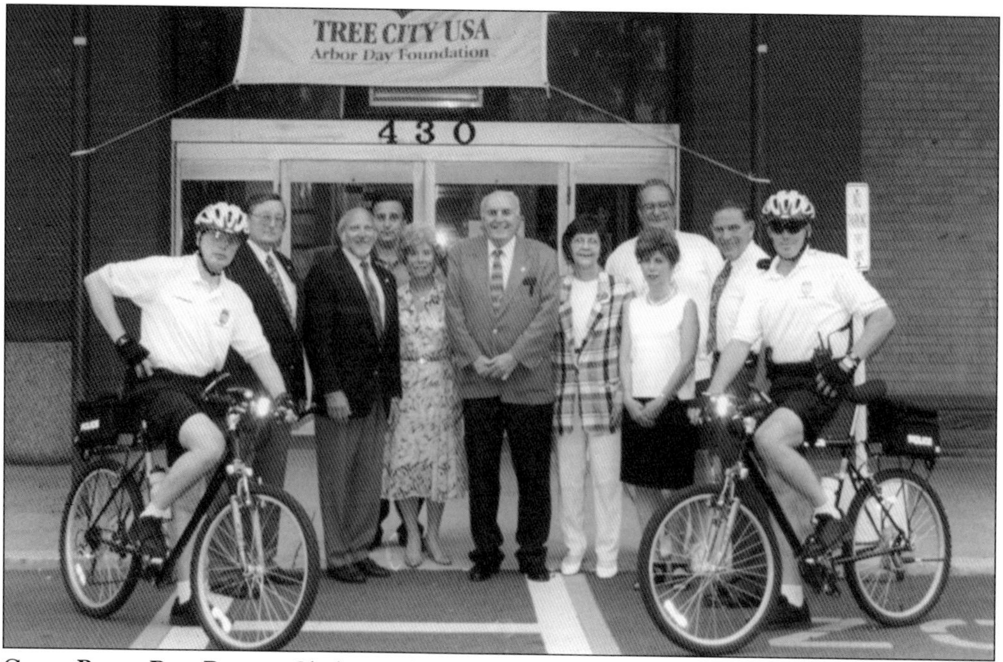

Clark Police Bike Patrol. Clark introduced a new bicycle patrol, as seen in this photograph with, from left to right, police officer Richard Hedenge, Councilman Rich Kazanowski, Mayor Robert Ellenport, Councilman Sal Bonaccorso, Councilwoman Dolores Memmer, Council Pres. Bill Kucher, Councilwoman Marie Soyka, Councilwoman Michele Cislo, Councilman Marty Ferrara, police chief Sandy Danco, and police officer James Pflug. (Courtesy of the Clark History Room.)

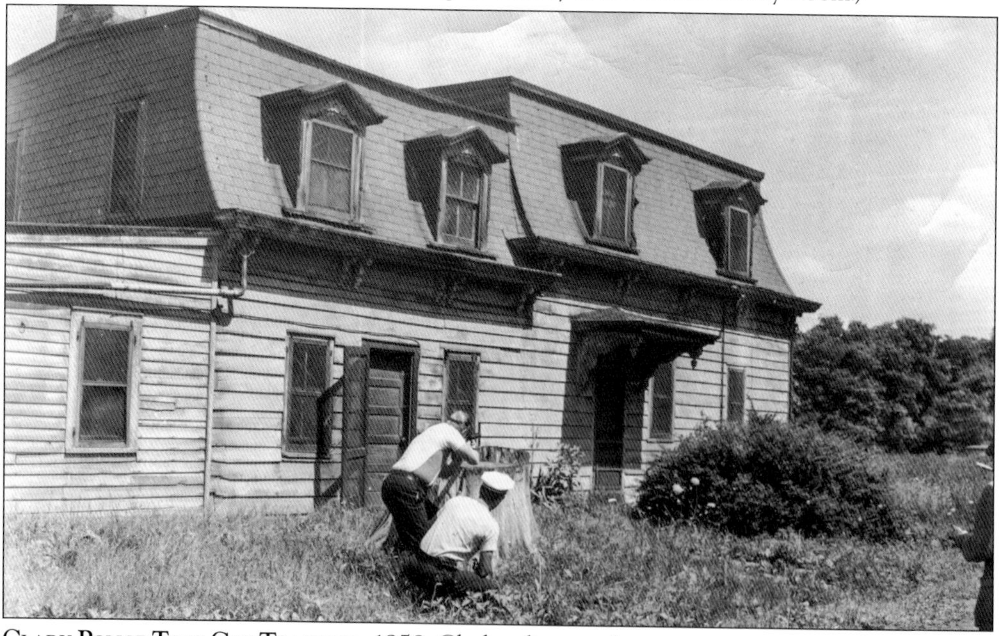

Clark Police Tear Gas Training, 1958. Clark police conduct tear gas training at the old Loeser Farm on Lake Avenue. It was common practice for the Clark Police and Fire Departments to hold training exercises on abandoned or soon-to-be-torn-down houses in the township. (Courtesy of the Clark History Room.)

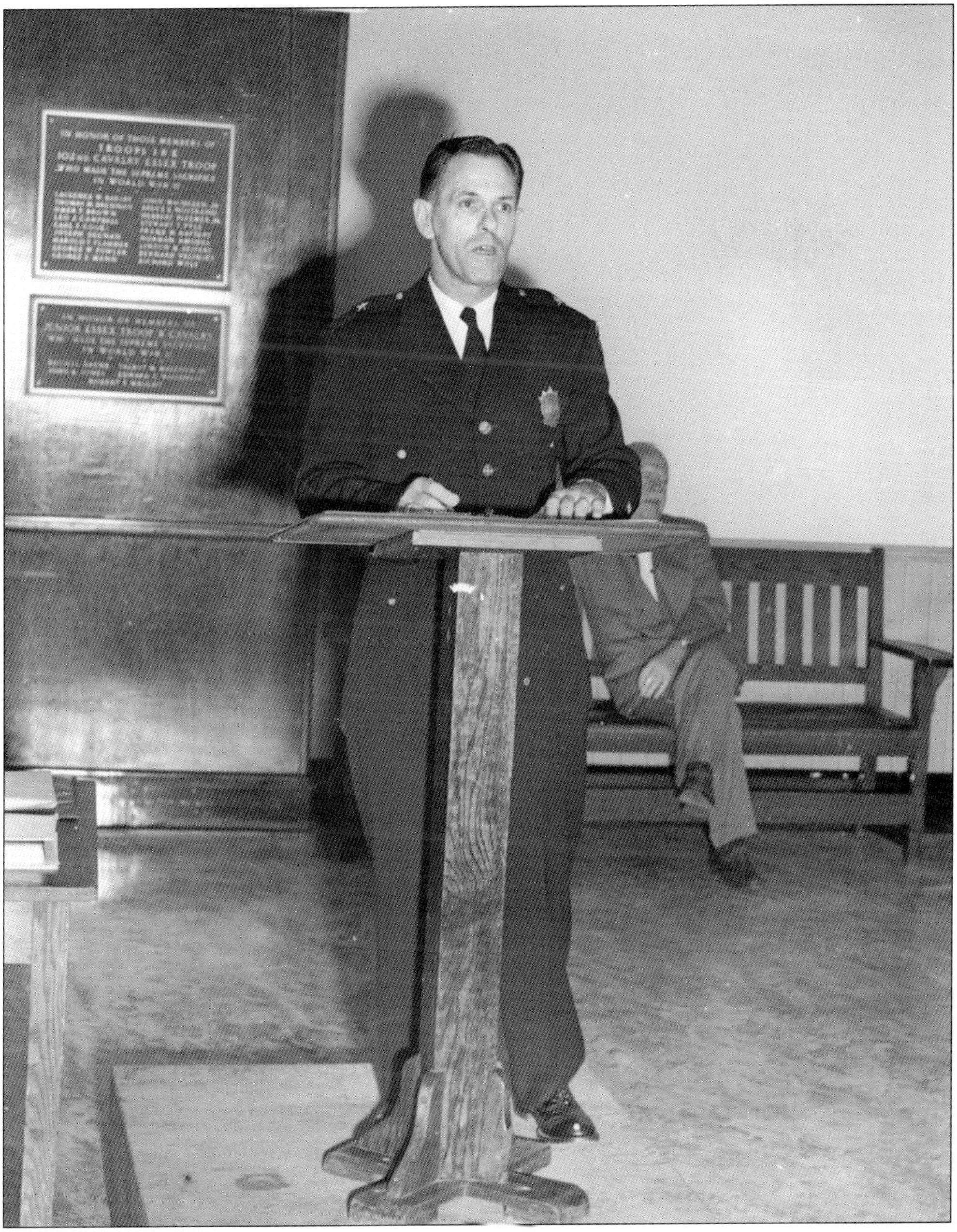

Police Chief William Muth. Muth served as the first full-time police chief in Clark from 1952 until his retirement in 1970. He is seen in this 1954 photograph at the state police headquarters giving a lecture on police procedure. (Courtesy of the Clark History Room.)

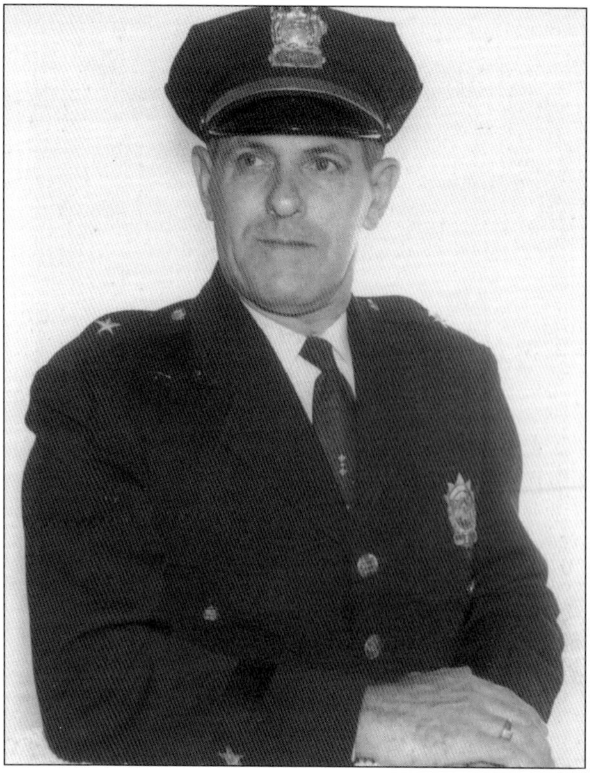

Police Chief William Muth and Police Chief Anthony P. Smar. Pictured at left is police chief William Muth, who served from 1952 to 1970. Below is a photograph of police chief Anthony P. Smar, who served from 1970 to 1989. (Both, courtesy of Clark History Room.)

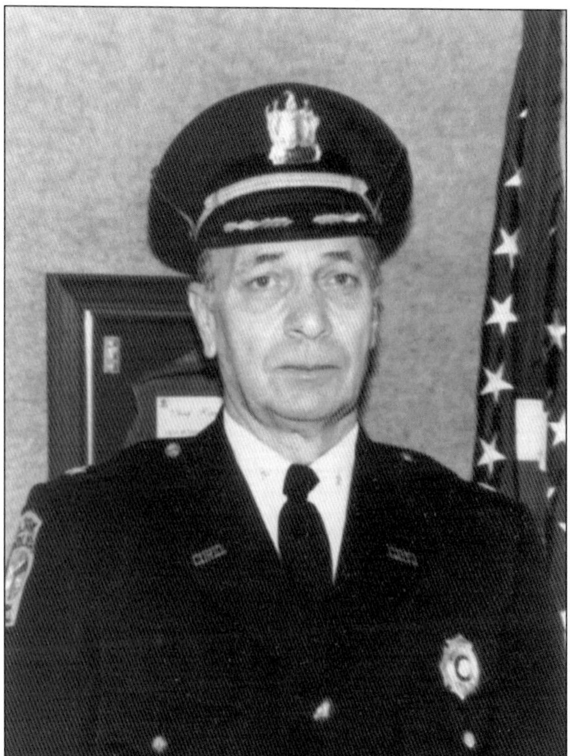

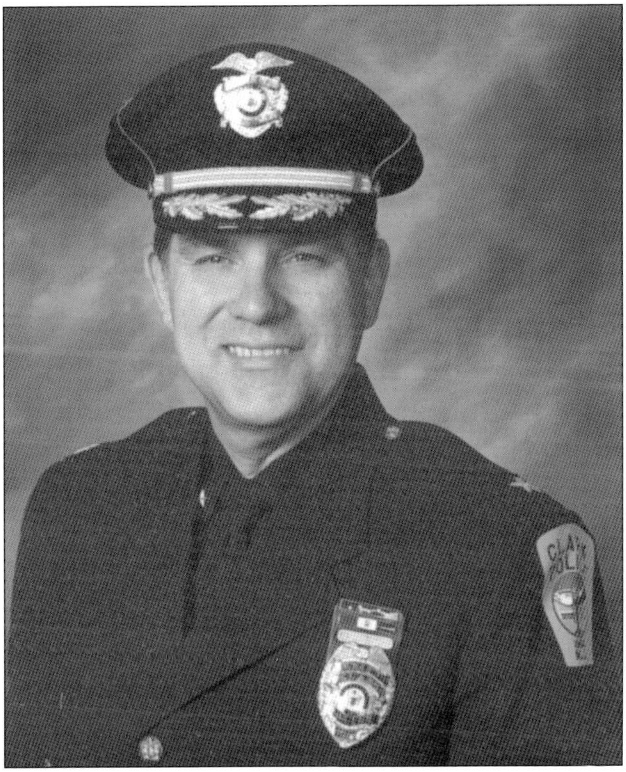

Police Chiefs Anton W. Danco Jr. and Dennis E. Connell Sr. At right is former police chief Anton W. Danco Jr., who served from 1989 to 2008. Seen below is police chief Dennis E. Connell Sr. who served from 2008 to 2011. (Both, courtesy of Clark History Room.)

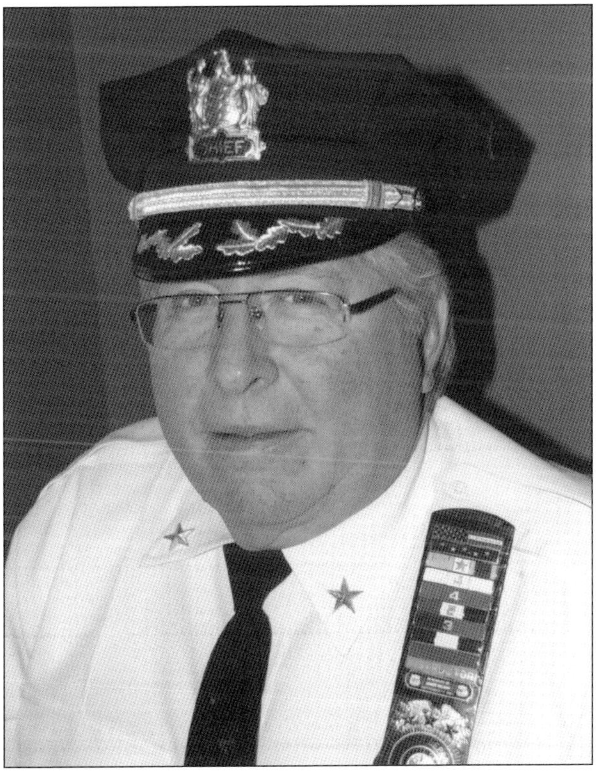

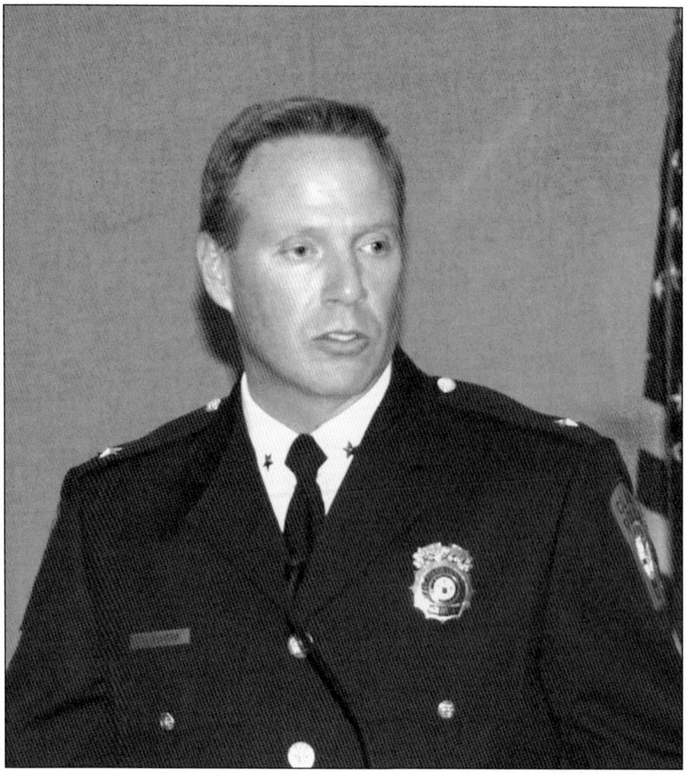

Police Chiefs Alan J. Sherb and Pedro Matos. Seen at left is police chief Alan J. Sherb, who served from 2011 to 2015. Chief Pedro Matos, seen below, entered the position in 2015. (Both, courtesy of Clark History Room.)

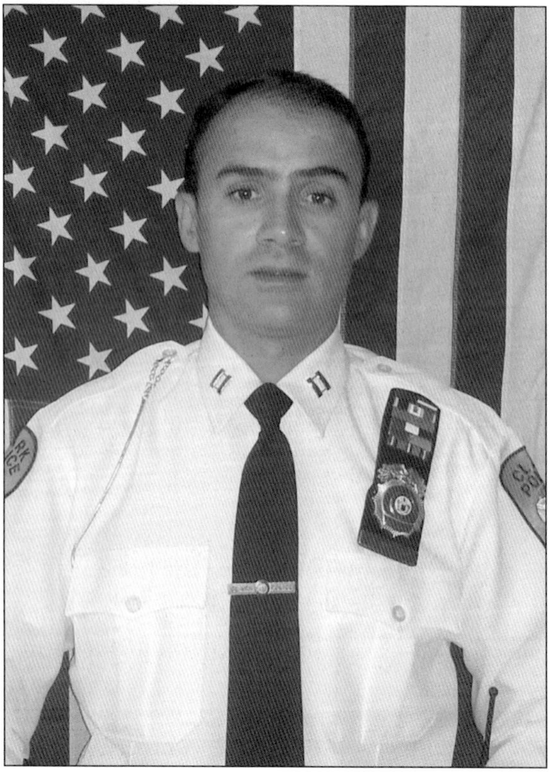

Four

July 4, 1971

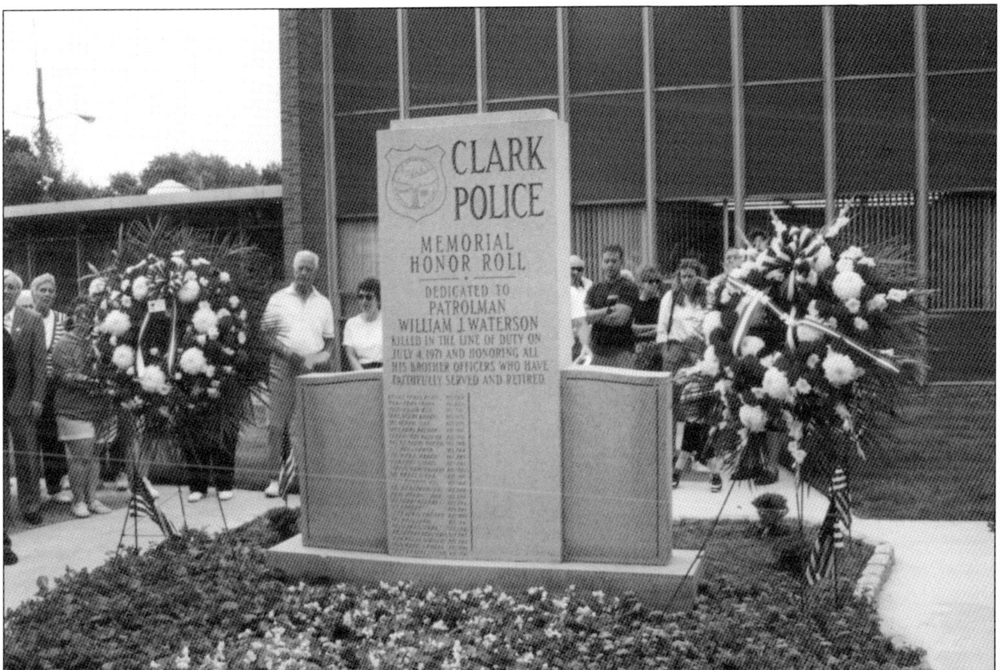

Memorial for Patrolman Waterson. The Clark Police Memorial Honor Roll is dedicated to Patrolman William "Billy" Waterson, the only Clark police officer to be killed in the line of duty. He died on July 4, 1971. (Courtesy of Victor DeMarzo.)

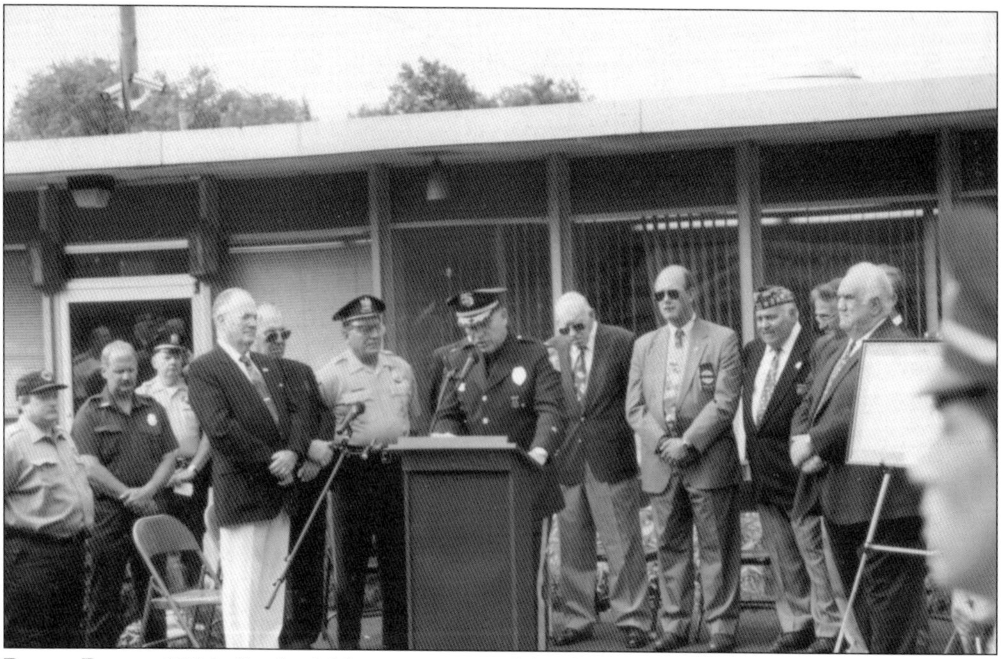

Police Plaza, 1996. On the 25th anniversary of the death of Patrolman Waterson, Clark PBA 125 rededicated the Waterson monument in front of the town's police headquarters. Shown here is police chief Anton "Sandy" Danco giving the opening remarks on July 4, 1996. (Courtesy of Victor DeMarzo.)

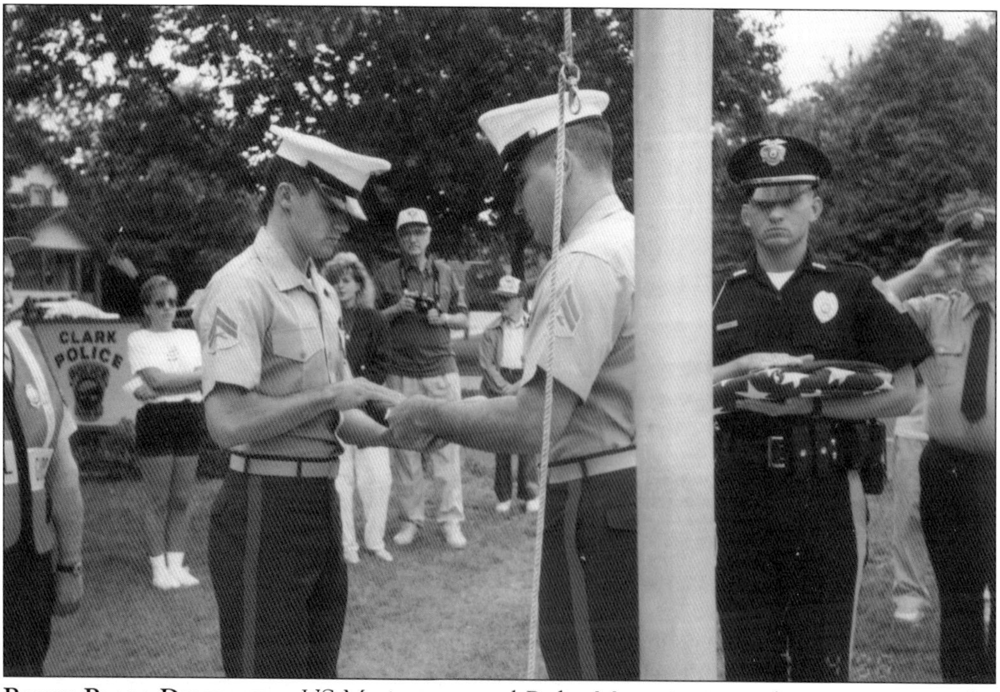

Police Plaza Dedication. US Marine corporal Pedro Matos is pictured prior to joining the Clark Police Department. He raises the American flag that was presented to the Waterson family. (Courtesy of Victor DeMarzo.)

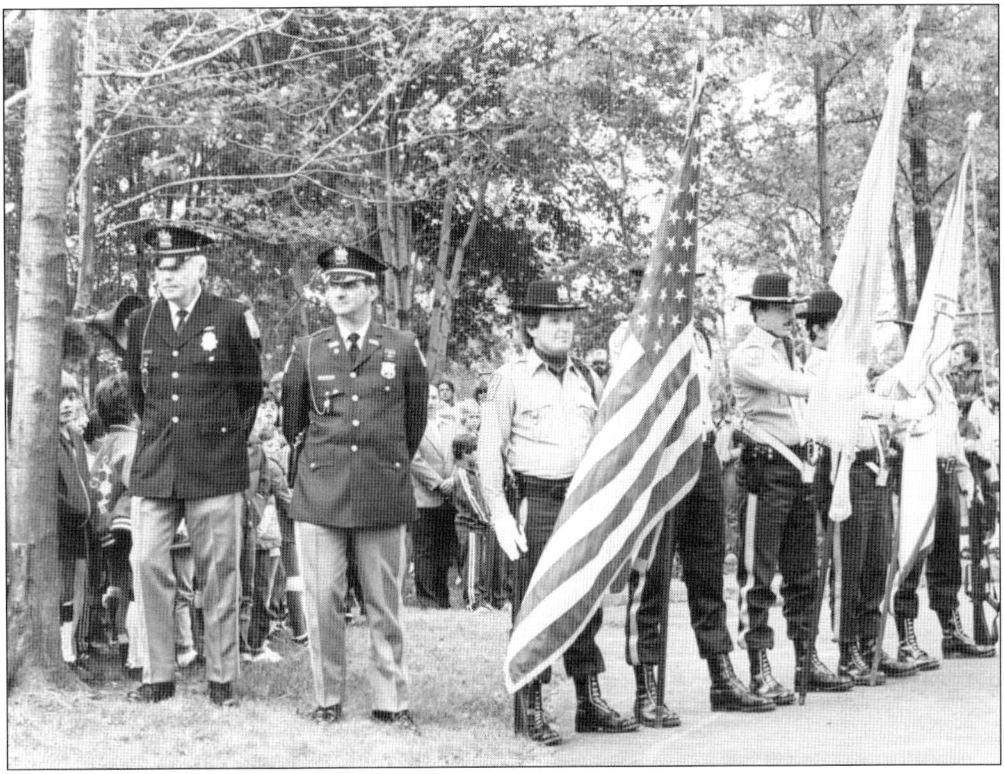

The Waterson Anniversary. In 1981, on the 10-year anniversary of the death of Patrolman Waterson, the Township of Clark and PBA 125 dedicated an athletic field at the end of Bartell Place in his memory. (Courtesy of Victor DeMarzo.)

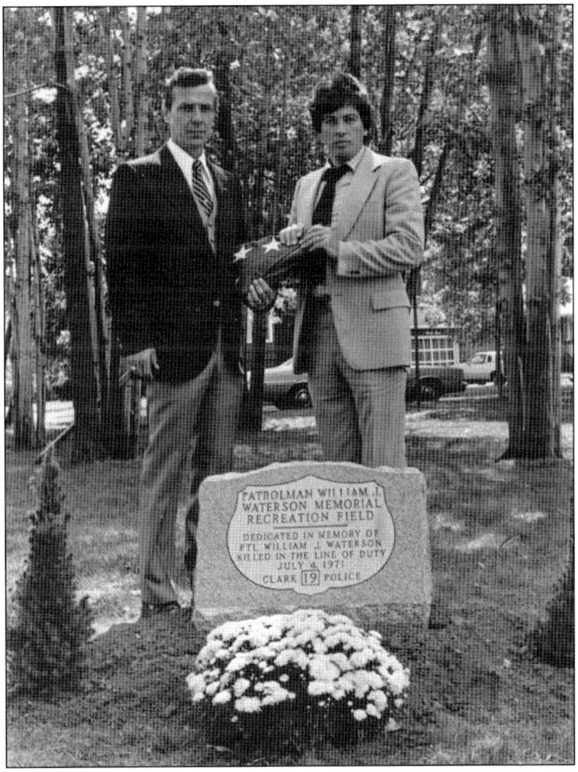

Waterson Field, 1981. In this photograph are the dedication marker and Clark police lieutenant Michael Kuch (left) and Clark police sergeant Robert Clark, a longtime friend of Billy Waterson, on July 4, 1981. (Courtesy of Victor DeMarzo.)

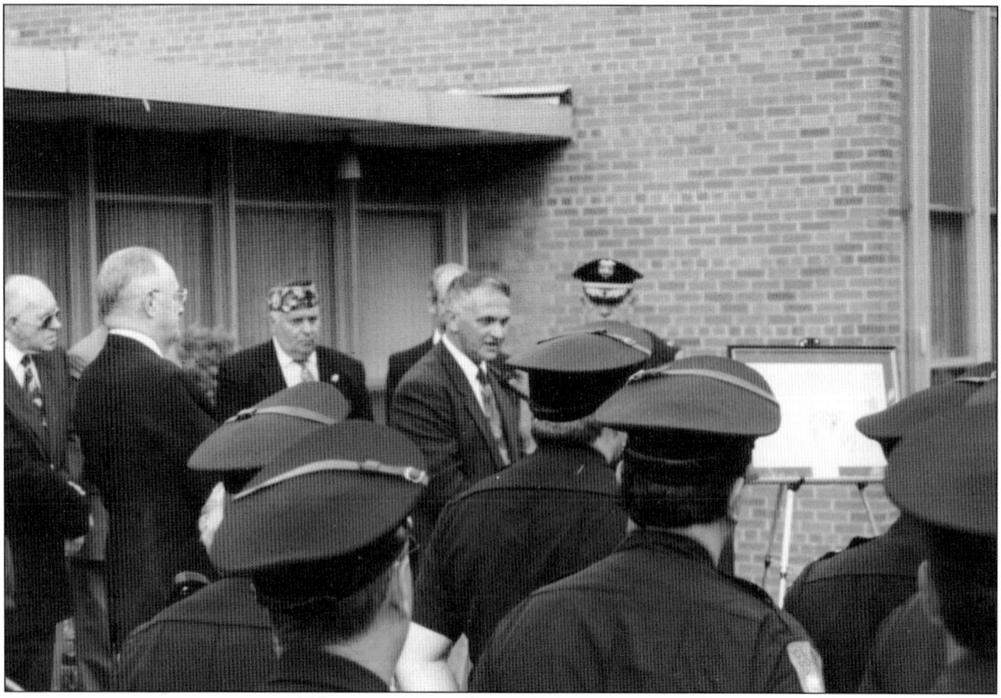

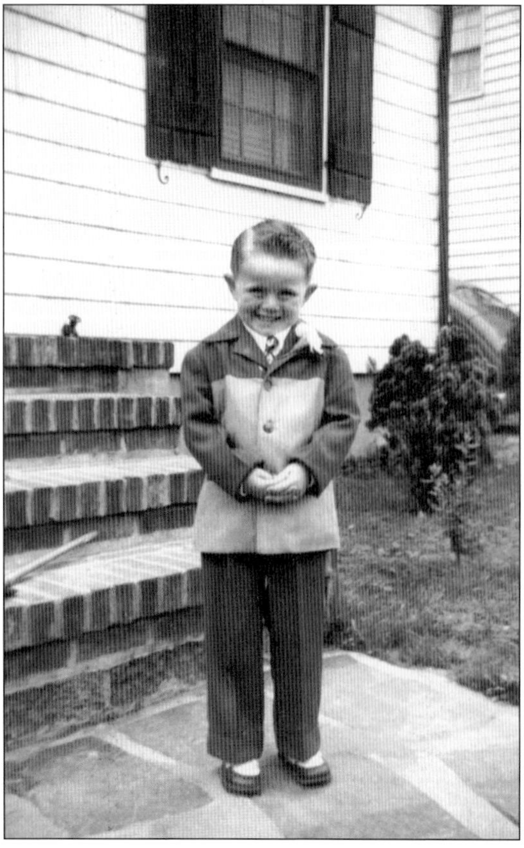

PBA 125 DEDICATION, 1996. PBA 125 president Victor DeMarzo, a retired police detective, led the project of creating the new police plaza to honor Patrolman Waterson and past Clark police officers. (Courtesy of Victor DeMarzo.)

BILLY WATERSON, 1951. Five-year-old Billy Waterson is pictured front of his childhood home at 7 Jeney Lane during Easter in 1951. (Courtesy of Jenny Waterson Black.)

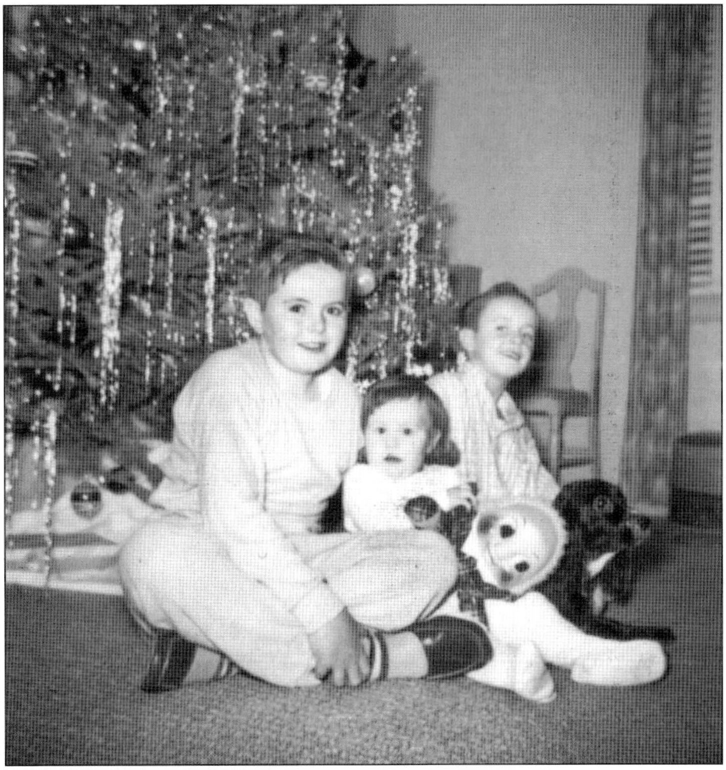

Christmas at the Watersons, 1953. Seen here from left to right are Billy Waterson, sister Jenny Waterson, and brother Edward Waterson. (Courtesy of Jenny Waterson Black.)

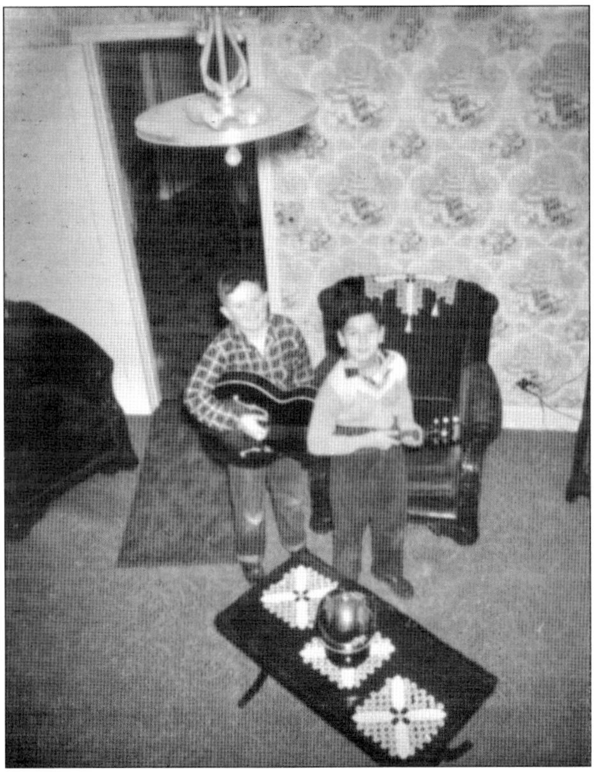

Dueling Guitars. Billy Waterson (left) and Joseph Lubrano rock the house during the musical craze of the mid-1950s (Courtesy of Jenny Waterson Black.)

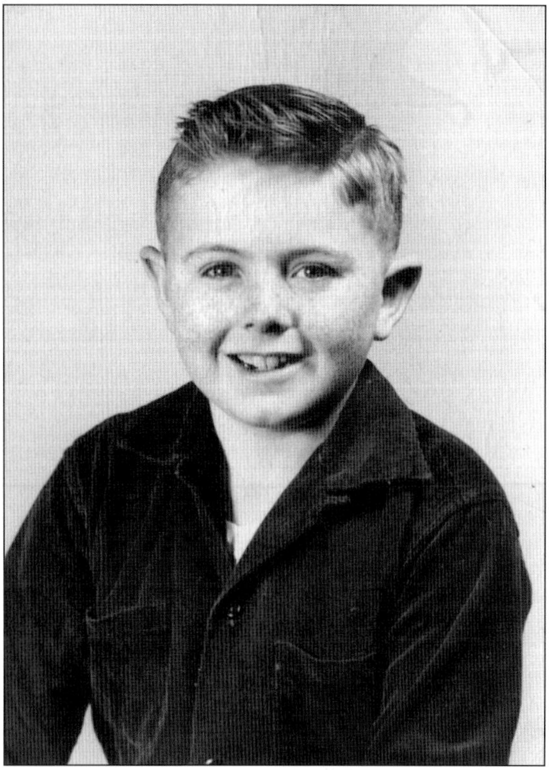

WILLIAM J . WATERSON. Shown here is Billy Waterson's sixth-grade photograph from Abraham Clark School. (Courtesy of Jenny Waterson Black.)

BILLY WATERSON, AGE 13. Billy Waterson is seen in this 1959 photograph at his home at 7 Janie Lane smiling with his pet dog Rex. (Courtesy of Jenny Waterson Black.)

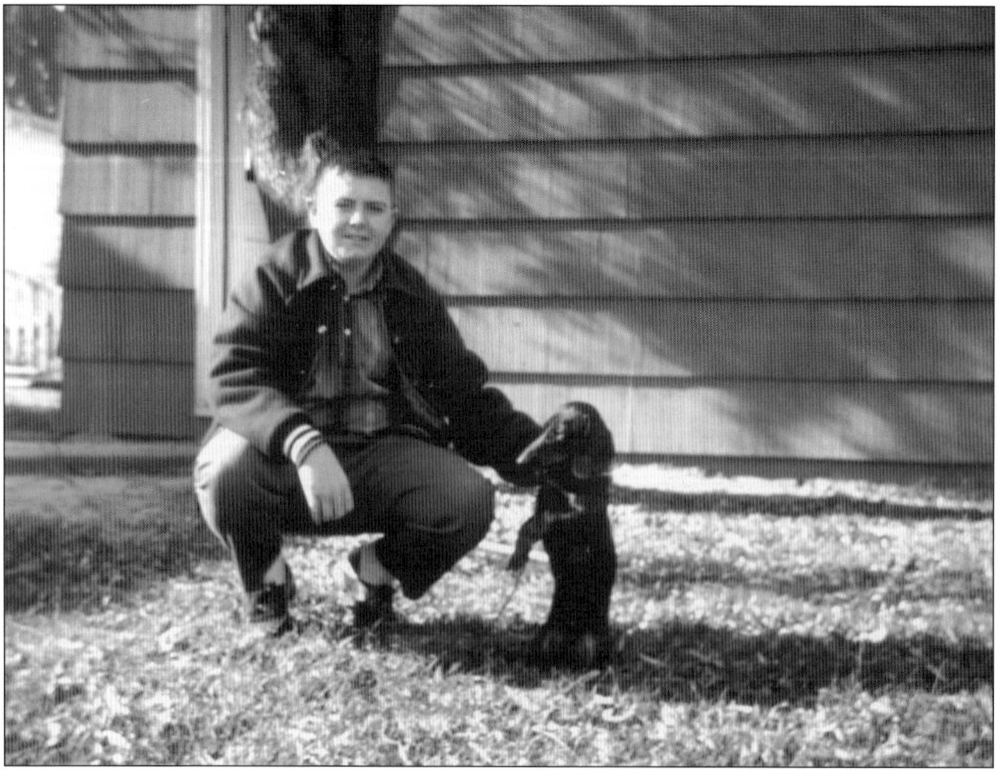

Eighth-Grade Graduation. This 1961 image shows Billy Waterson graduating from Charles H. Brewer School in Clark, New Jersey. (Courtesy of Jenny Waterson Black.)

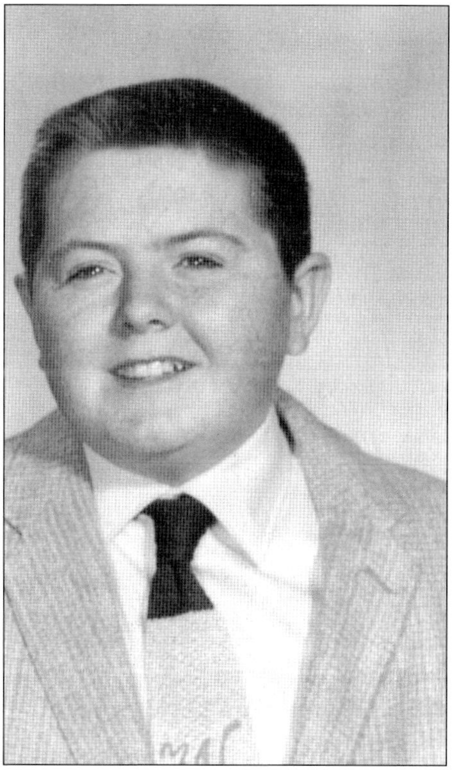

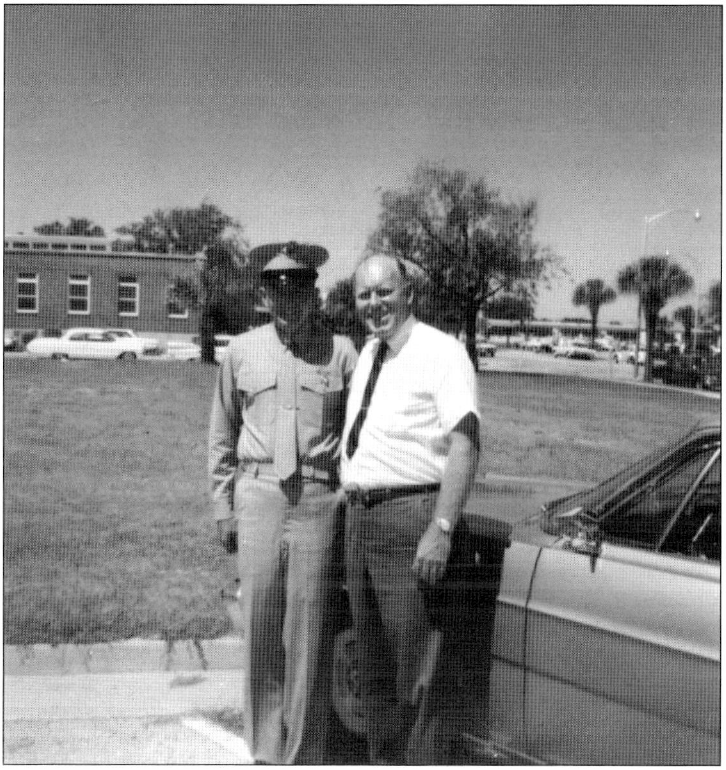

US Marine Private First Class William J. Waterson. Upon graduating from Arthur L. Johnson High School in 1965, Billy joined the US Marines. He is seen here with his father, Capt. John Waterson, after he completed basic training in the spring of 1966. In September 1966, Billy was sent to Vietnam. (Courtesy of Jenny Waterson Black.)

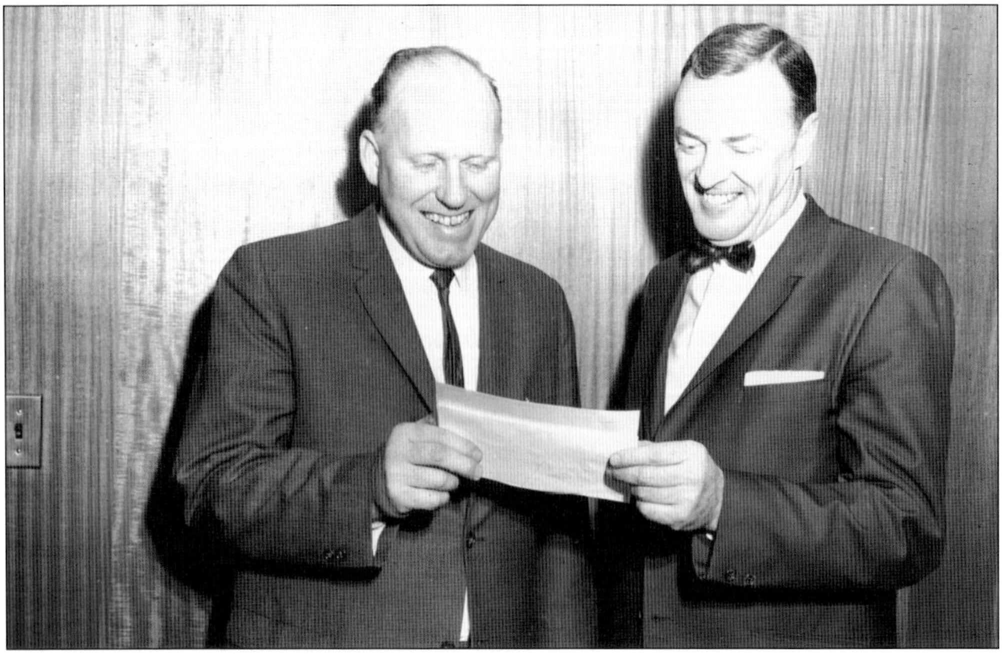

Captain Waterson and Mayor Maguire. Capt. John Waterson (left) and Mayor William Maguire are seen here accepting a contribution to the community's fundraising drive in support of troops from Clark that were serving in foreign wars. (Courtesy of Jenny Waterson Black.)

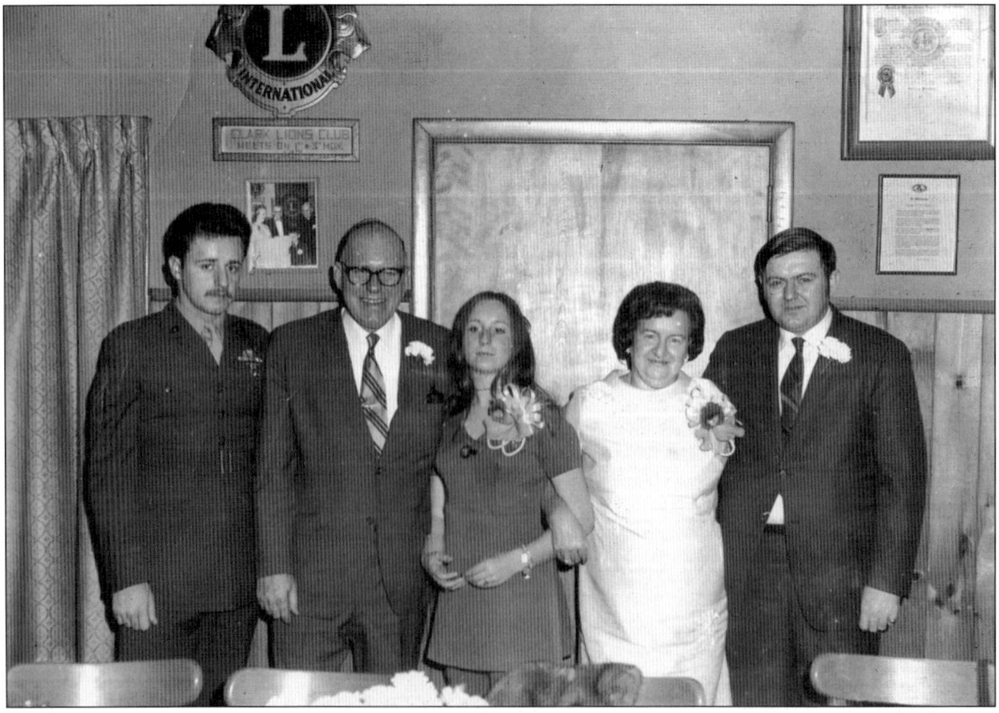

Waterson Family. Seen in this 1969 photograph are, from left to right, Edward Waterson, Capt. John Waterson, Jenny Waterson, Edna Waterson, and Billy Waterson. (Courtesy of Jenny Waterson Black.)

Billy and Jenny. In the fall of 1964, Billy Waterson was a member of the Arthur L. Johnson football team. Billy is seen here after a victory is picking up his sister, Jenny. (Courtesy of Jenny Waterson Black.)

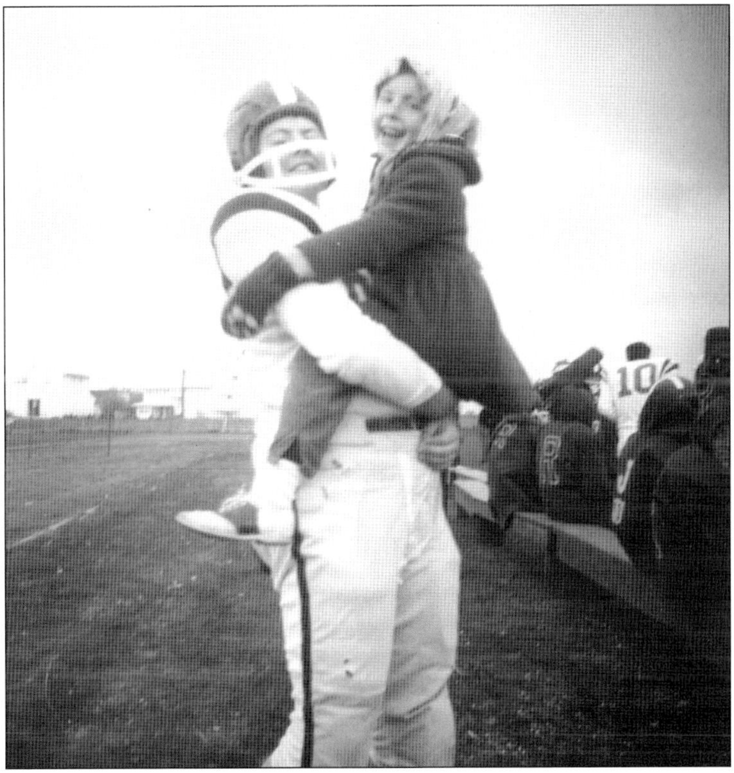

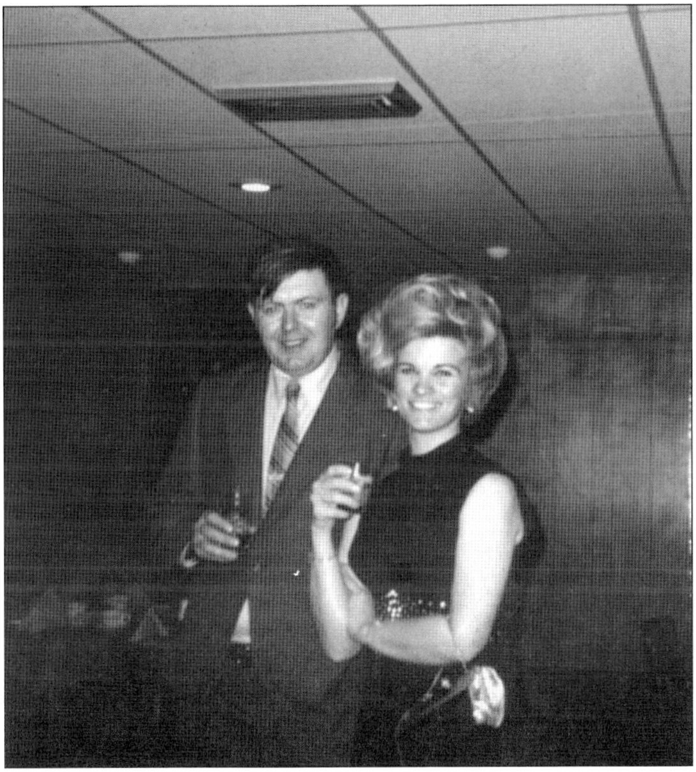

Billy Waterson and Veronica Scott. After returning from Vietnam in early 1969, Billy Waterson joined the Clark Township Police Department and became engaged to local girl Veronica Scott. (Courtesy of Jenny Waterson Black.)

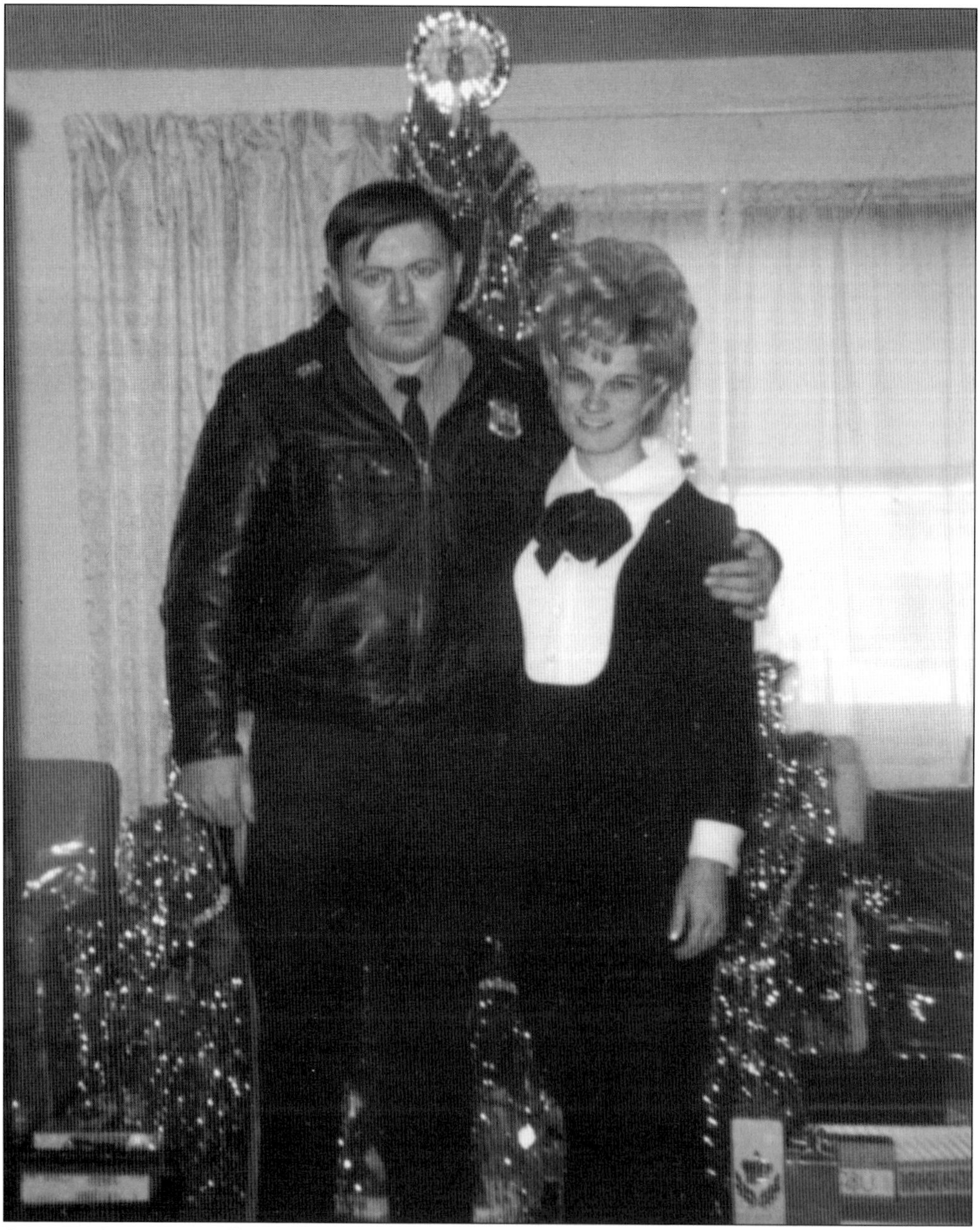

CHRISTMAS, 1970. William Waterson, age 24, and his fiancée, Veronica Scott, stand in front of the Waterson Christmas tree in 1970. (Courtesy of Jenny Waterson Black.)

Five

CLARK VOLUNTEER EMERGENCY SQUAD

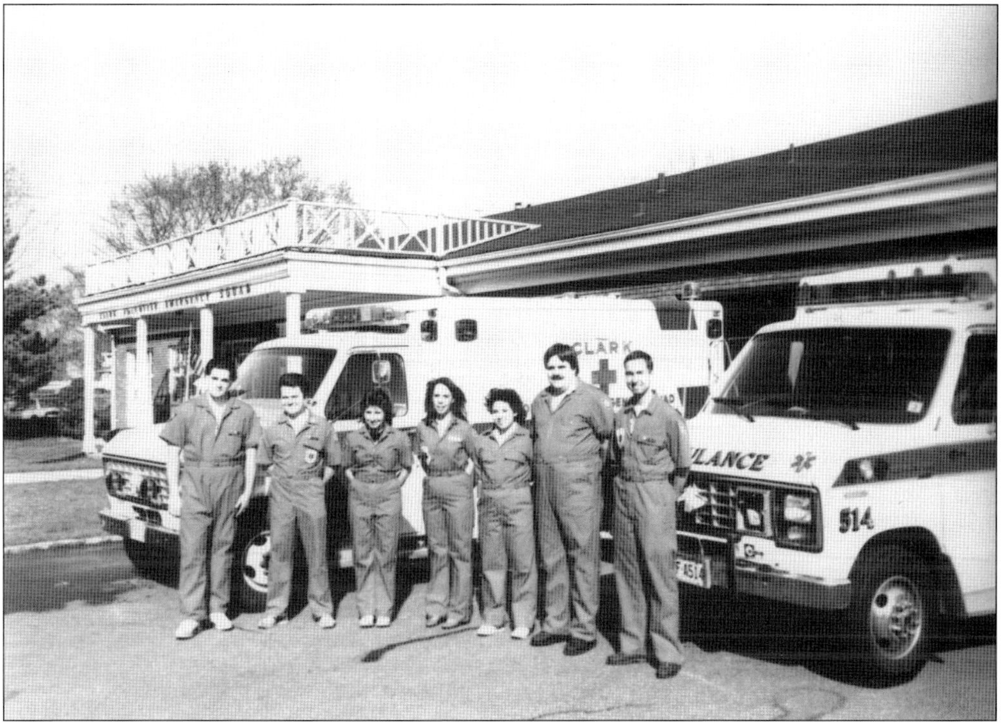

CLARK VOLUNTEER EMERGENCY SQUAD, 1992. Members of the 1992 Clark Volunteer Emergency Squad stand in front of the Raritan Road Squad House. Seen in this image are, from left to right, Randy Schwartz, Peter Watson, Anne Marie Krok, Laurie Flood, Pres. Beth Long, Gary Long, and Mike Prail. (Courtesy of the Clark Volunteer Emergency Squad.)

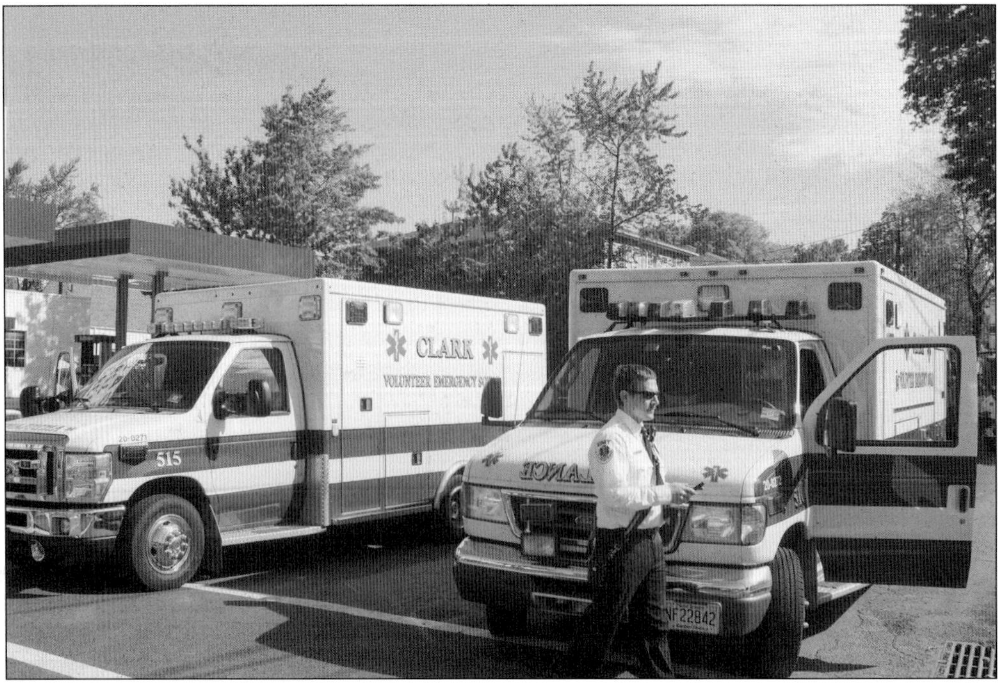

First Responders. Clark Volunteer Emergency Squad Ambulances 515 and 516 are a call away when the cry for help sounds. This is a 2005 photograph of the volunteer squad at a community event. (Courtesy of the Clark Volunteer Emergency Squad.)

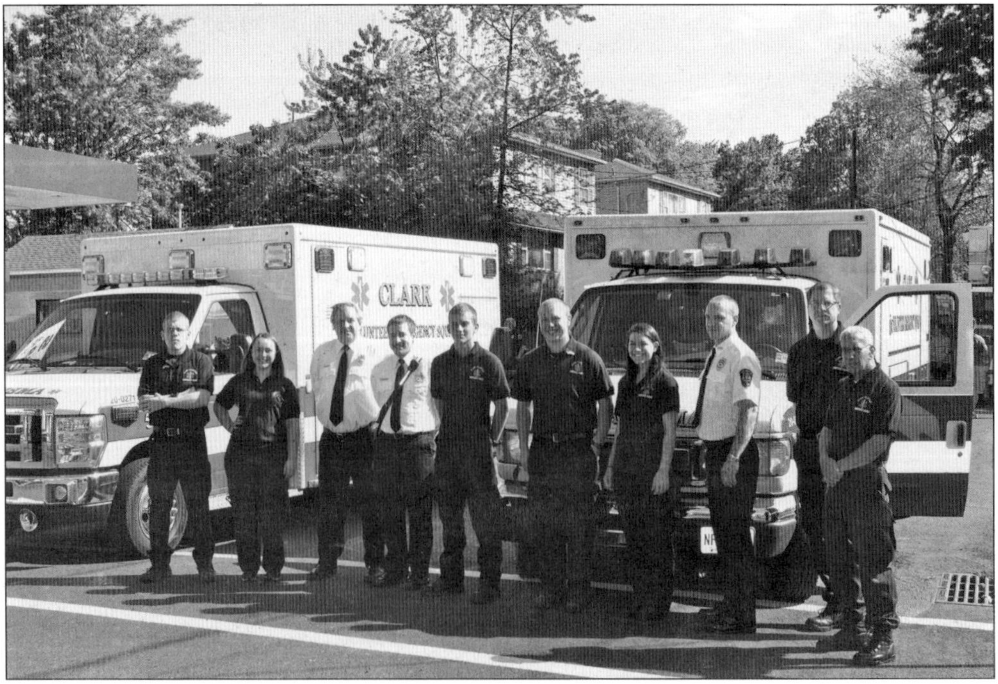

Clark Volunteer Emergency Squad, 2012. Included in this picture are Gerald Pobuta, Katherine Hicks, Michael Hajkowski, and Pres. Ron Weslowski, members of the 2012 Clark Volunteer Emergency Squad. (Courtesy of the Clark Volunteer Emergency Squad.)

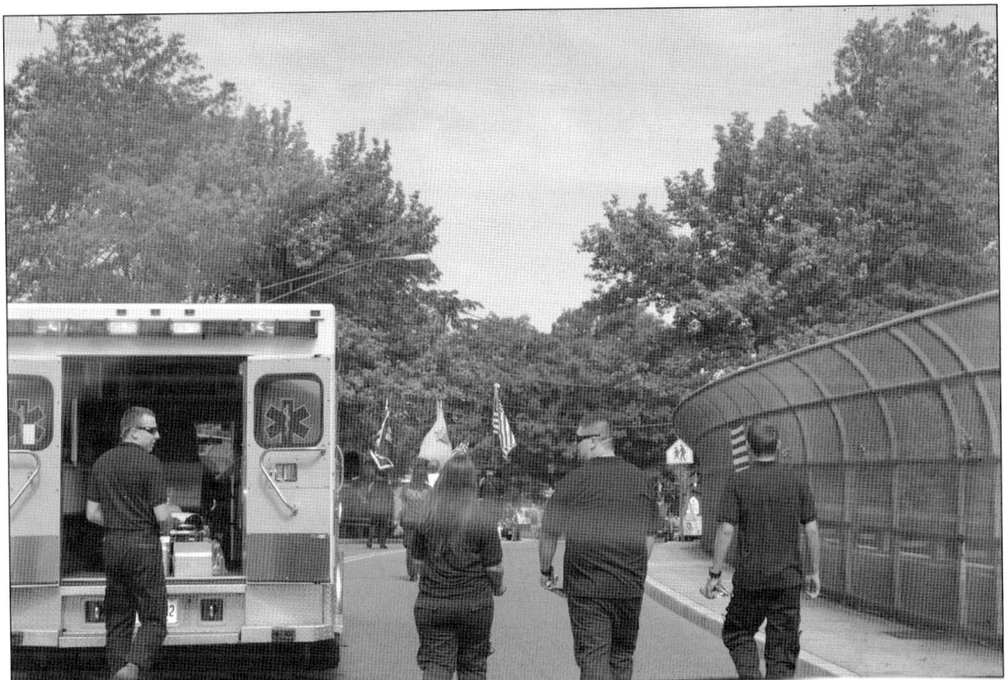

Clark Volunteer Emergency Squad, 2014. The members of the 2014 Clark Volunteer Emergency Squad led field commander Ryan Wakstein's march in the township's annual Memorial Day parade, following ambulance 516. (Courtesy of the Clark Volunteer Emergency Squad.)

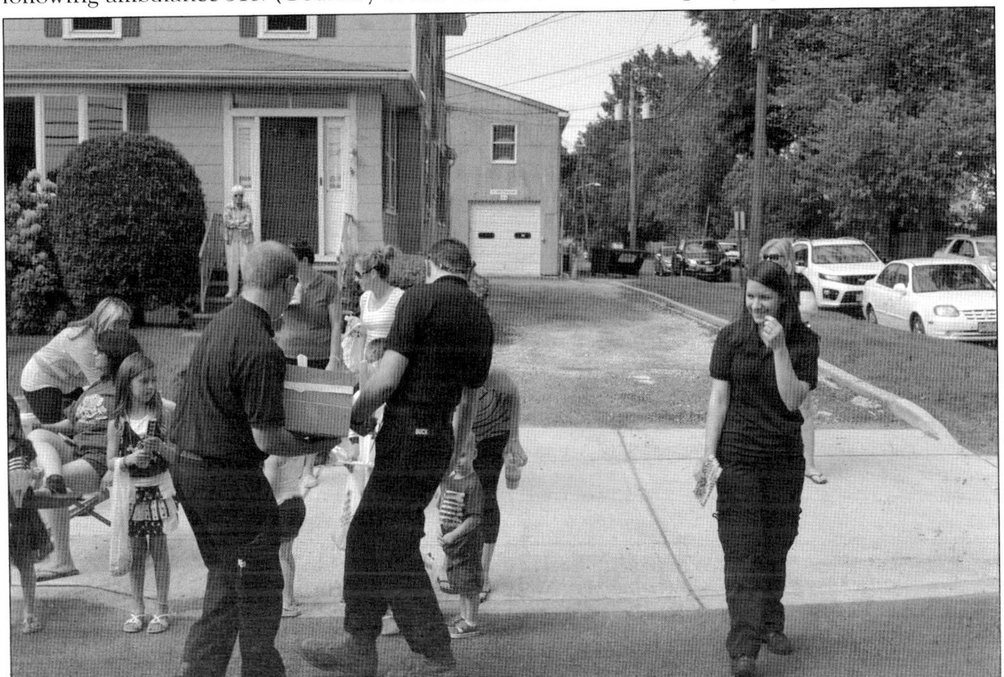

Memorial Day Parade 2012. Members of the Clark Volunteer Emergency Squad participate in the Memorial Day parade. Here they are giving out free ice cream to the children of Clark. (Courtesy of the Clark Volunteer Emergency Squad.)

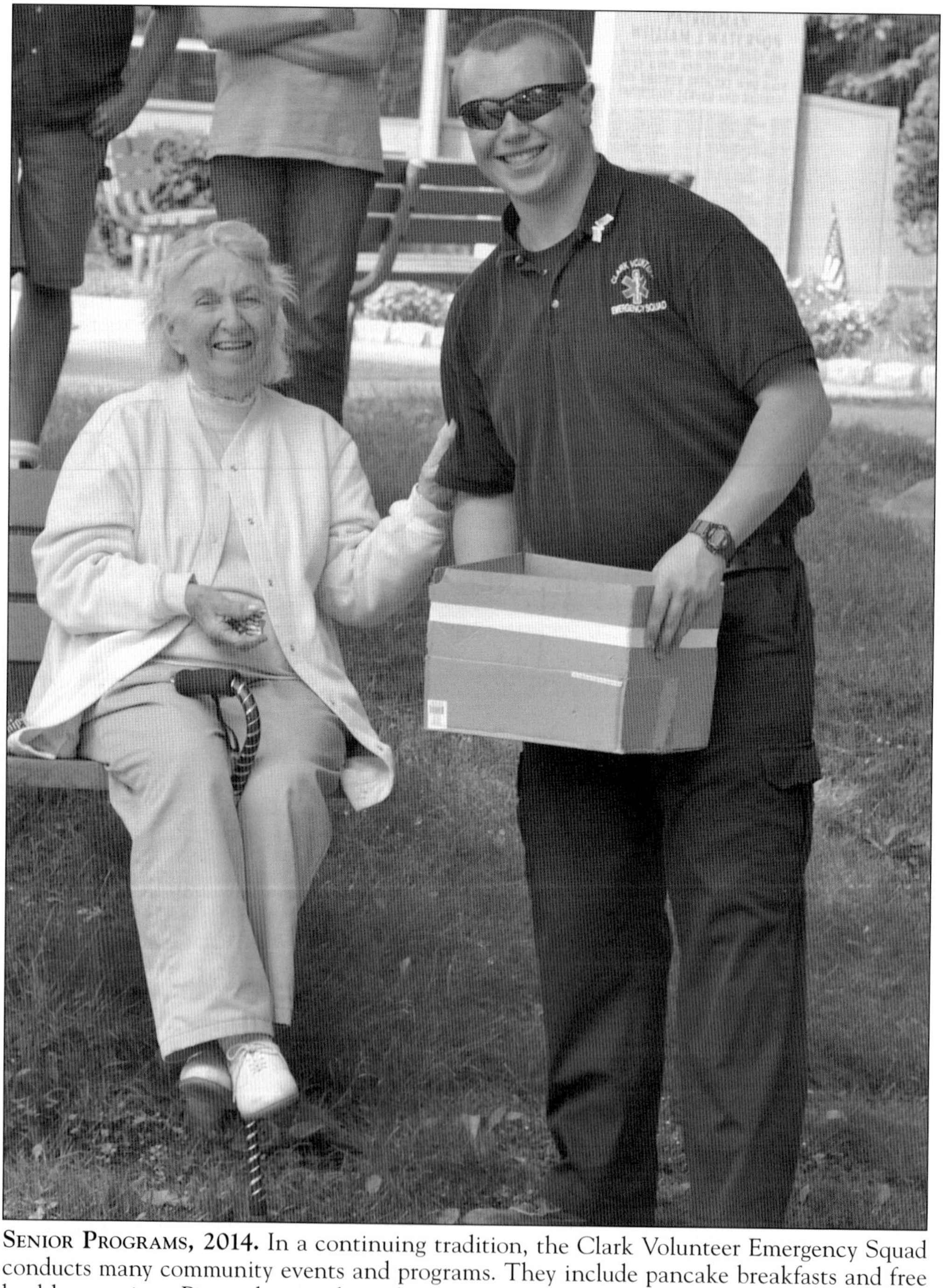

Senior Programs, 2014. In a continuing tradition, the Clark Volunteer Emergency Squad conducts many community events and programs. They include pancake breakfasts and free health screenings. Pictured is squad member Danny Sheldon bringing water to Margaret Kehoe. (Courtesy of the Clark Volunteer Emergency Squad.)

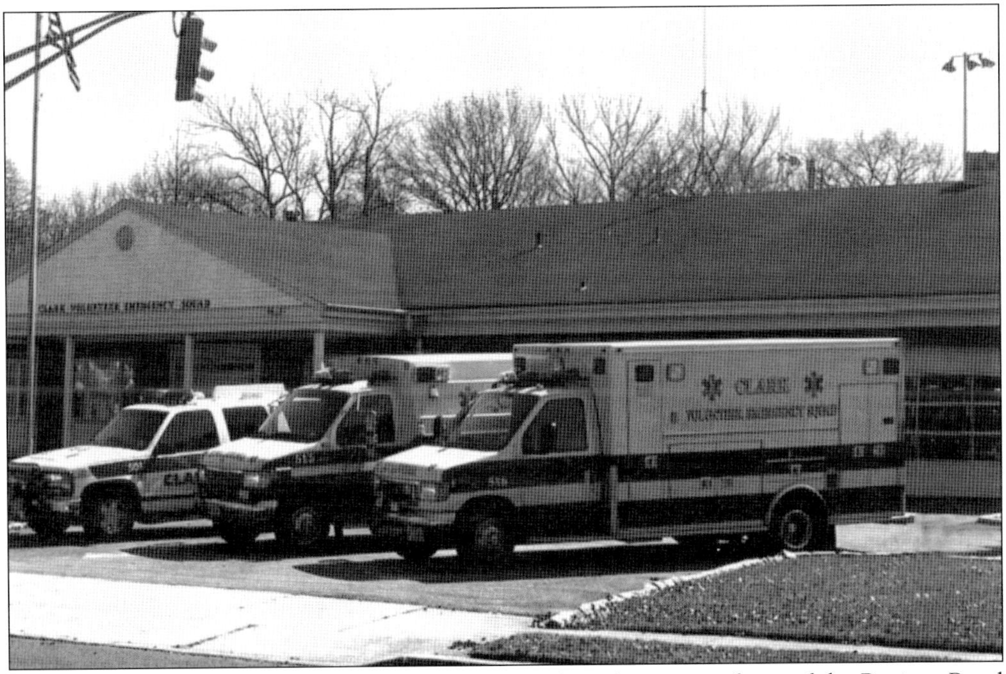

Raritan Road Squad House and Automobiles. Squad rigs sit in front of the Raritan Road Squad House during the 1990s. From left to right are the 1992 Chevrolet Suburban SUV Command Vehicle, Ambulance 515, and Ambulance 516. (Courtesy of the Clark Volunteer Emergency Squad.)

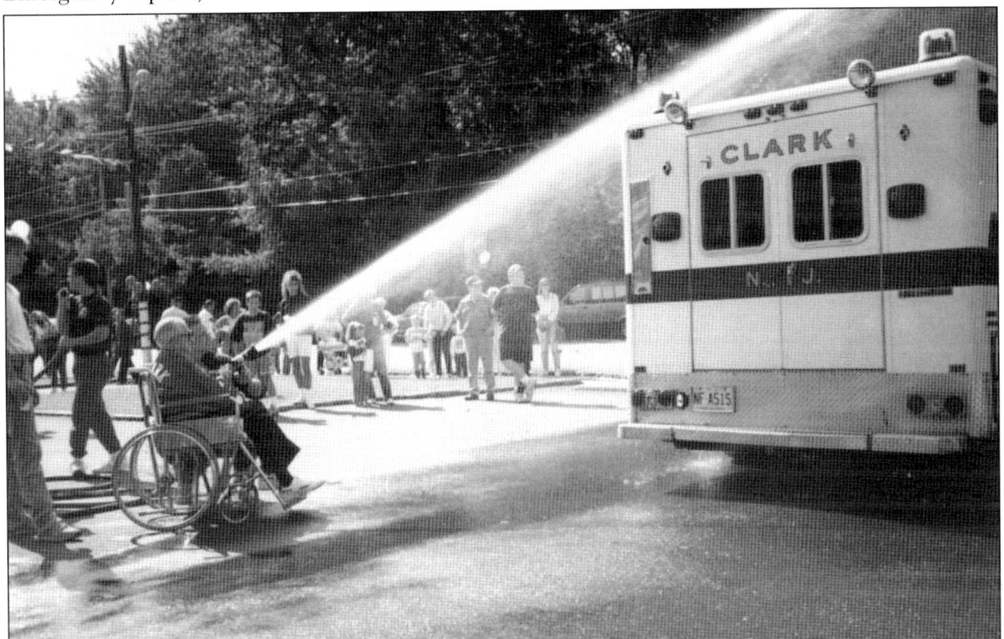

Clark Volunteer Emergency Squad Wet Down. In 2006, the Clark Volunteer Emergency Squad members and residents came out to an old-fashioned open house and wet down the first aid squad's ambulance 515. (Courtesy of the Clark Volunteer Emergency Squad.)

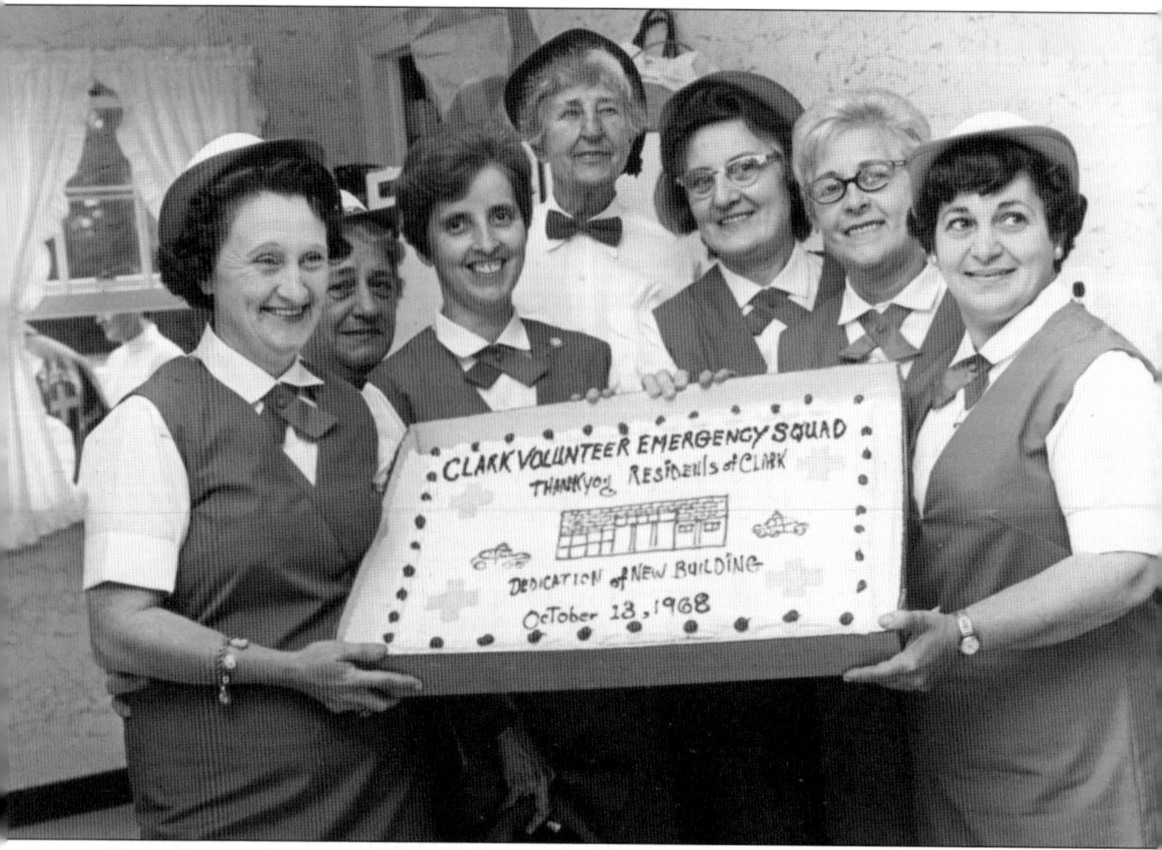

CLARK LADIES AUXILIARY. The Clark Ladies Auxiliary presents the cake for the dedication of the Raritan Road Squad House on October 13, 1968. The Clark Ladies Auxiliary is considered the backbone of the emergency community. (Courtesy of the Clark Volunteer Emergency Squad.)

Six

Clark Volunteer Fire Department

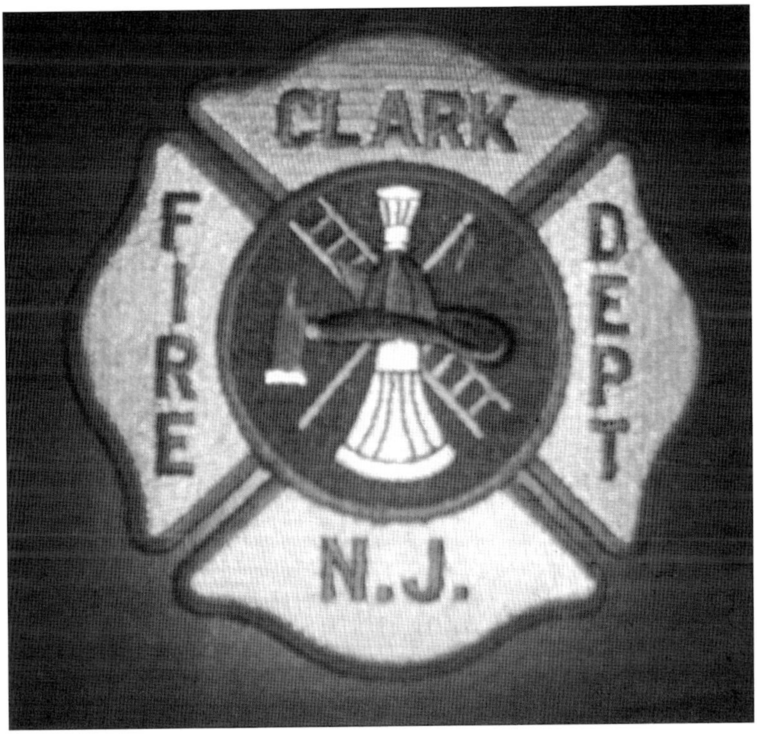

Fire Department Seal. Pictured is the Clark Fire Department's seal, which all members on the Clark Fire Department wear on their uniforms at all times while on duty. (Courtesy of the Clark Volunteer Fire Department.)

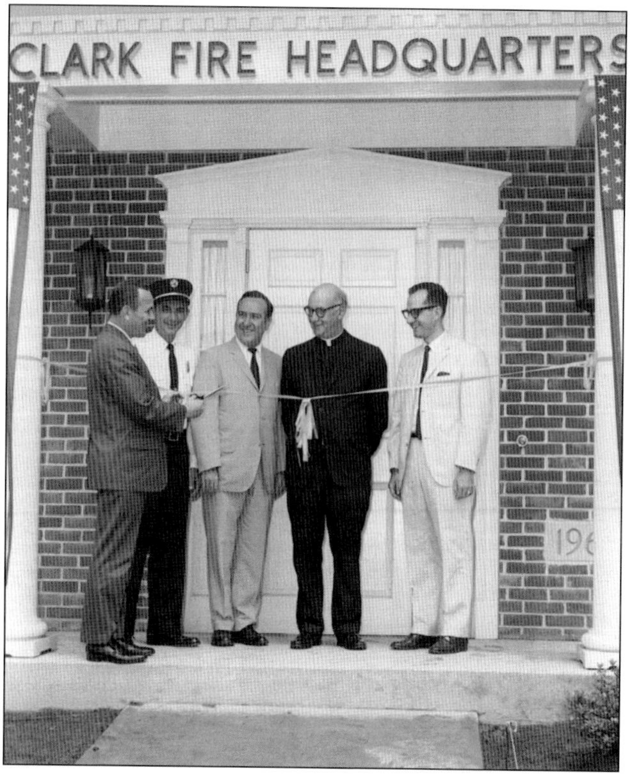

Broadway Firehouse. This photograph shows the Broadway firehouse dedication in June 1969. This was Clark's first modern fire department headquarters and was state of the art in being able to house four pieces of apparatus. Seen here are, from left to right, Mayor Thomas Kaczmark, fire chief Robert Volpe, unidentified, Fr. Denis Whalen, and New Jersey senator Frank McDermet. (Courtesy of the Clark Volunteer Fire Department.)

1964 LeFrance Pumper. The 1964 LeFrance pumper was placed into service in June 1964. It is here outside of the Westfield Avenue firehouse. (Courtesy of the Clark Volunteer Fire Department.)

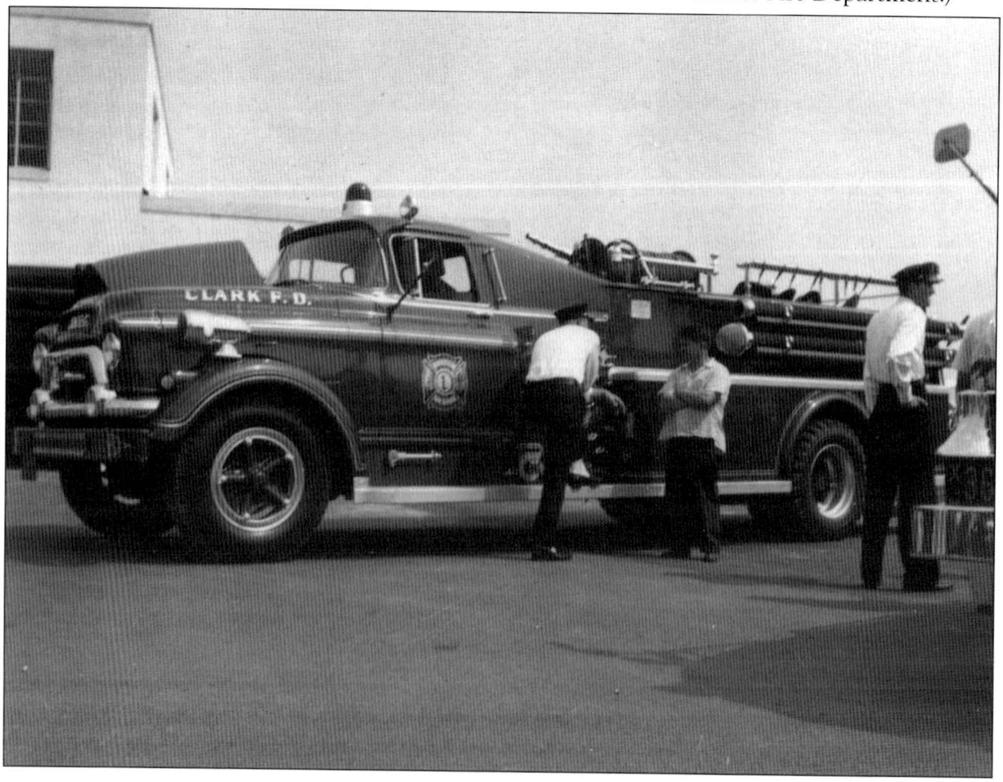

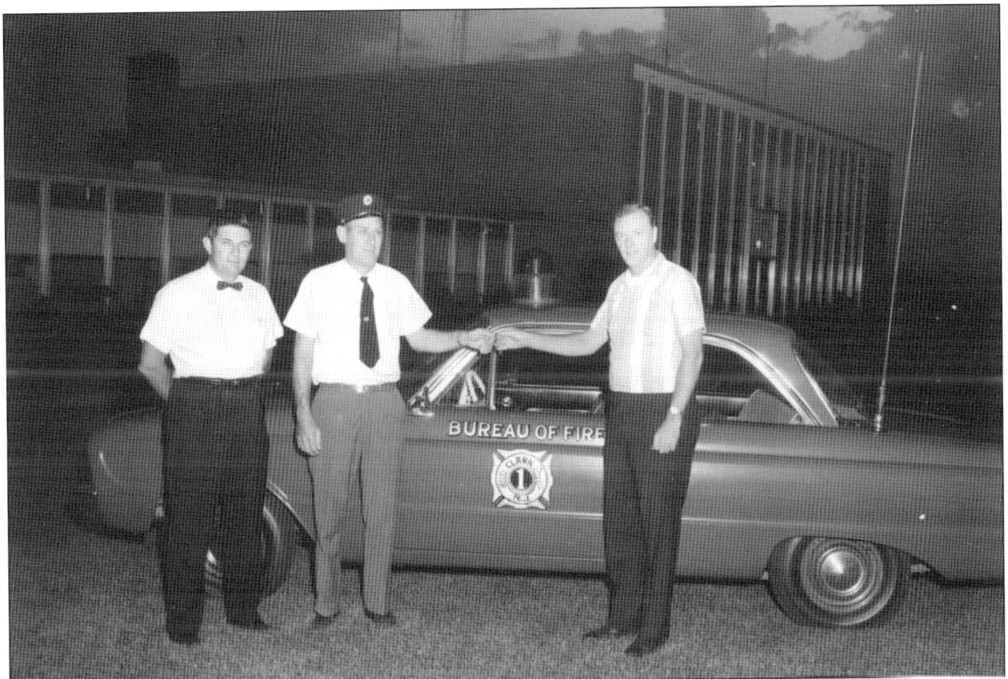

1961 Ford Falcon. This is the 1961 Ford Falcon fire bureau vehicle that was in use by the fire department. Pictured from left to right are public safety director Charles Grunder, fire chief Frank Bihon, and Mayor William Maguire. (Courtesy of the Clark Volunteer Fire Department.)

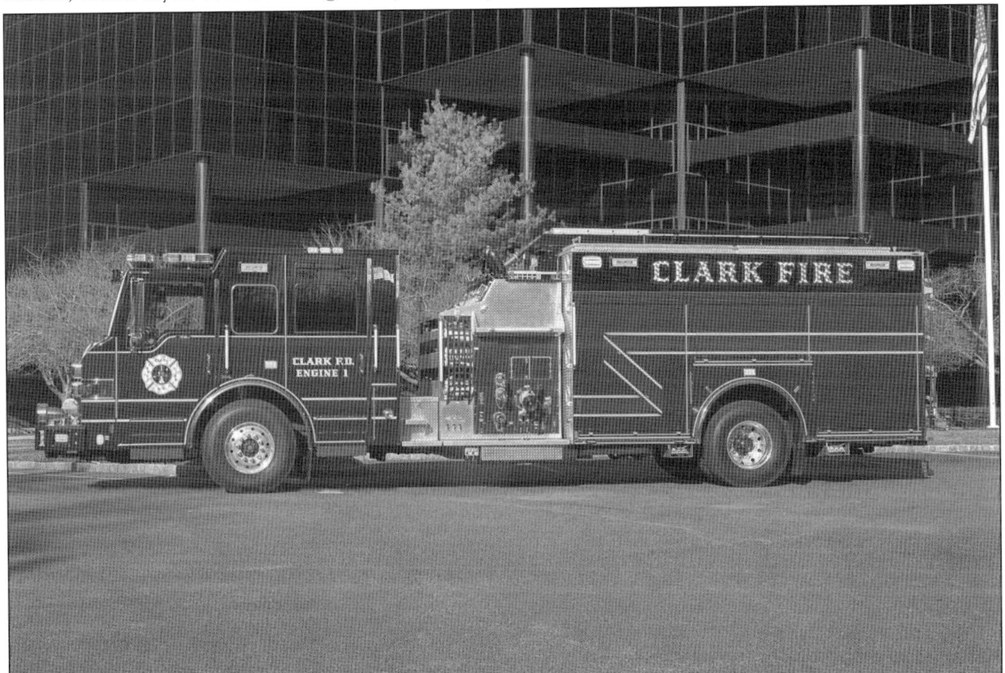

2015 Engine No. 4 Pierce Velocity. The 2015 Engine No. 4 Pierce Velocity pumper is the newest addition to the Clark Volunteer Fire Department. (Courtesy of the Clark Volunteer Fire Department.)

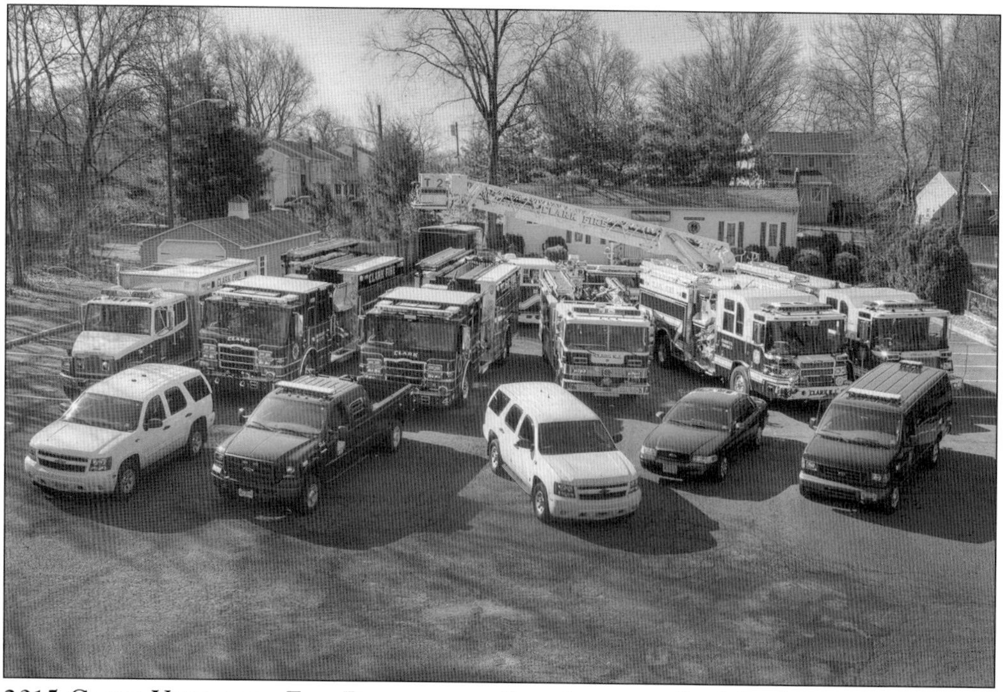

2015 Clark Volunteer Fire Department. Seen here are all of the department vehicles in use for the Clark Volunteer Fire Department in 2015. (Courtesy of the Clark Volunteer Fire Department.)

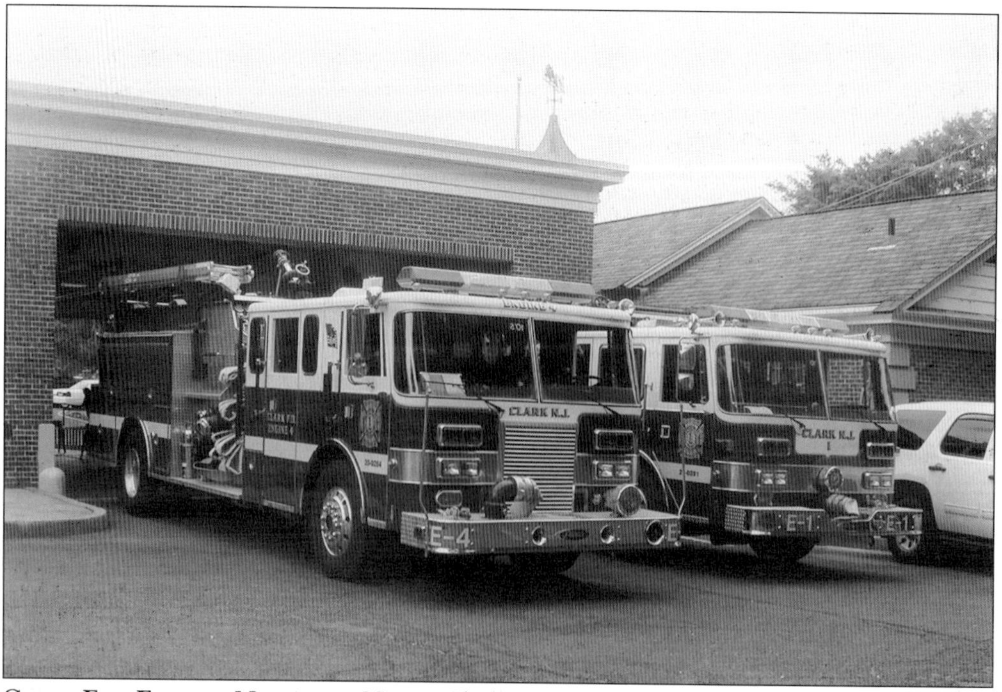

Clark Fire Engines No. 4 and No. 1. Clark Fire Engines No. 4 and No. 1 are pictured at the Broadway firehouse. Both engines were retired in 2015. (Courtesy of the Clark Volunteer Fire Department.)

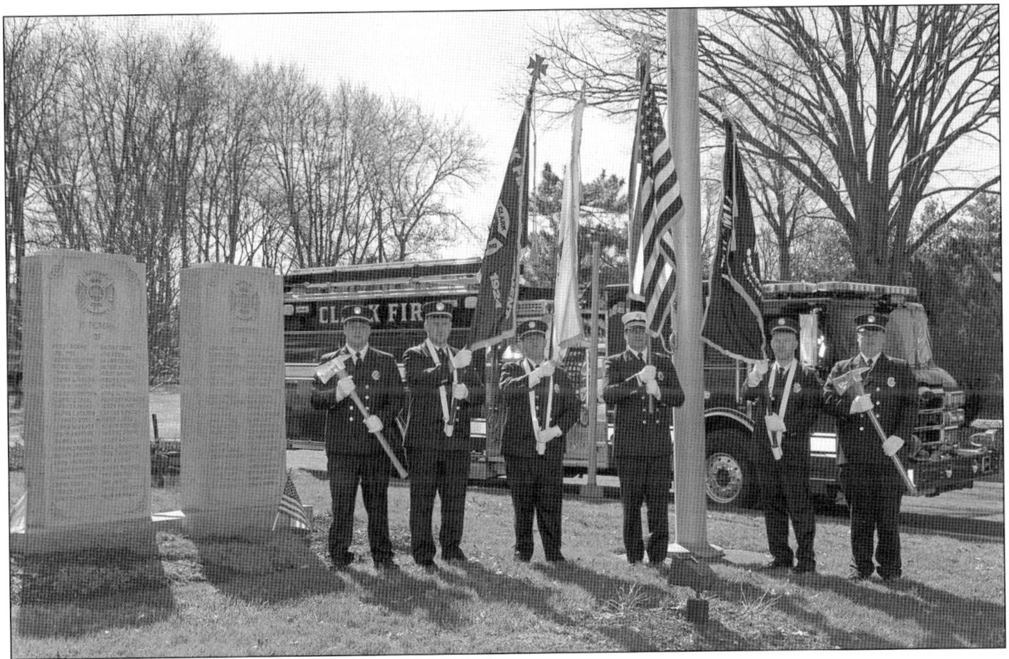

Clark Volunteer Fire Department Honor Guard. The Clark Volunteer Fire Department Honor Guard conducts a memorial service on September 11, 2014. It took place in front of the department's Broadway firehouse at the department's Firemen's Memorial. (Courtesy of the Clark Volunteer Fire Department.)

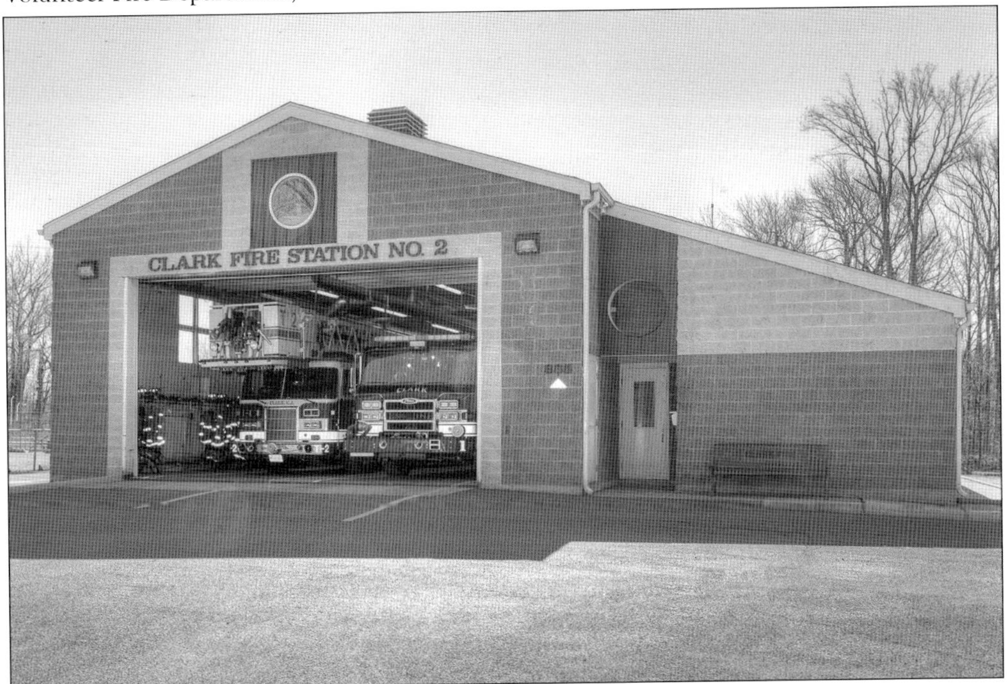

Clark Fire Station No. 2. Seen in this 2014 photograph is Clark Fire Station No. 2, which was dedicated in 1989. It currently serves the southern section of Clark. (Courtesy of the Clark Volunteer Fire Department.)

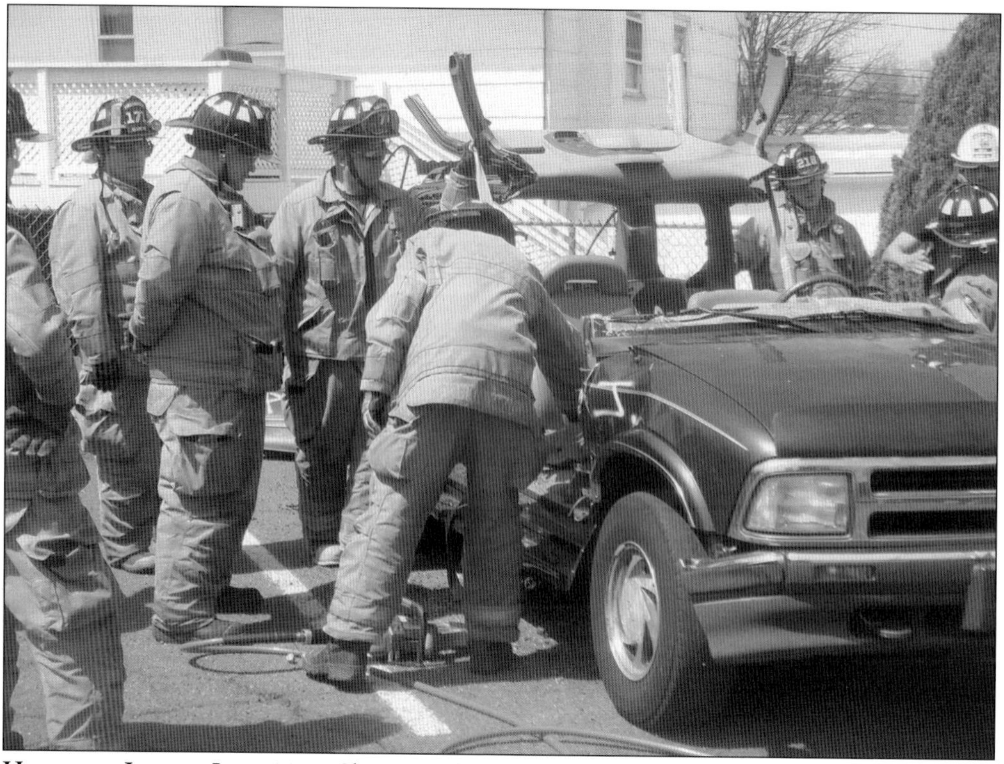

Holmatro Jaws of Life, 2013. Shown in this photograph are Clark firefighters conducting an exercise on a 1996 Chevrolet Blazer. This exercise shows the proper use of the Holmatro Jaws of Life to aid a trapped accident victim. (Courtesy of the Clark Volunteer Fire Department.)

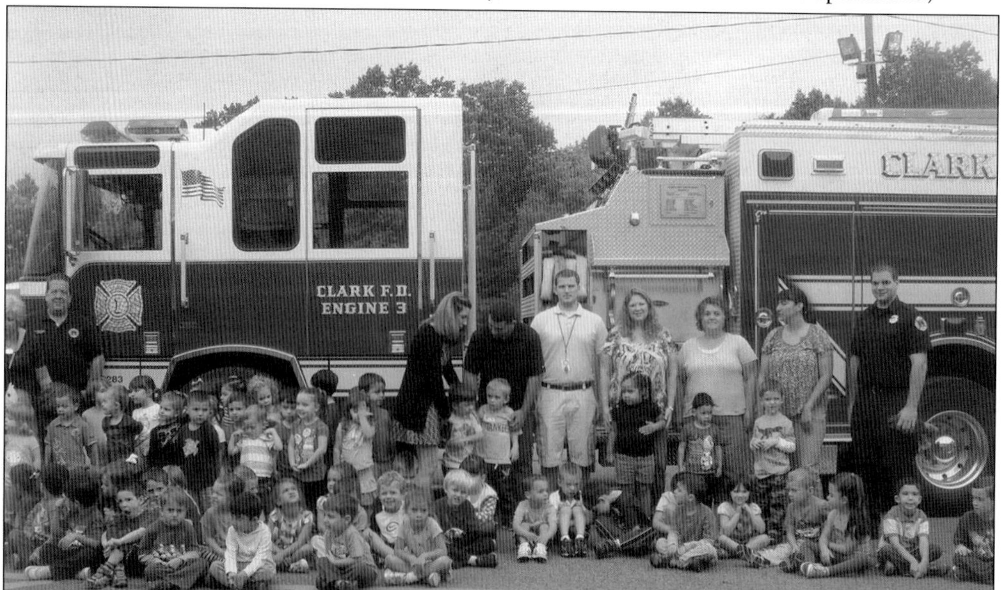

Clark Fire Prevention Week, 2010. In a continual effort to educate the children of Clark, the department opens up both firehouses and vehicles as an education program for youth of the township. (Courtesy of the Clark Volunteer Fire Department.)

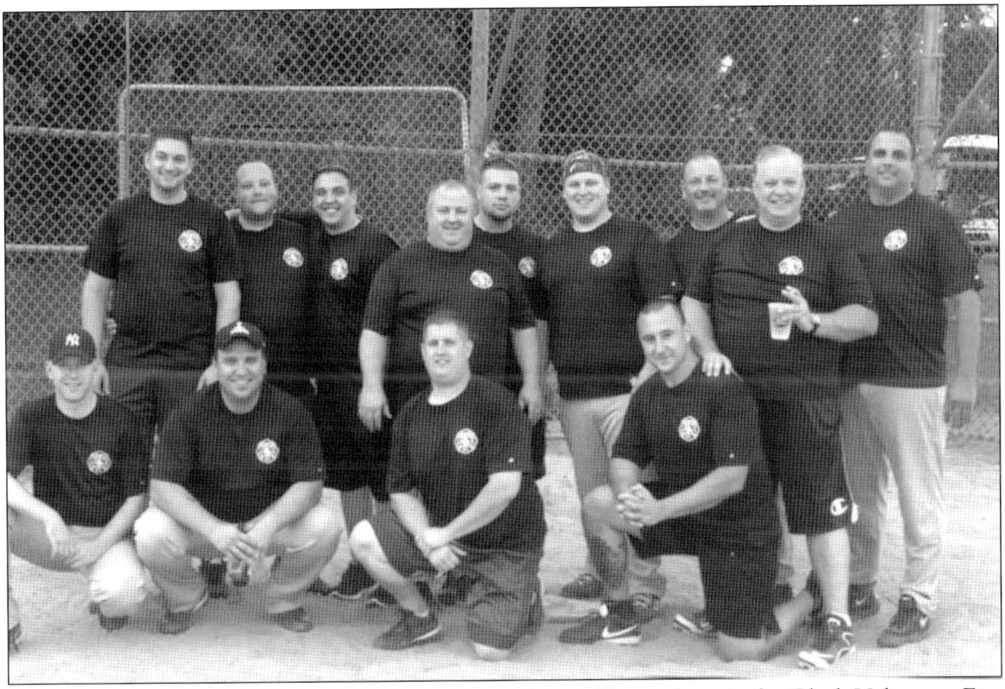

CLARK VOLUNTEER FIRE DEPARTMENT SOFTBALL TEAM. Shown here is the Clark Volunteer Fire Department's softball team. The team poses for a photograph while taking a break from fighting fires. (Courtesy of the Clark Volunteer Fire Department.)

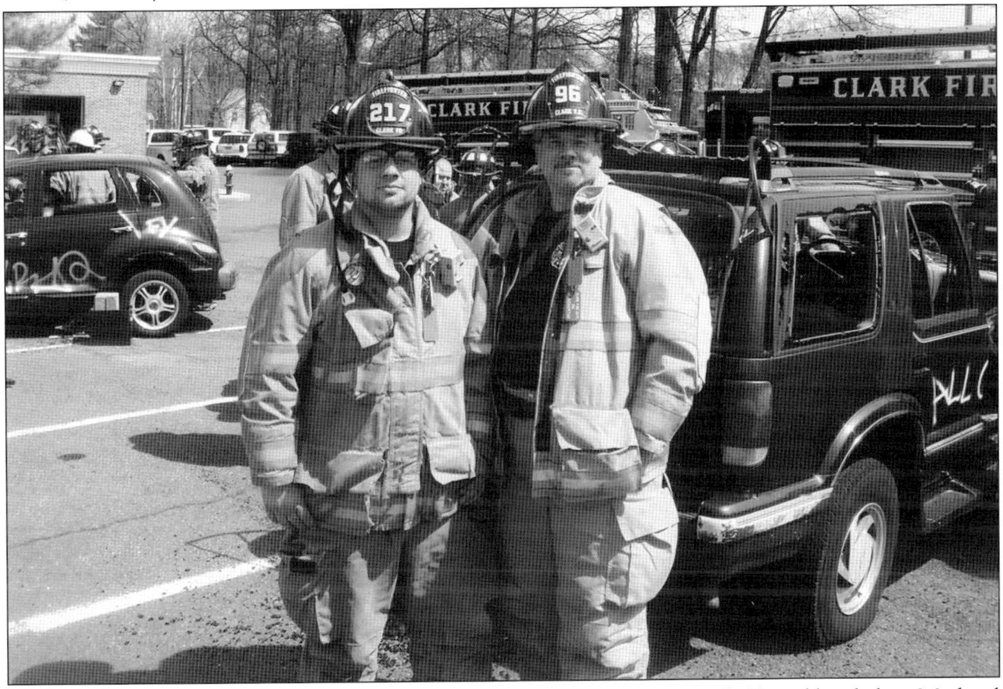

FATHER AND SON. The Clark firefighters seen here are Adam Nenortis (left) and his father, Michael Nenortis. They are a rare father-and-son combination in firefighting community. (Courtesy of the Clark Volunteer Fire Department.)

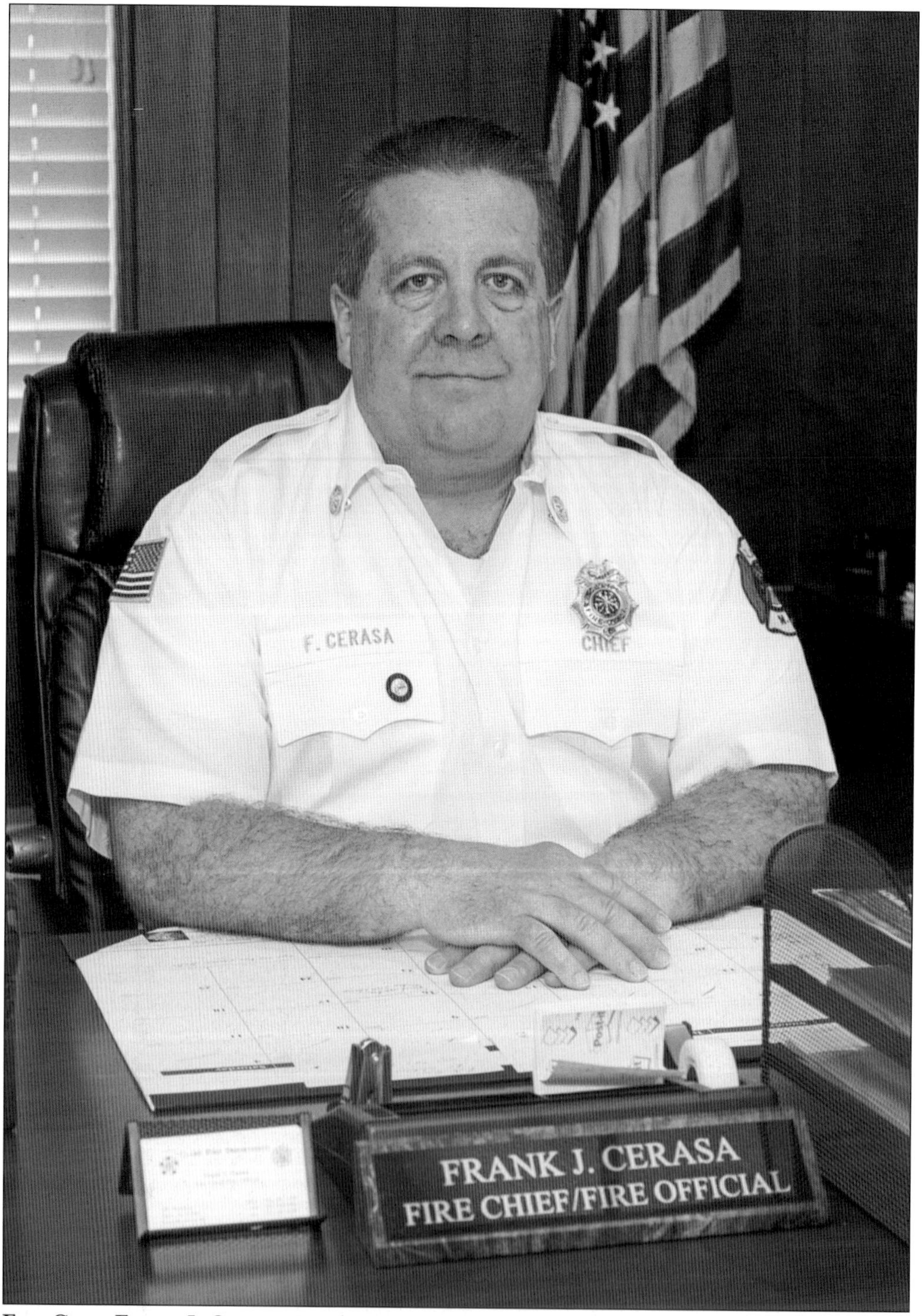

Fire Chief Frank J. Cerasa. Frank J. Cerasa, a lifelong resident of Clark, has been a member of the Clark Fire Department since 1984. Cerasa served as chief in 1993 and 1994, and he will be the first full-time chief in the department's history beginning in 2015. (Courtesy of the Clark Volunteer Fire Department.)

Seven

SCHOOL DAYS

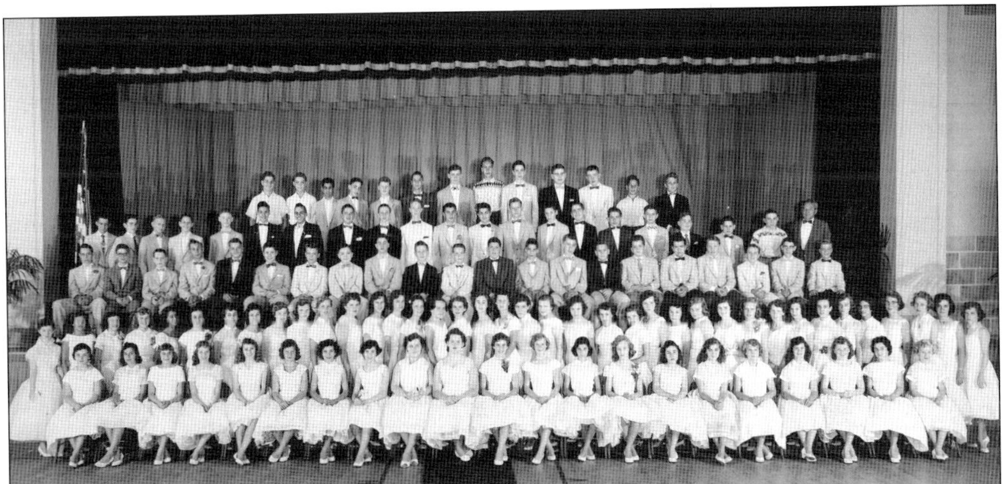

CHARLES H. BREWER SCHOOL CLASS OF 1961. Charles H. Brewer School is located at 430 Westfield Avenue. It opened in 1949 and closed its doors in June 1982. This photograph shows the eighth-grade graduates of June 1961. (Courtesy of the Clark History Room.)

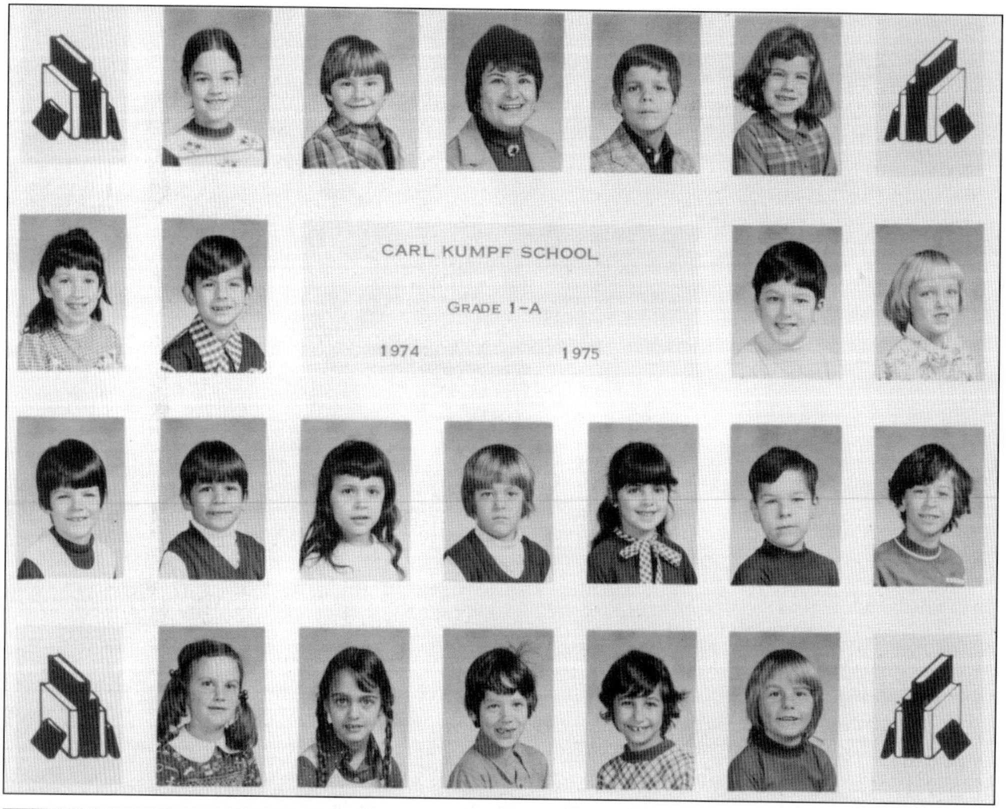

CARL KUMPF SCHOOL. This photograph shows teacher Ginny Warneck's first-grade class at Carl Kumpf School. The children are six-year-old Clark students in the 1974–1975 school year. (Courtesy of the Clark History Room.)

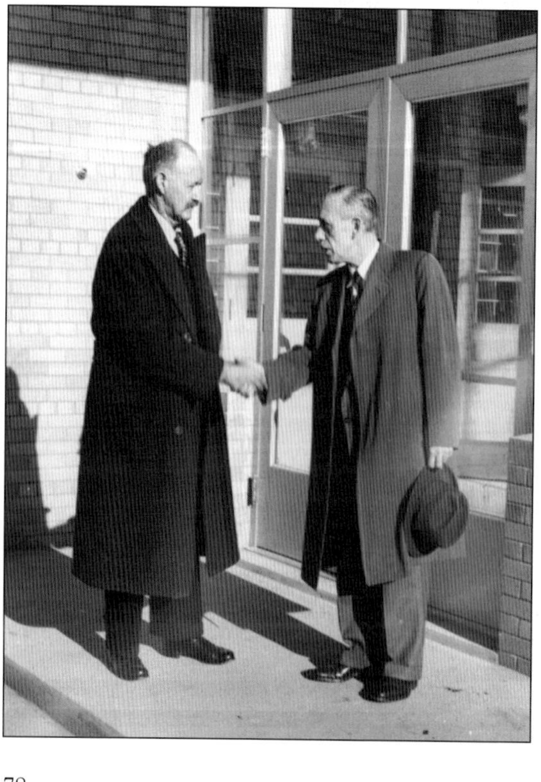

FOUNDERS IN CLARK EDUCATION. Founders of the Clark Board of Education are shown in this 1951 photograph. Shown are Charles H. Brewer (left) and Oliver Resch, president of the Clark Board of Education, whose efforts helped build the foundation of the Clark Public School System. (Courtesy of the Clark History Room.)

Awards Night, 1952. Clark principal Frank K. Hehnly of Charles H. Brewer School accepts an award at a board of education meeting in June 1952 along with board of education president Oliver Resch. (Courtesy of the Clark History Room.)

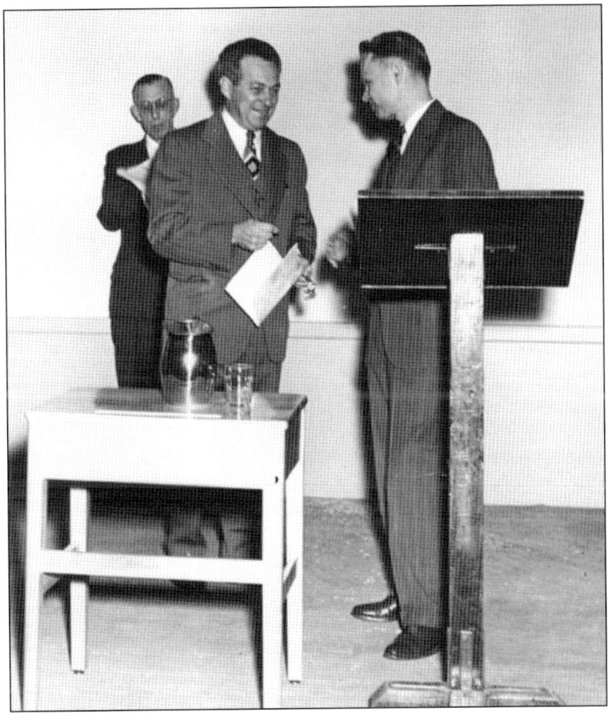

Founders Days at Abraham Clark. Third-grade children perform in a school Founder's Day pageant at Abraham Clark School in 1974. (Courtesy of the Clark History Room.)

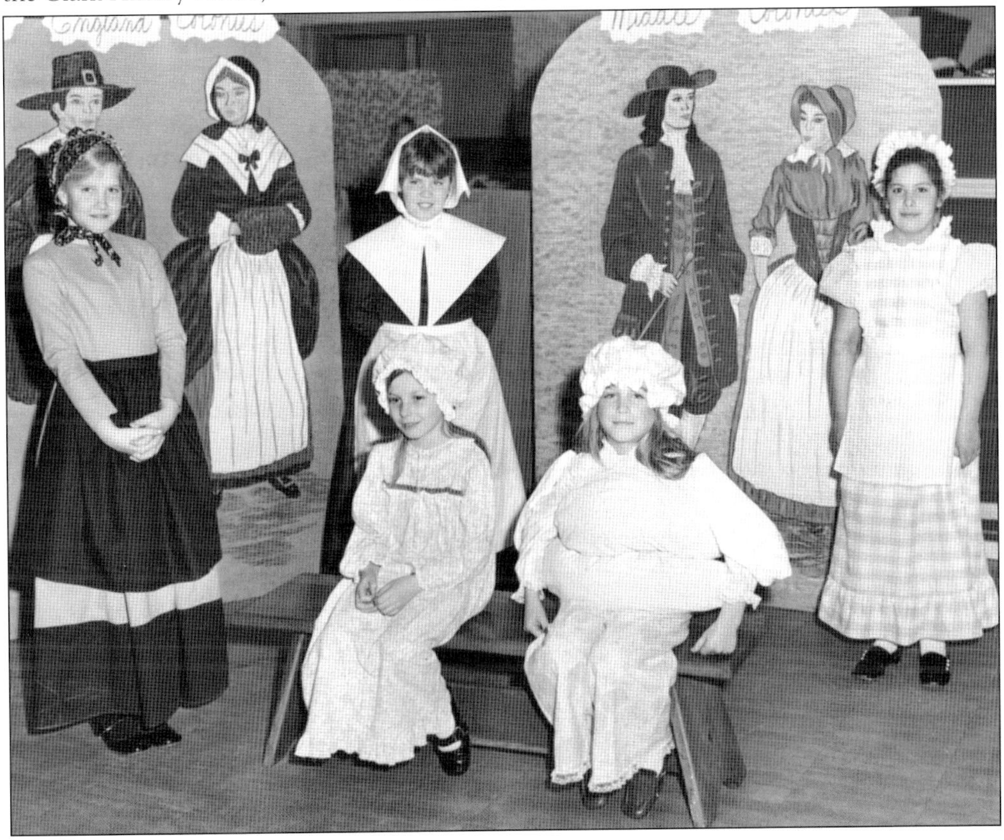

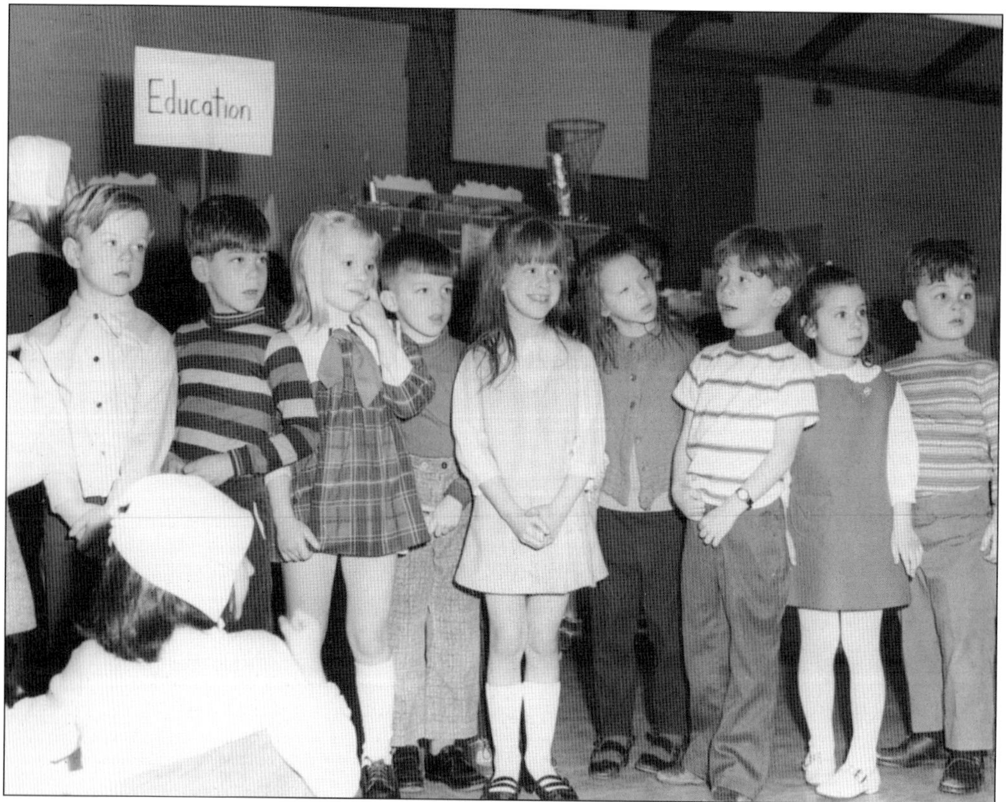

CHILDREN OF CLARK. Pictured here are the children of Clark in an Abraham Clark assembly under the direction of school principal Caesar Marone in 1972. (Courtesy of the Clark History Room.)

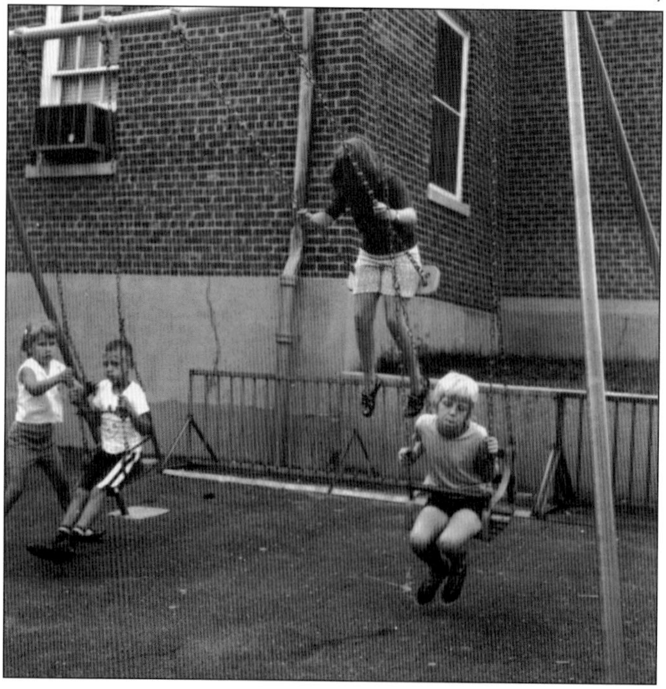

RECESS AT ABRAHAM CLARK SCHOOL. Recess at Abraham Clark School takes an hour for lunch and playtime on the swings in the back courtyard, as seen in this 1972 photograph. (Courtesy of the Clark History Room.)

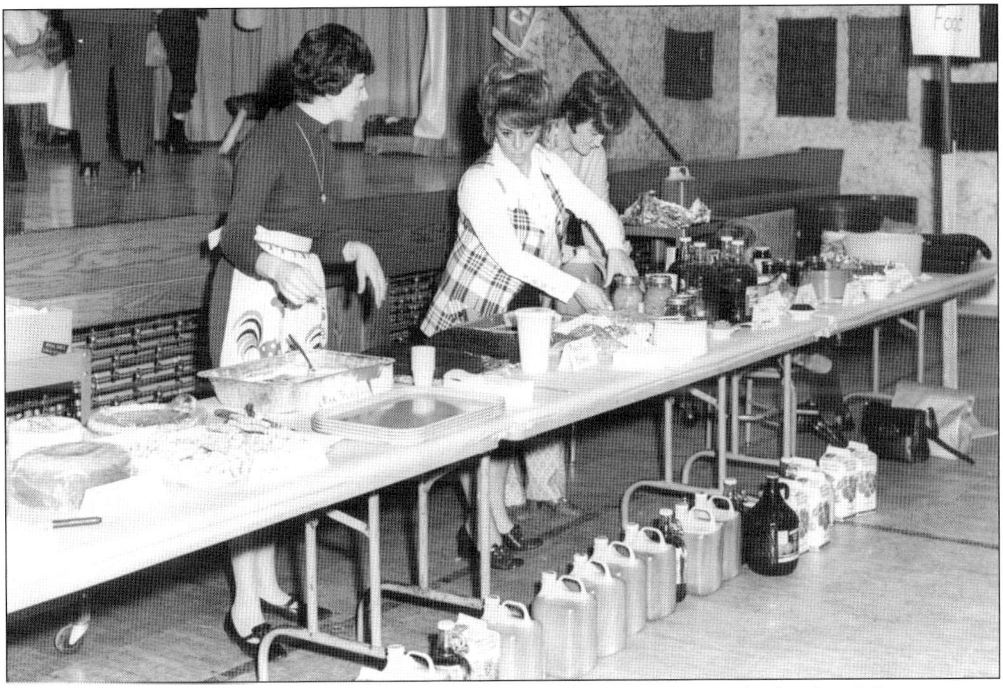

Abraham Clark PTA. The Abraham Clark PTA mothers prepare snacks for the children during a holiday pageant in 1973. School PTA moms were instrumental in aiding teachers with many of the programs and after-school activities. (Courtesy of the Clark History Room.)

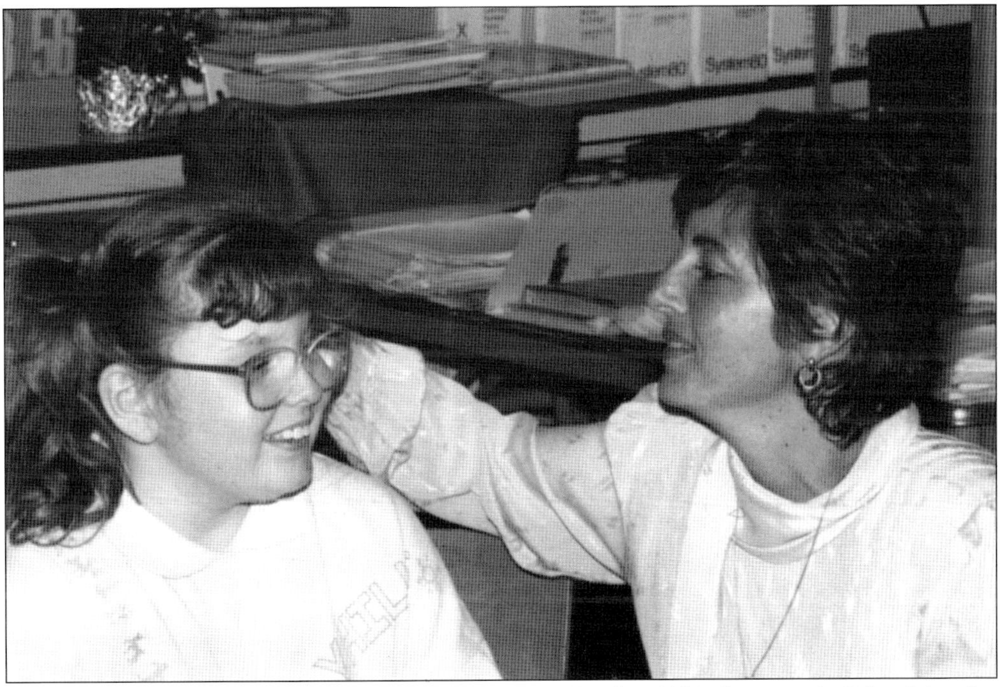

Helping a Child along the Path of Knowledge. In this 1970 photograph, Edna Isbrecht, a second-grade teacher at Carl H. Kumpf School, checks on the needs of one of her students. (Courtesy of the Clark History Room.)

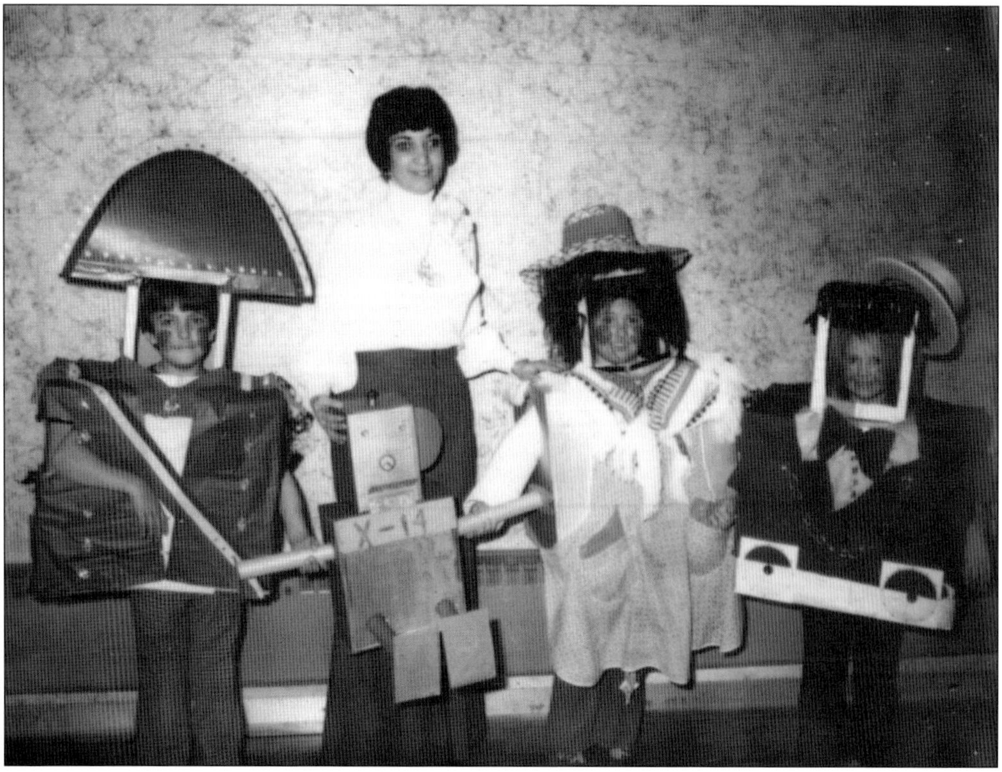

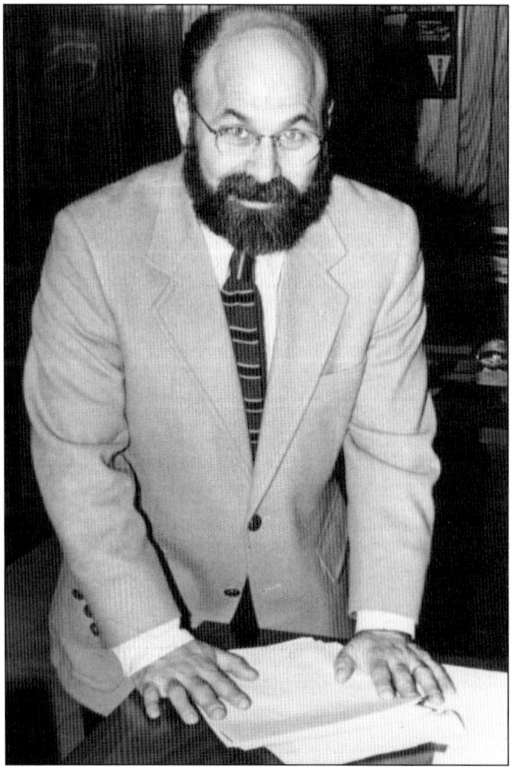

HALLOWEEN, 1973. Shown here is the first-prize winner for best group competition in the 1973 Halloween contest at Abraham Clark School. (Courtesy of the Clark History Room.)

DR. PAUL J. ORTENZIO. Dr. Ortenzio was the superintendent of the Clark Public School System from 1986 until 2006. He was one of the most powerful and controversial leaders in the history of the Clark Public School System. (Courtesy of the Clark History Room.)

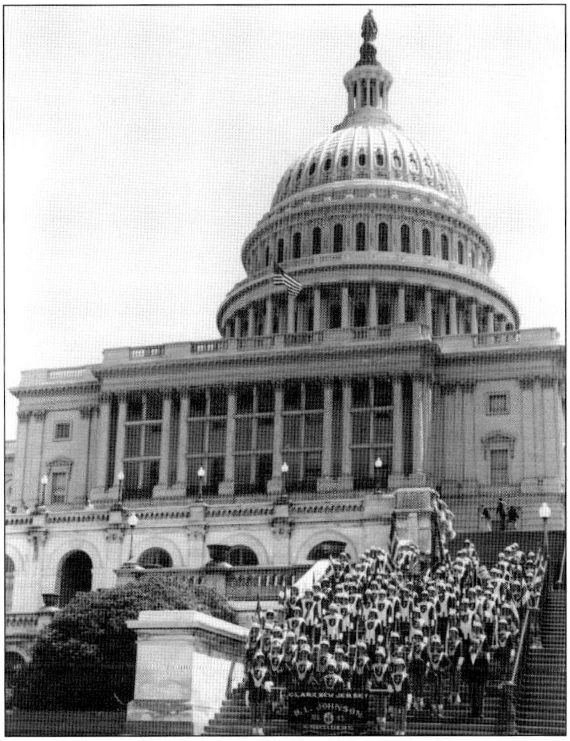

THE BAND AT THE CAPITOL. The Arthur L. Johnson High School band and color guard perform at the nation's capitol in a band competition in April 1978. (Courtesy of Steve Deara.)

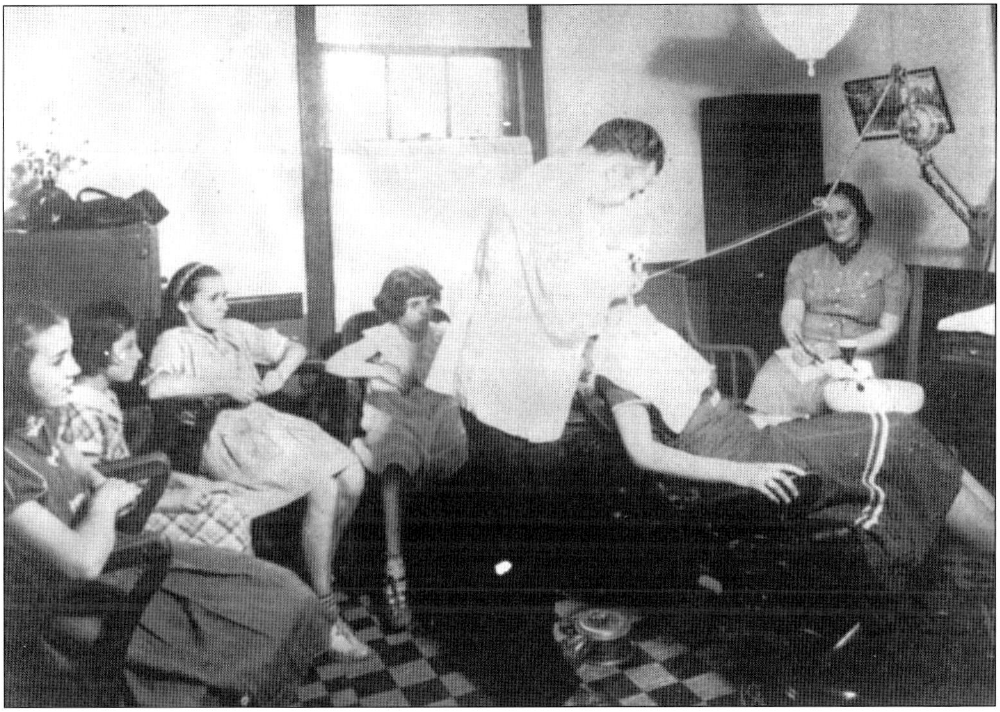

THE SCHOOL DENTIST, 1948. The school dentist was common at the Abraham Clark School, which provided free dental care to Clark students with parental permission in 1948. (Courtesy of the Clark History Room.)

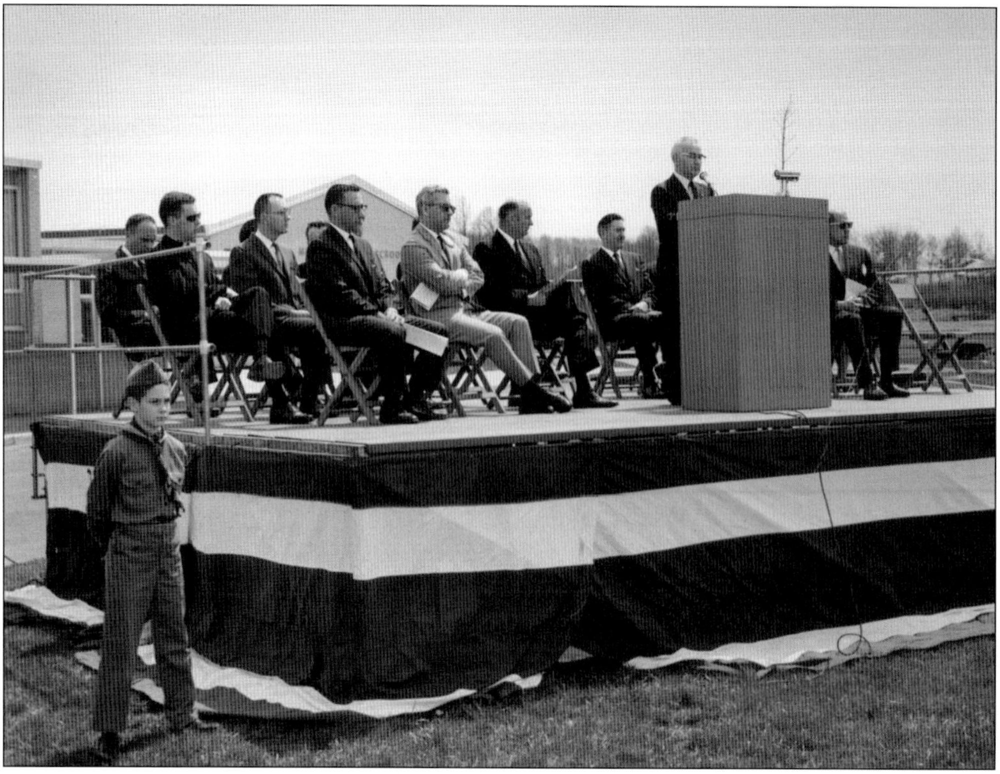

MILDRED TERRACE SCHOOL DEDICATION. Mildred Terrace School was dedicated in June 1967 due to the rapid expansion of population in the 1960s. A new school was needed, and the Mildred Terrace School was erected. Its name would be changed in September 1972 with the sudden death of school superintendent Dr. Carl H. Kumpf. (Courtesy of the Clark History Room.)

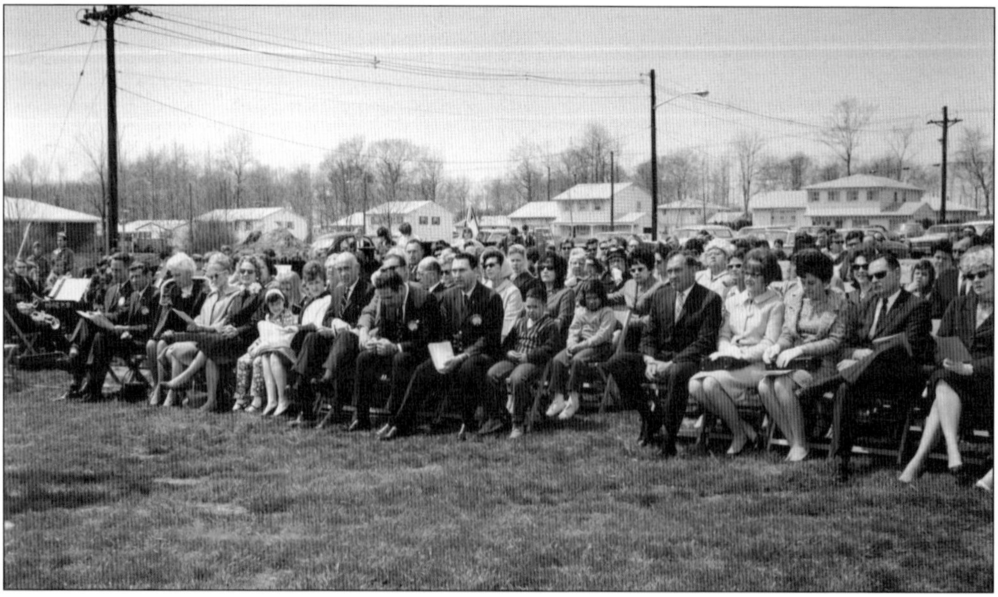

MILDRED TERRACE DEDICATION. Shown here are township and school board officials and residents celebrating a new school in June 1967. (Courtesy of the Clark History Room.)

Eight

Our Town

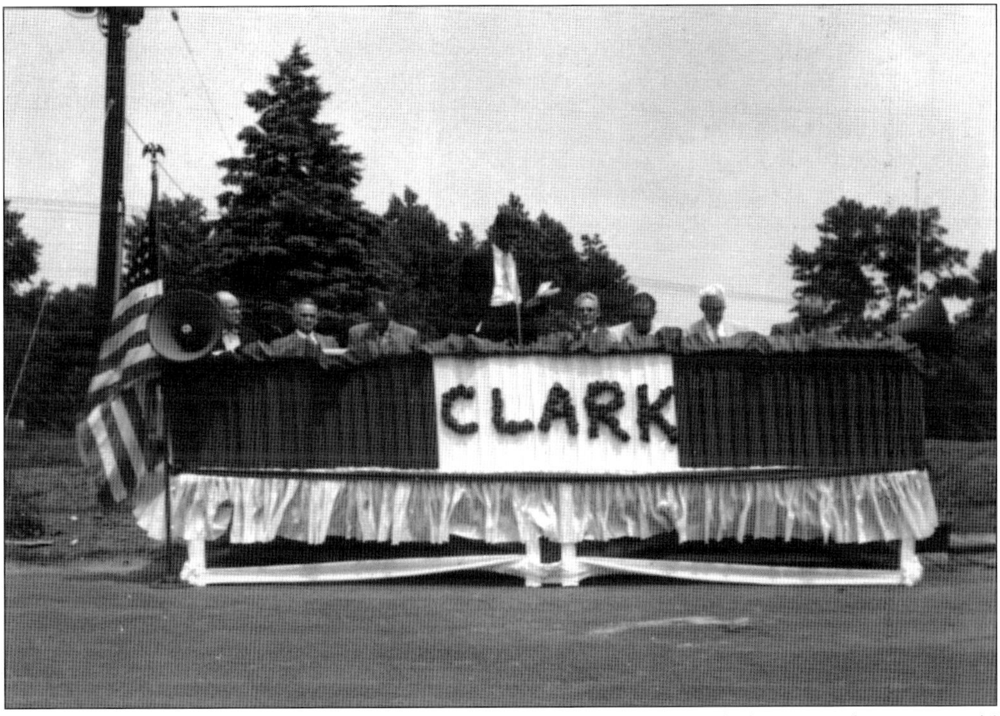

Clark Municipal Building Dedication, 1958. As the township of Clark grew in the post–World War II era, the growing population of its residents needed expanded municipal offices and police headquarters. In 1957, with public support and a referendum, a new municipal complex was constructed at 315 Westfield Avenue. Its formal dedication took place on June 22, 1958. Seen on the reviewing stand are Clark mayor John O'Connor and members of the township committee. (Courtesy of the Clark History Room.)

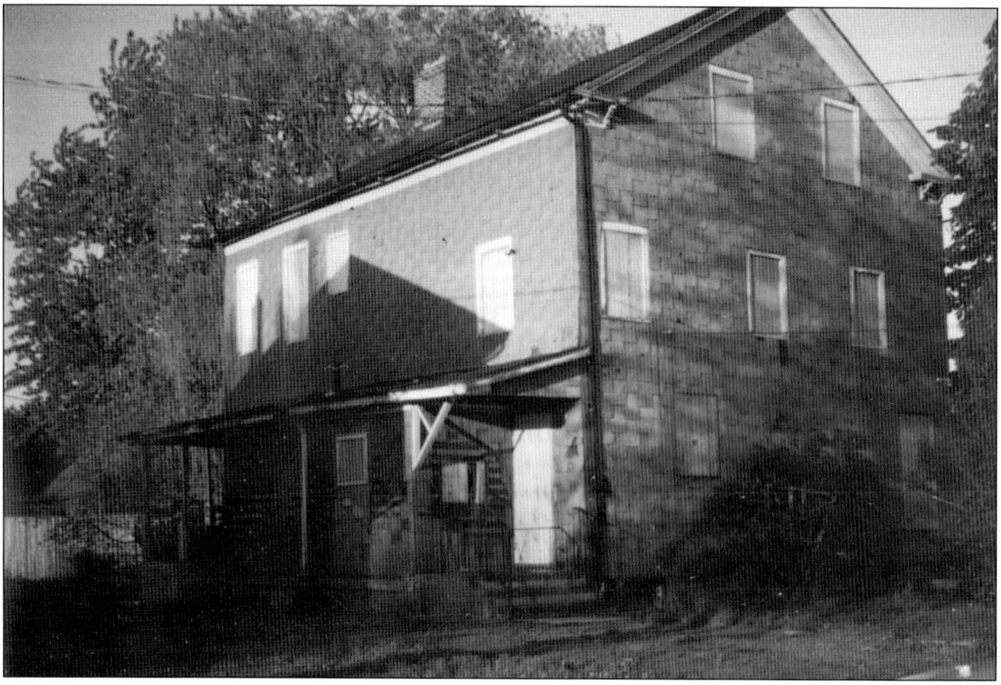

The Ritter Home. The Ritter home was located at the end of present-day Stanton Street, facing Madison Hill Road. The home dates back to the mid-19th century and was owned by the Ritters, a family well known for also owning most of Westfield Avenue—one of Clark's most historic streets—between the 1880s and 1940s. This photograph of the home was taken in 1968, a year before it was razed. (Courtesy of the Clark History Room.)

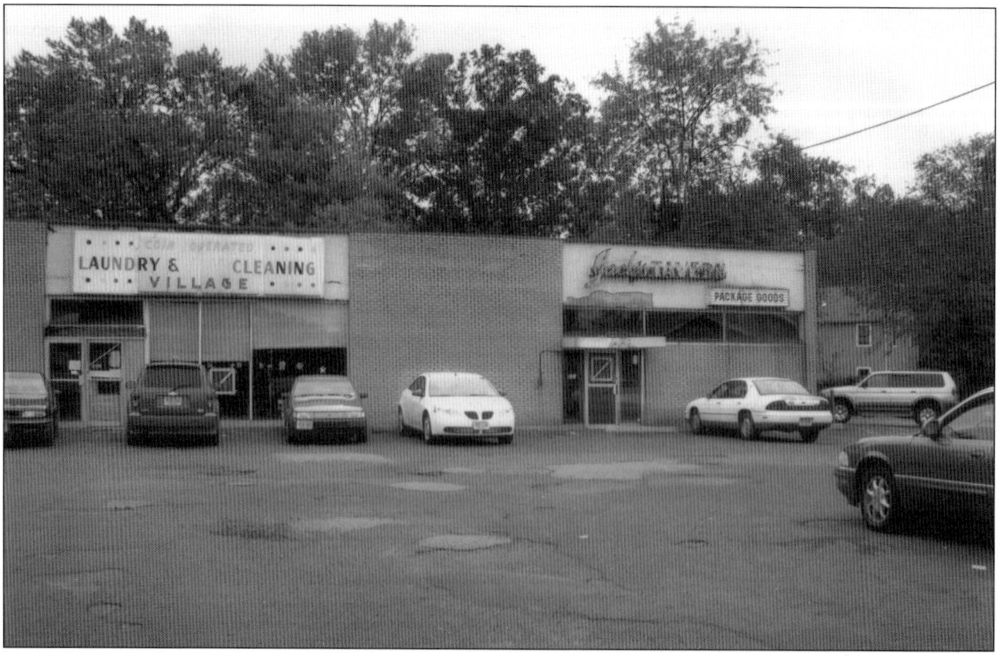

Jack's Tavern and Laundromat. Pictured is Jack's Tavern & Laundromat prior to its closing in 1999. This building was constructed in 1961 and razed in 2011. (Courtesy of Richard Seng.)

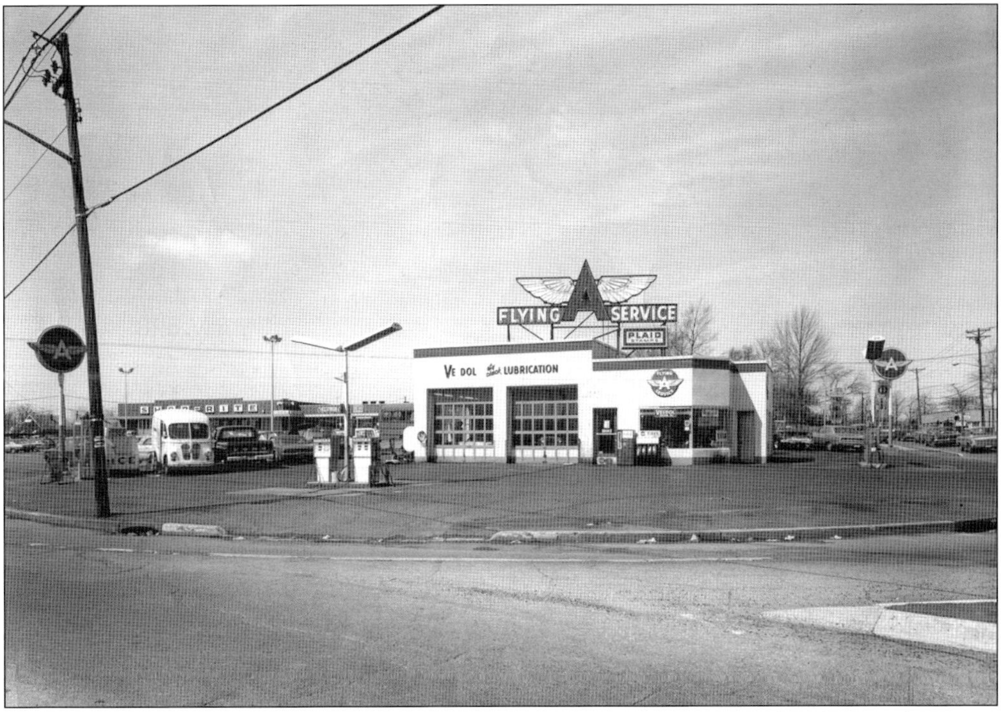

SARAFINS FLYING-A-SERVICE STATION. At the intersection of Raritan Road and Central Avenue was Sarafins Flying-A-Service Station, which was built in 1957. It received a new neighbor in 1961 with the addition of a Shop Rite. The photograph below was taken on August 6, 1958, and shows the station at the height of its popularity, prior to the construction of Shop Rite. At the rear of the station is Miller Farm. (Both, courtesy of John Sarafin.)

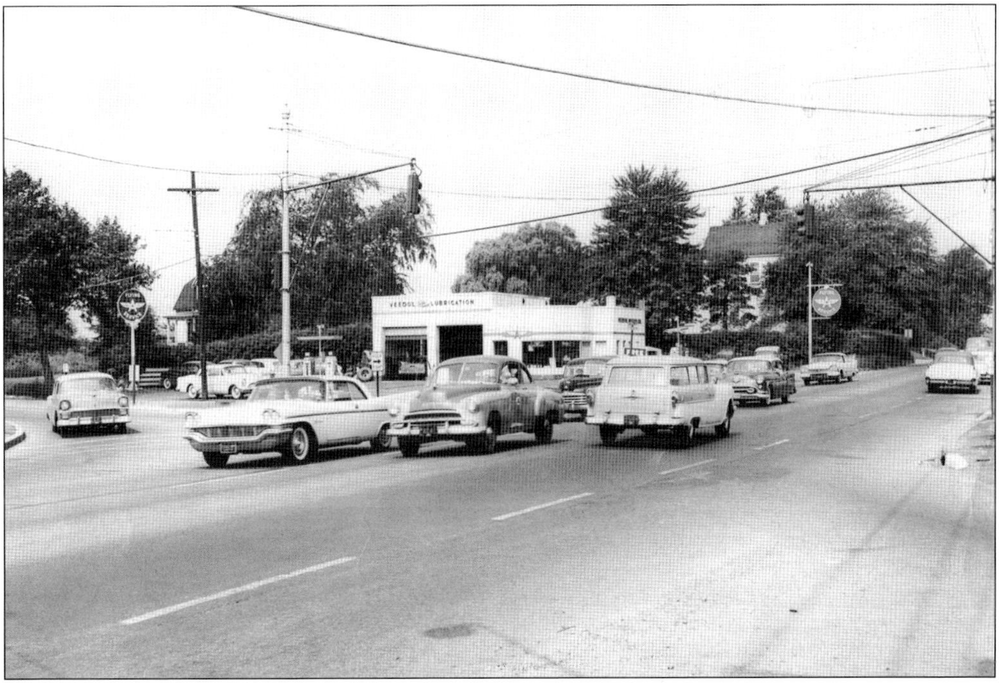

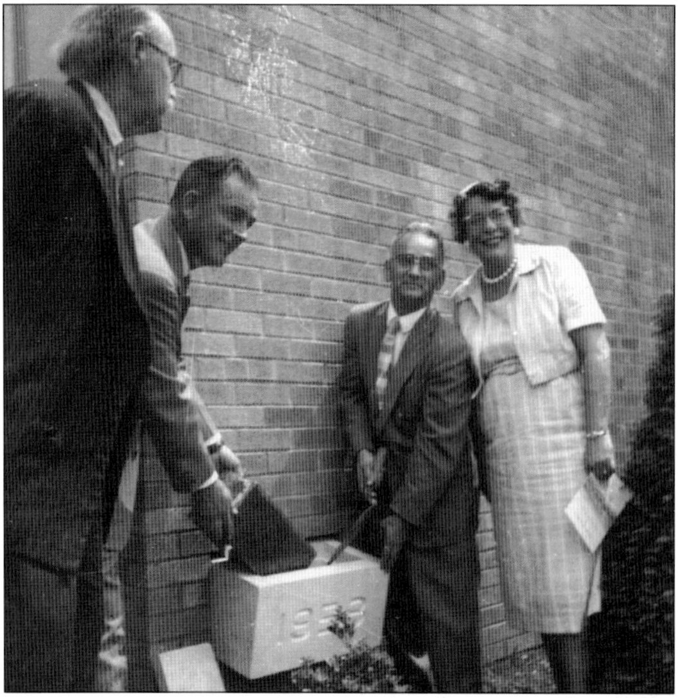

Laying the Cornerstone, 1958. From left to right, Charles Brewer, committeeman John O'Connor, Mayor Jay Stemmer, and Congresswoman Florence P. Dwyer set the cornerstone of the Clark Municipal Building at 315 Westfield Avenue. (Courtesy of the Clark History Room.)

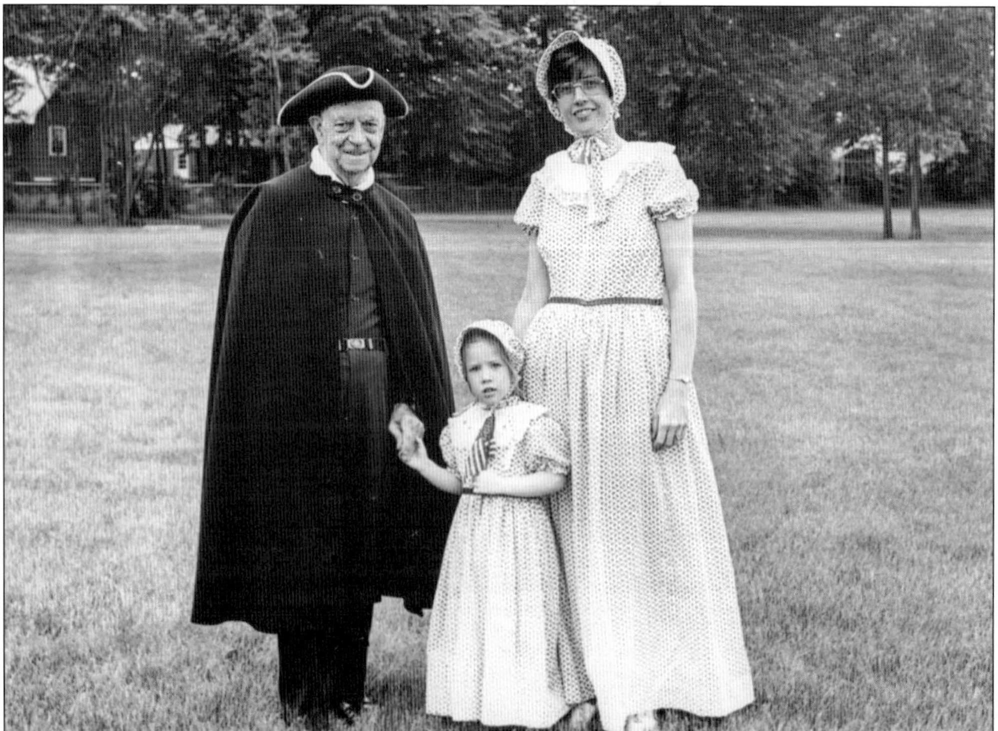

Clark's Patriot. Clark patriot Edward Ayers greets residents during the July 4, 1976, Bicentennial celebration. It was held at the high school. Ayers was codirector of the Bicentennial events and a founder of the Clark Public Library. (Courtesy of the Clark History Room.)

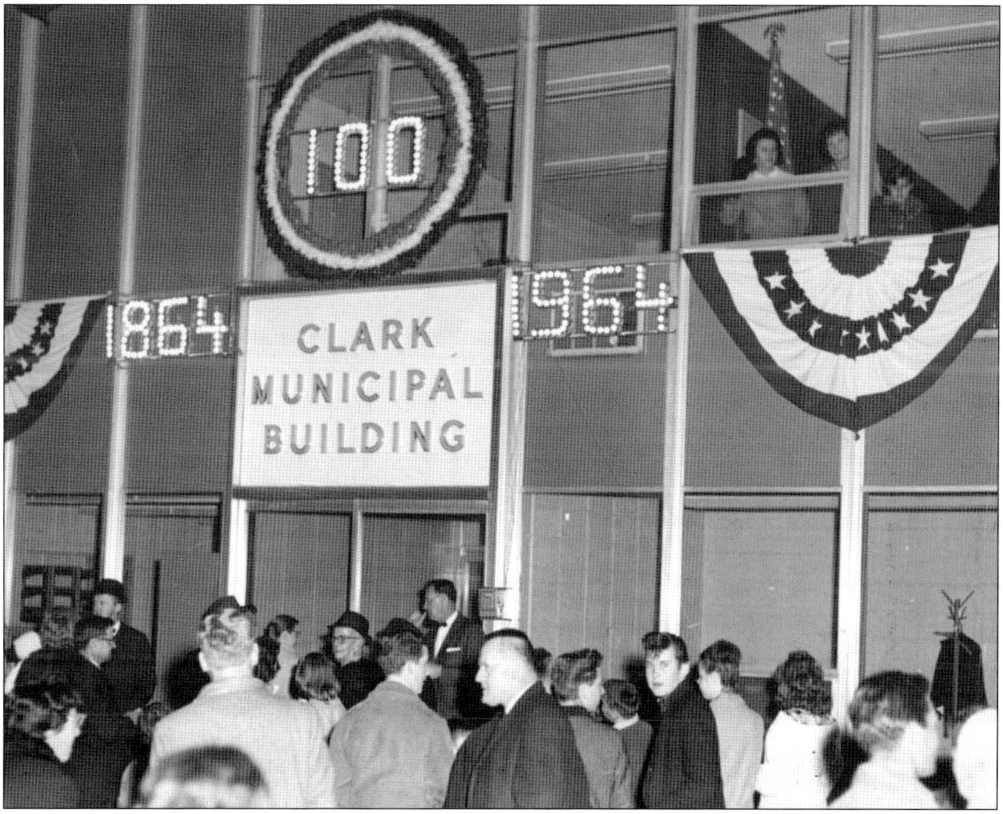

CLARK CENTENNIAL, 1964. The township held a rally and dedication on February 15, 1964, to start the 100th-anniversary celebration at town hall. (Courtesy of the Clark History Room.)

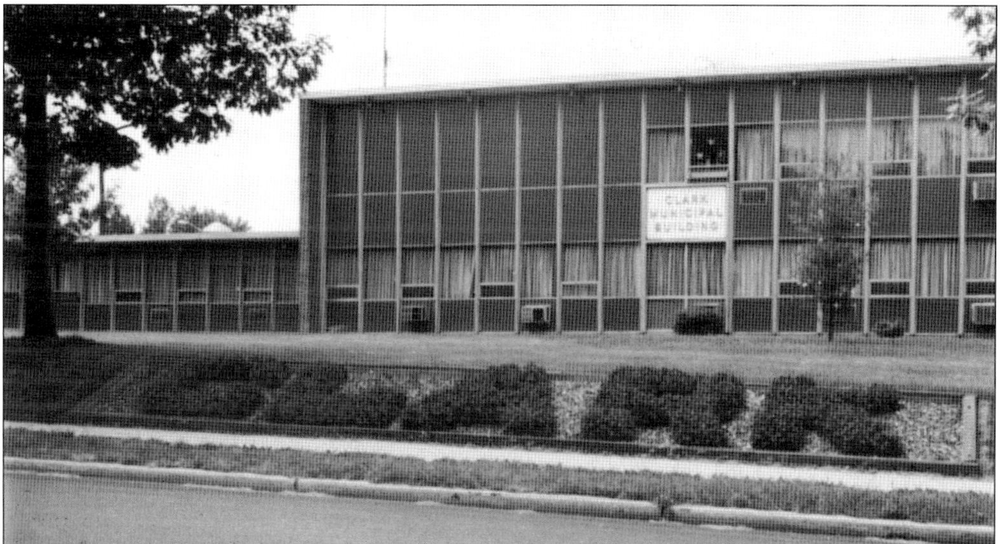

CLARK TOWN HALL, 1976. This 1976 picture of Clark Town Hall shows a Bicentennial flower display of the township's name that was created by the members of the Clark Garden Club. (Courtesy of the Clark History Room.)

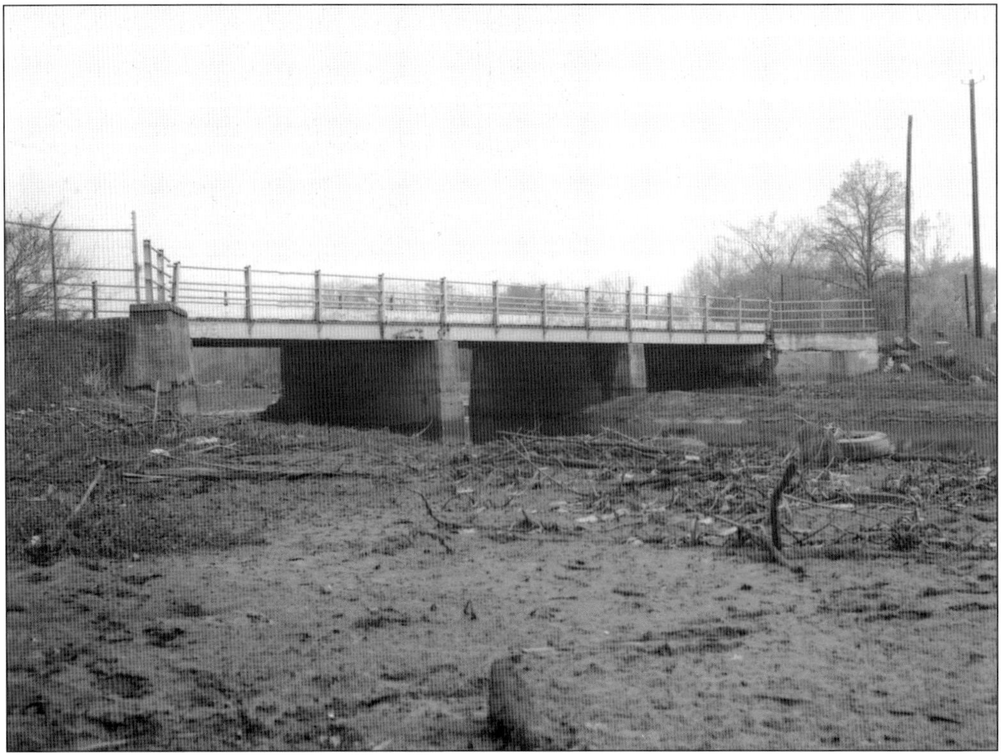

DROUGHT OF 1977. One of the worst droughts to hit Central New Jersey happened in 1977. Its affect is seen in this photograph, taken from the Raritan Road Bridge looking east. (Courtesy of the Clark History Room.)

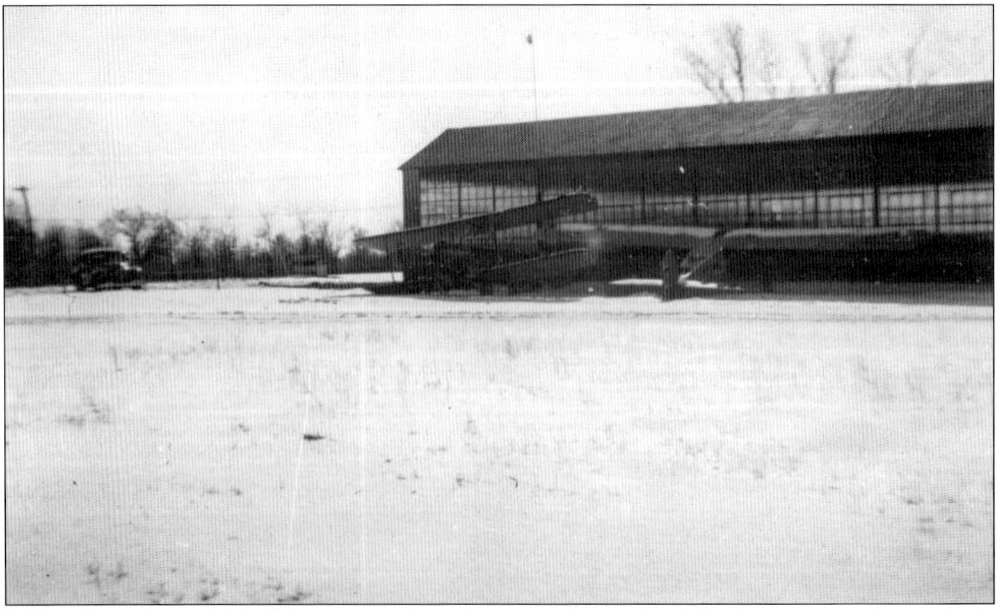

WESTFIELD AIRPORT, 1940. Westfield Airport was located along Lake Avenue on the border with Colonia, with all of the airport and runways located in Clark. It operated from 1920 until 1958, when it closed; it became Drexel Hill in 1963. (Courtesy of Robert LeDuc.)

Post–World War II Clark. In Clark, from 1946 to 1956, many farmers began selling their land to developers to meet the need for housing. Along with the GI Bill, it helped new Clark residents take steps to save money. One way to cut costs was by cutting their children's hair themselves. (Courtesy of the Frank family.)

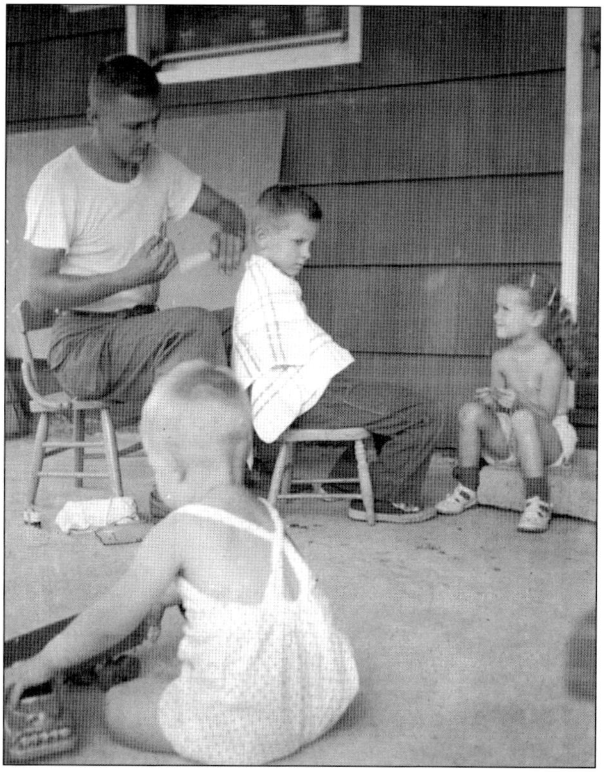

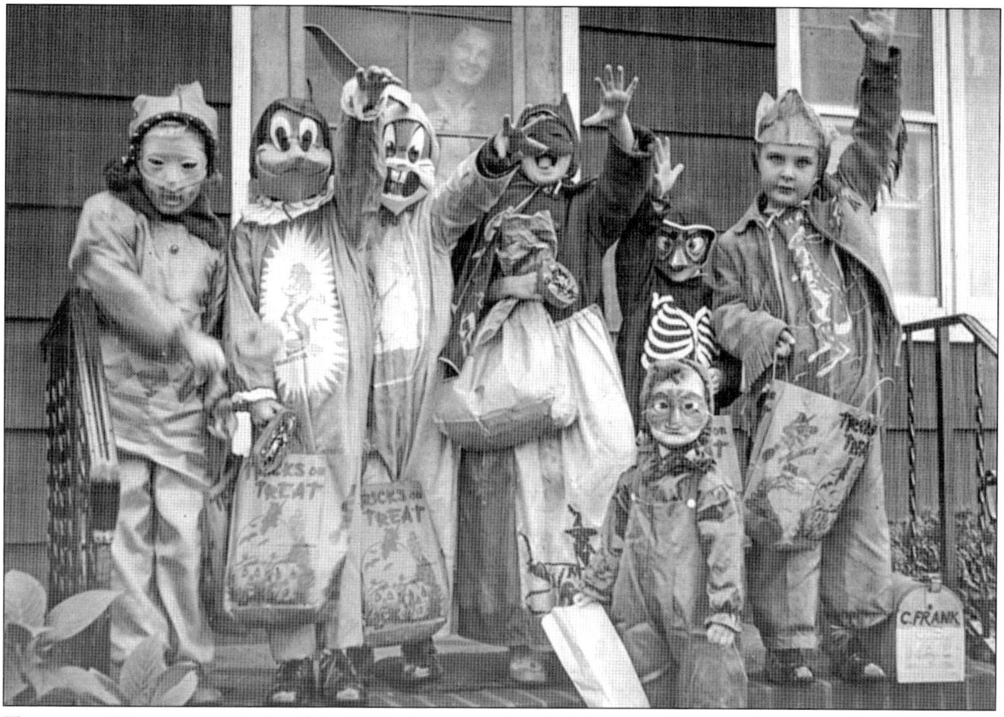

Trick or Treat, 1956. In this 1956 photograph, children go door-to-door searching for their Halloween treats along Wendell Place. (Courtesy of the Frank family.)

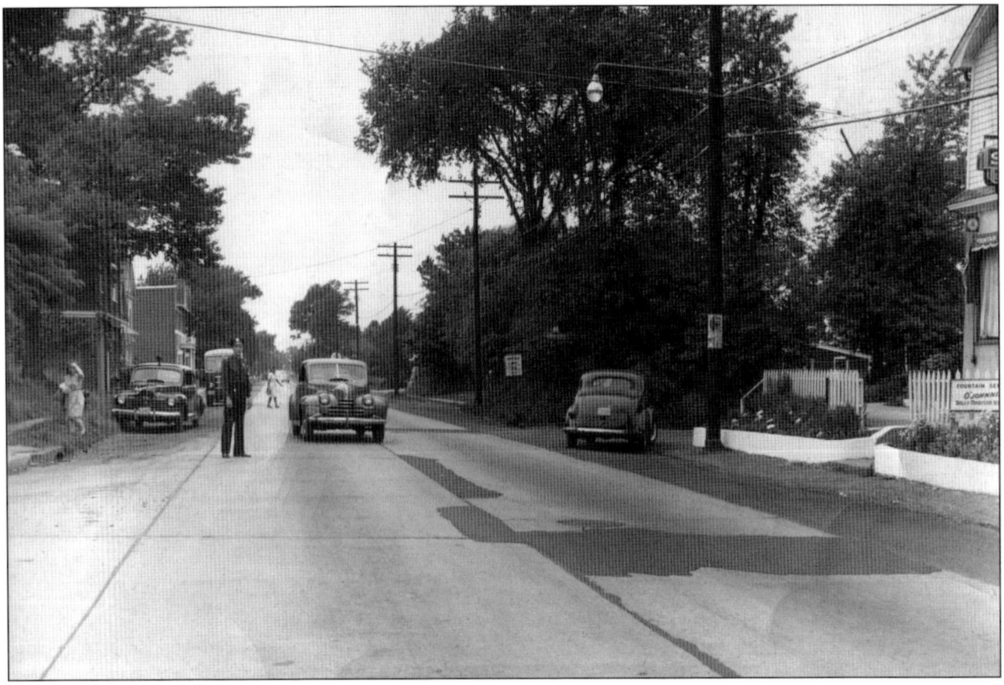

WESTFIELD AVENUE, 1946. In this 1946 photograph, taken facing west, is the Madison Hill Road intersection at the Rahway border. On the right is the original O'Johnnie's soda shop. (Courtesy of the Clark History Room.)

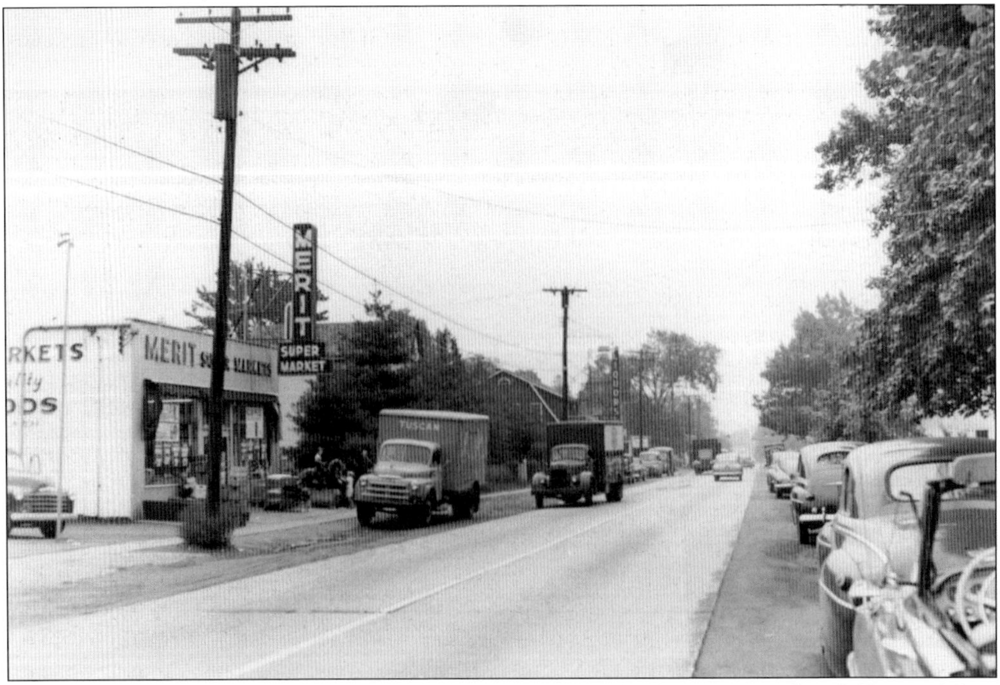

WESTFIELD AVENUE, 1954. In this 1954 photograph, taken looking east, is the Eli Kazaws Merit Food Town, which was a landmark along the Westfield Avenue corridor. (Courtesy of the Clark History Room.)

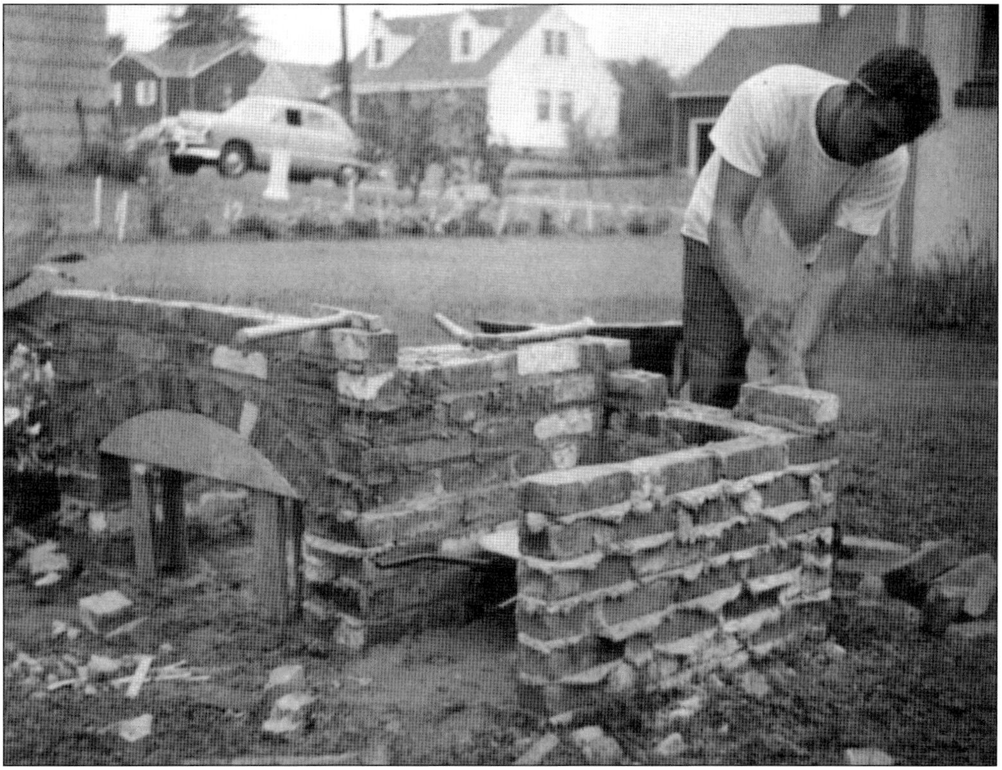

Building the American Dream. New Clark resident Carl Frank, a recent Army veteran, purchased a new home on Wendell Place (with help of the GI Bill) and worked on the weekends to build a family barbecue in his backyard in 1954. (Courtesy of the Frank family.)

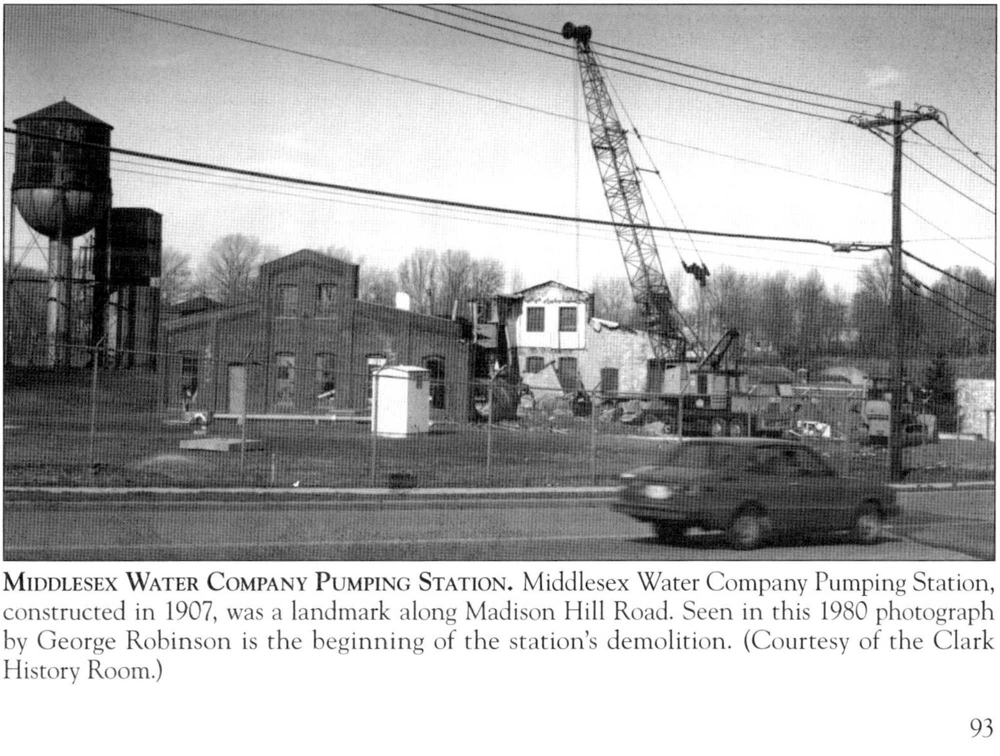

Middlesex Water Company Pumping Station. Middlesex Water Company Pumping Station, constructed in 1907, was a landmark along Madison Hill Road. Seen in this 1980 photograph by George Robinson is the beginning of the station's demolition. (Courtesy of the Clark History Room.)

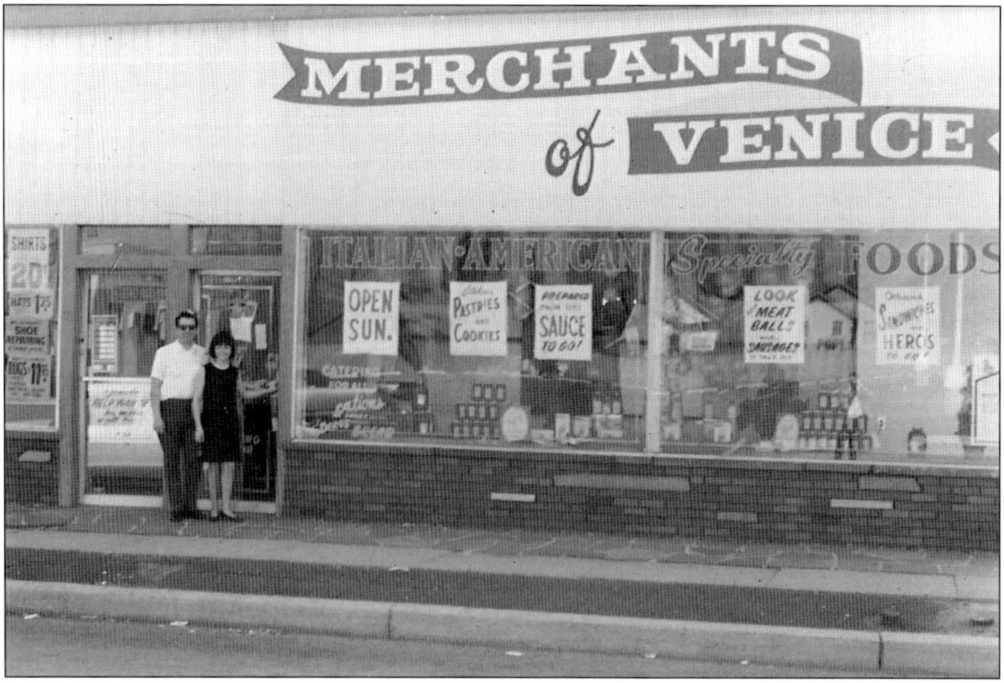

Merchants of Venice. From 1967 to 1995, this Clark landmark catered to the township, providing residents with homemade hot and cold Italian sandwiches. Seen in front of the store on opening day are Chet George and Grace George. (Courtesy of Joe Pisapia.)

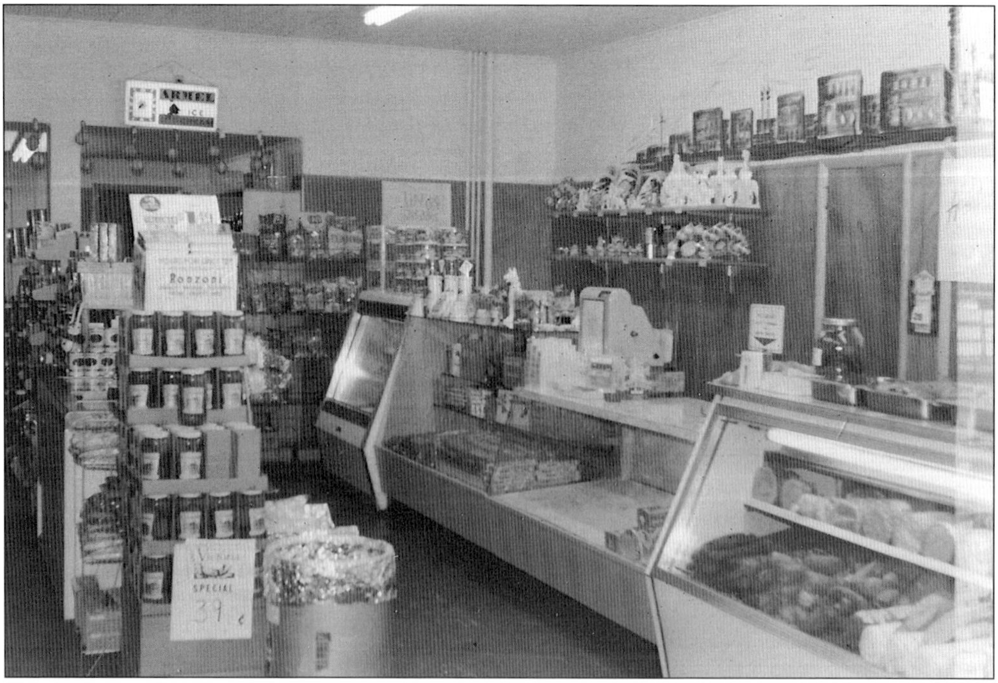

Inside Merchants of Venice. This photograph was taken on opening day at Merchants of Venice, located on Westfield Avenue in Clark, New Jersey This landmark was a mainstay for Clark residents at lunchtime and for family parties. (Courtesy of Joe Pisapia.)

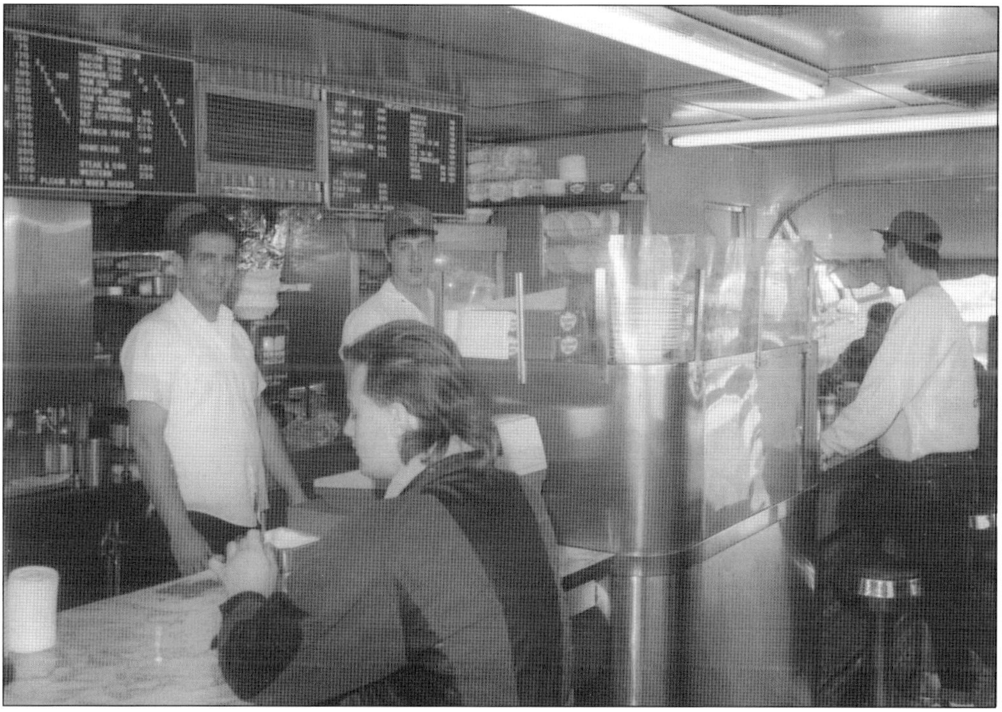

THE WHITE DIAMOND. The White Diamond restaurant opened in 1946. The original landmark stood on the corner of Raritan Road and Central Avenue until 1994, when it was razed to erected the new building seen in this photograph, taken by Denis Connell. (Courtesy of Denis Connell Sr.)

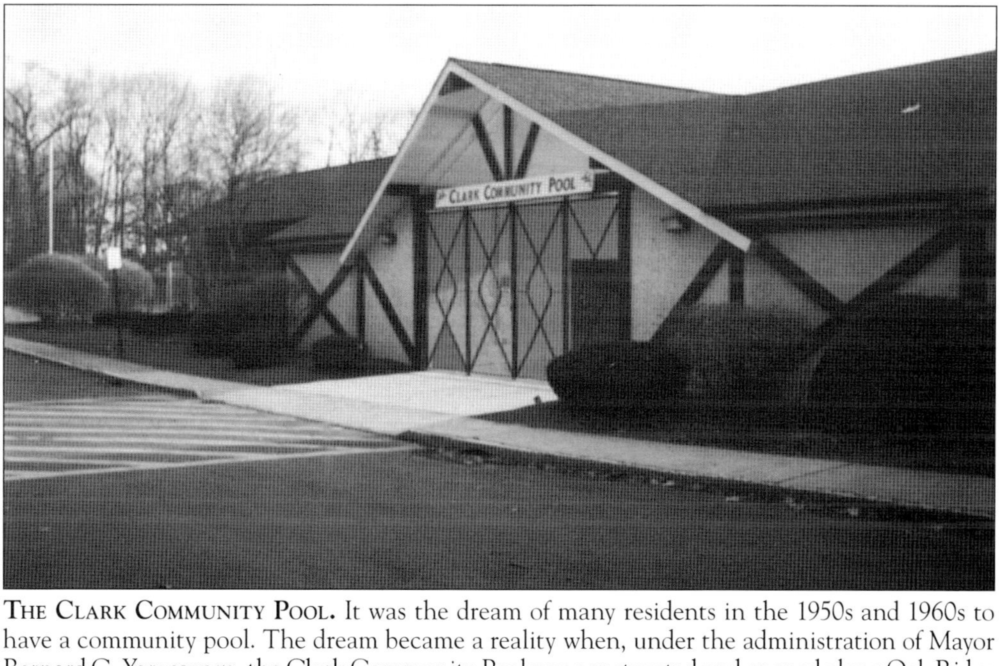

THE CLARK COMMUNITY POOL. It was the dream of many residents in the 1950s and 1960s to have a community pool. The dream became a reality when, under the administration of Mayor Bernard G. Yarusavage, the Clark Community Pool was constructed and opened along Oak Ridge Road in 1974. (Courtesy of the Clark History Room.)

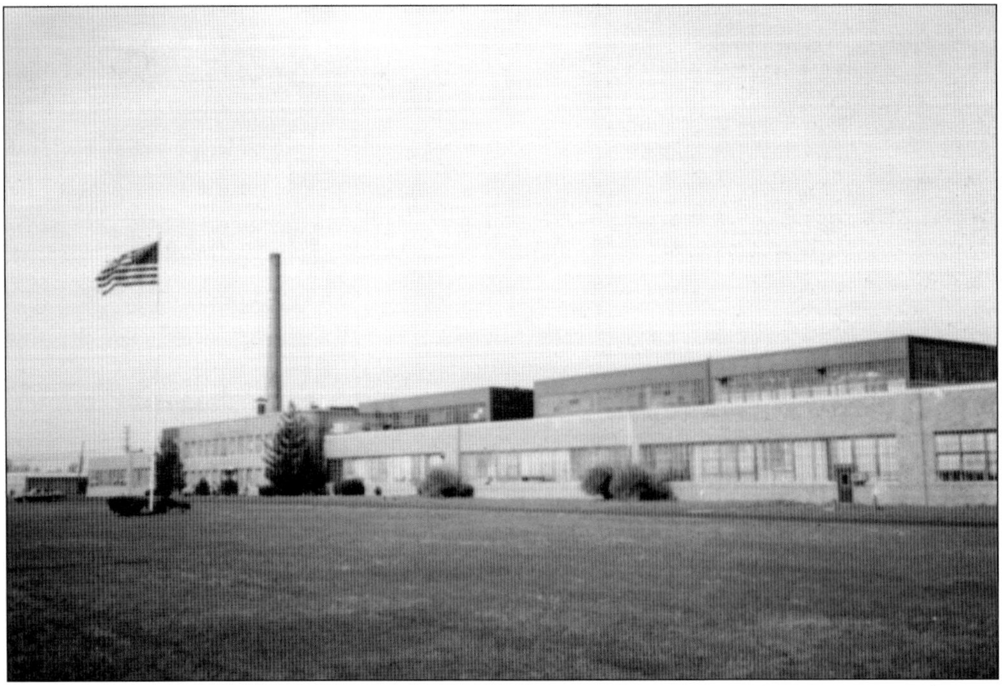

Hyatt Roller Bearing. This factory was located along Raritan Road from 1931 until 1987, when it closed. It made roller bearings for GM automobiles, providing employment for may local residents. (Courtesy of the Clark History Room.)

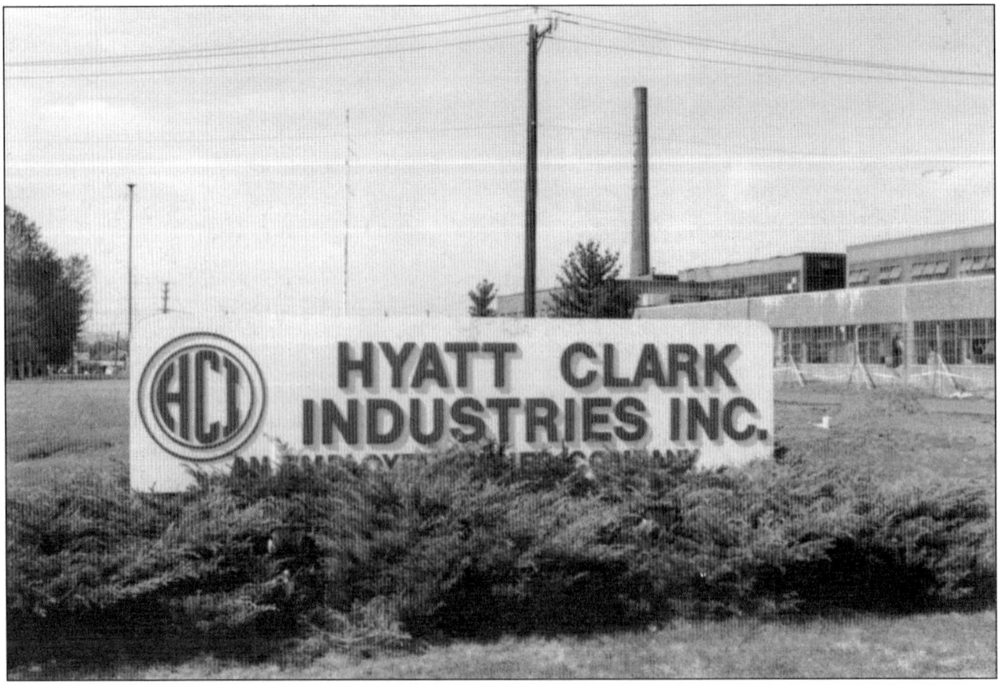

Hyatt Clark Industries, 1981. In 1981, GM announced it intended to close Hyatt Roller Bearing Company. The closing was stopped when employees stepped in and purchased the plant and created Hyatt Clark. It remained in business until 1987. (Courtesy of the Clark History Room.)

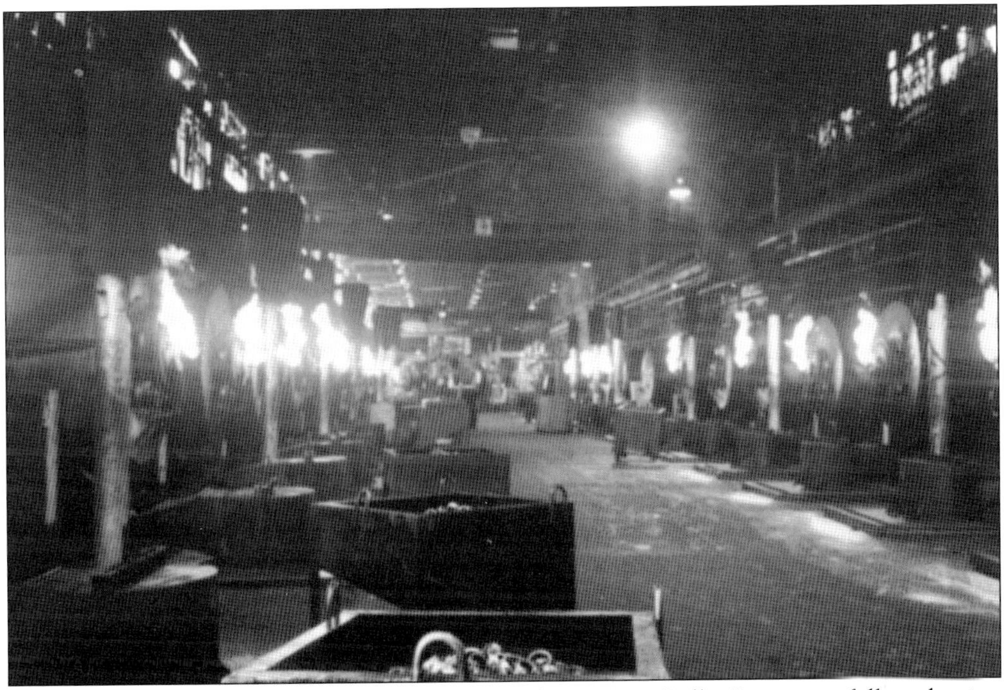

Hyatt Roller Bearing, 1976. This photograph shows Hyatt Roller Bearing in full production with all 24 furnaces in operation. This plant employed day and night shifts and worked on a 24-hour schedule. (Courtesy of the Clark History Room.)

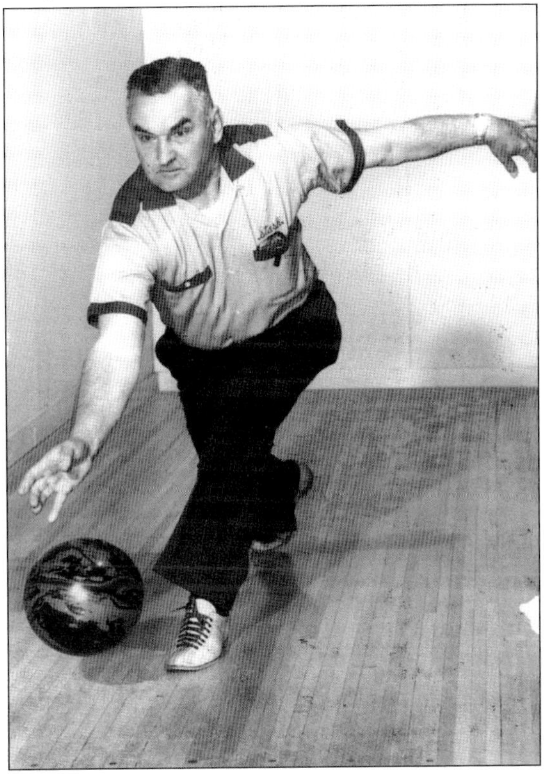

Bowling on Westfield Avenue, 1955. Longtime resident Mike Versosky bowls a 300 game at Augie Tavern and Bowling Alley. The two-lane bowling facility was a popular tavern and bowling alley in the 1940s and 1950s. (Courtesy of the Marhold family.)

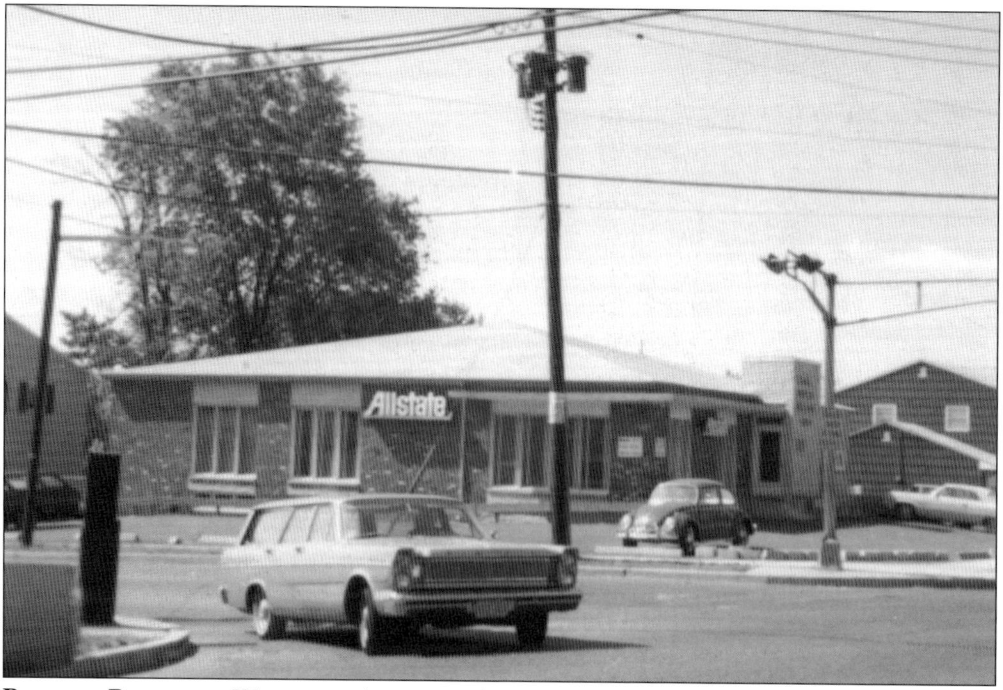

RARITAN ROAD AND WESTFIELD AVENUE. The intersection pictured here in 1965 shows the recent change of a residential home being torn down for a new commercial building. (Courtesy of the Clark History Room.)

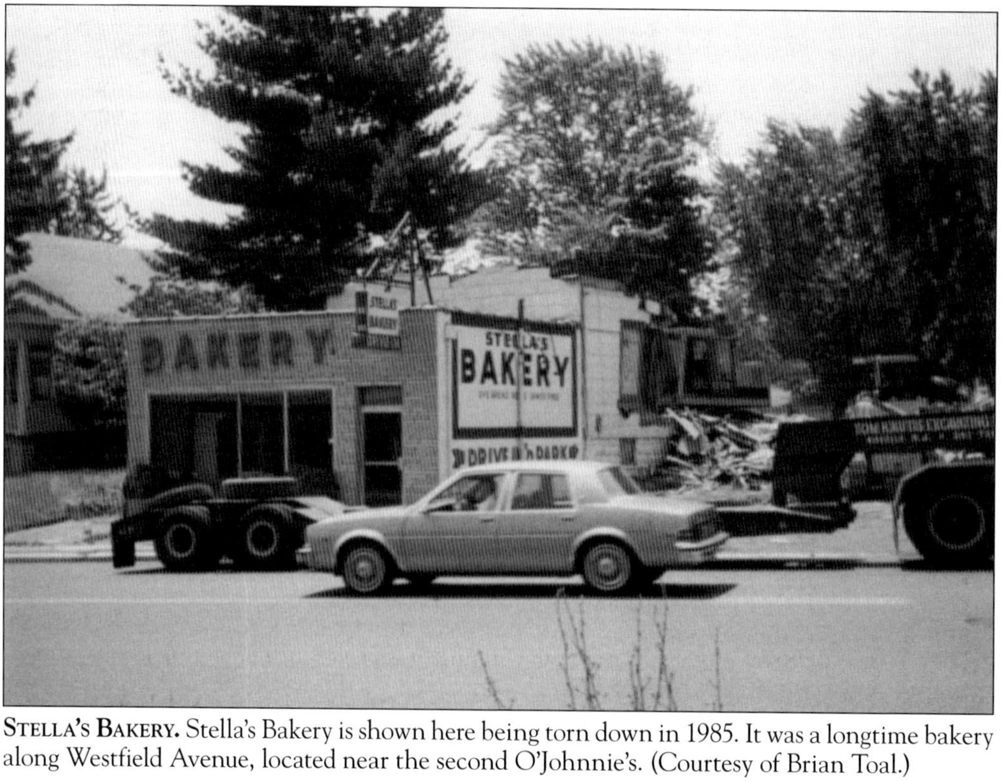

STELLA'S BAKERY. Stella's Bakery is shown here being torn down in 1985. It was a longtime bakery along Westfield Avenue, located near the second O'Johnnie's. (Courtesy of Brian Toal.)

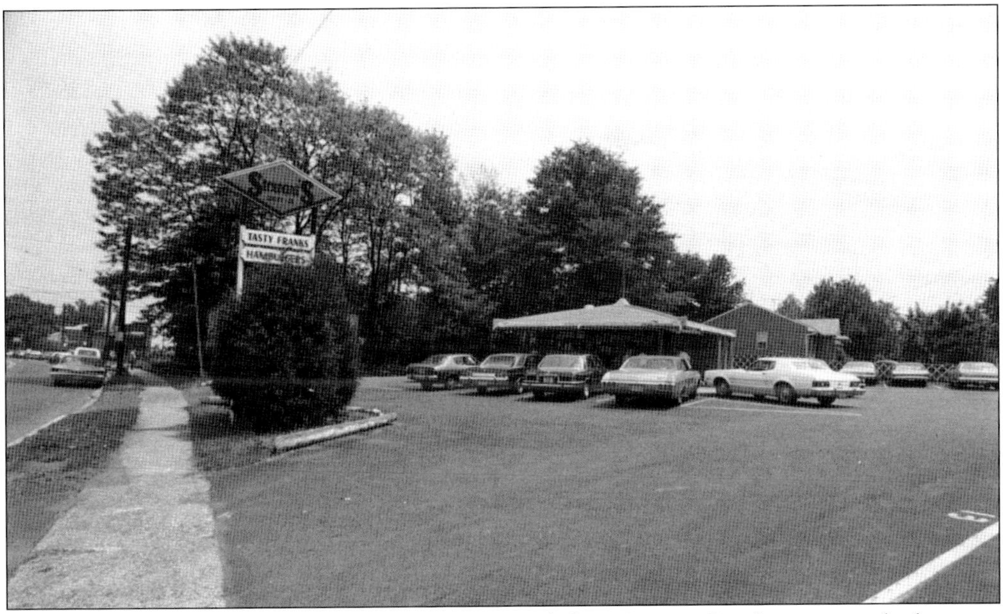

Stewart's Root Beer Stand. This building, located along Raritan Road, was a popular hangout spot for high school students in the late 1970s. It closed in 1986 and became Clark Bar-B-Que. (Courtesy of the Clark History Room.)

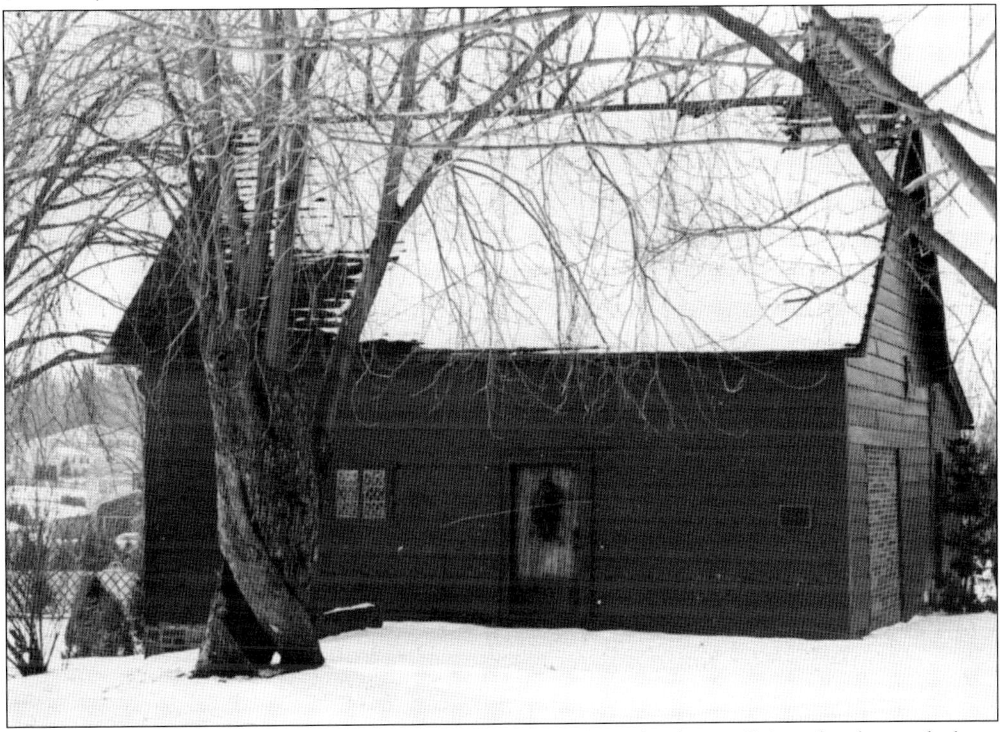

Dr. William Robinson Plantation. This building dates back to 1690 and is located along Madison Hill Road. This was the first homestead in the territory that became Clark Township. Currently under the direction of Scott McCabe and the Clark Historical Society, it is a home faithfully restored to its original 17th-century design. (Courtesy of the Clark History Room.)

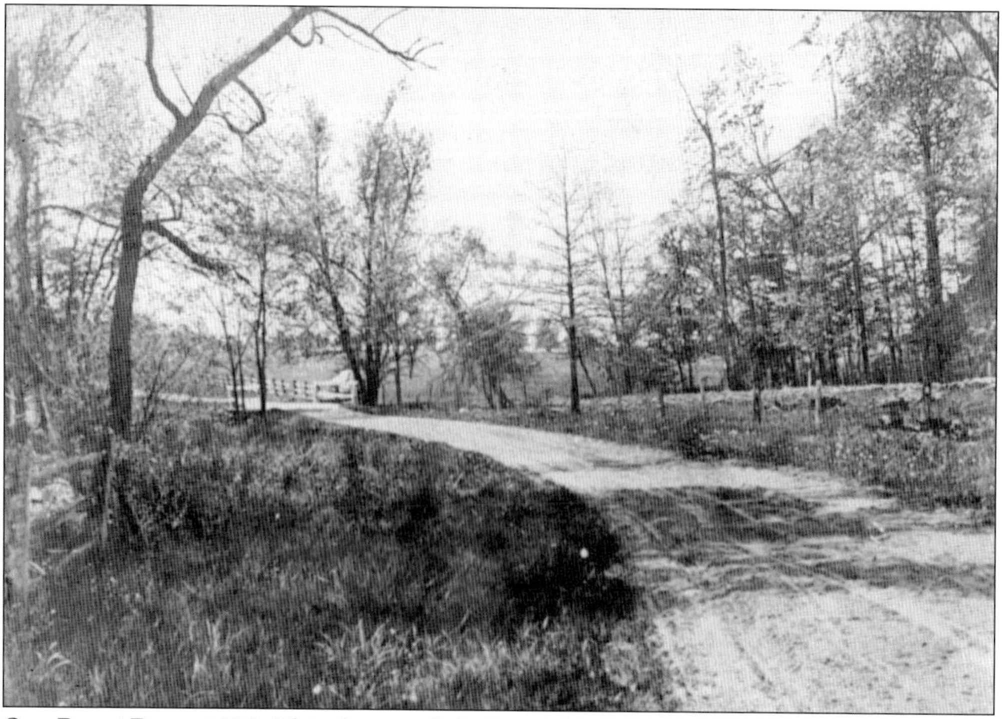

Oak Ridge Road, 1870. This photograph looks south along Oak Ridge Road, a dirt one-lane farm road, in 1870. (Courtesy of the Clark History Room.)

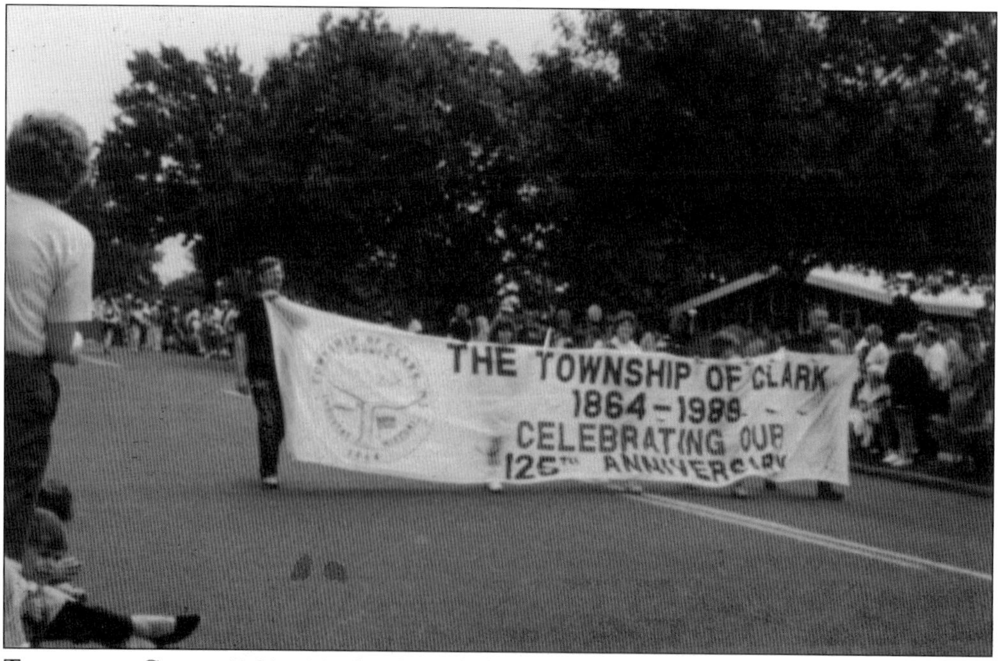

Township of Clark, 1864–1989. In 1989, Clark Township held its 125th-anniversary celebration with events like the one seen here. This parade took place on September 17, 1989. Holding the banner is, from left to right, Robert Yelenowsky, Sharon Biss, Karen Yelenowsky, and Paul Biss. (Courtesy of the Clark History Room.)

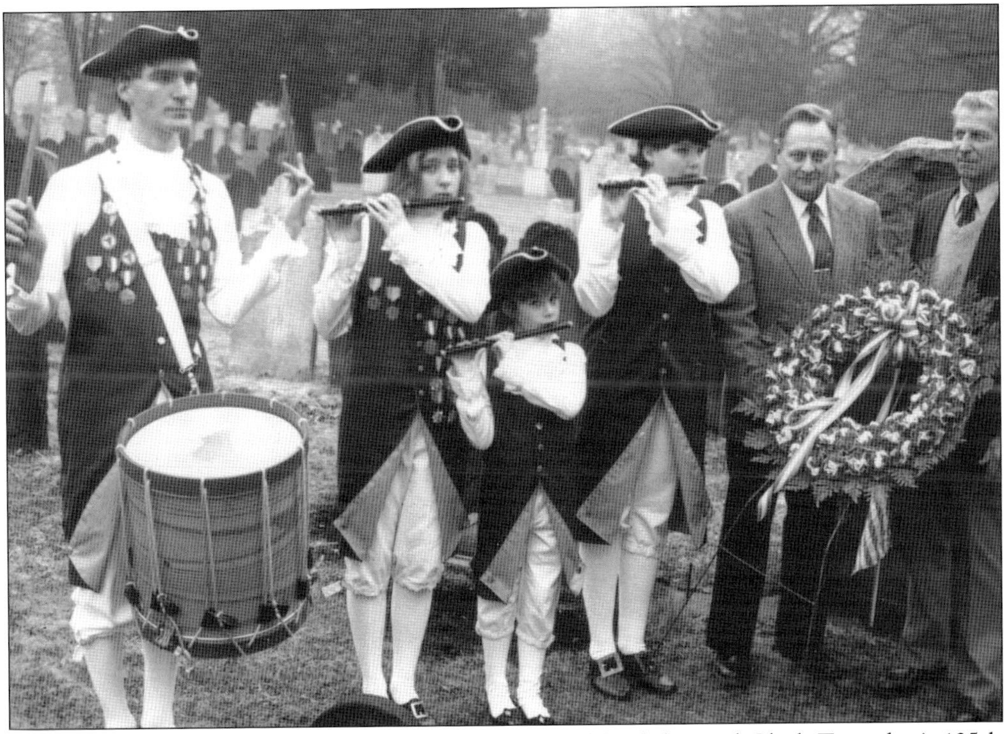

February 15, 1989. Marking Abraham Clark's 263rd birthday and Clark Township's 125th anniversary, Clark mayor Bernard G. Yarusavage (second from right) and Councilman Joseph Rybak lay a wreath at the grave of the township namesake in Rahway Cemetery. They are joined by members of the Westfield Fife and Drum Corps. (Courtesy of Dr. Denis Connell Sr.)

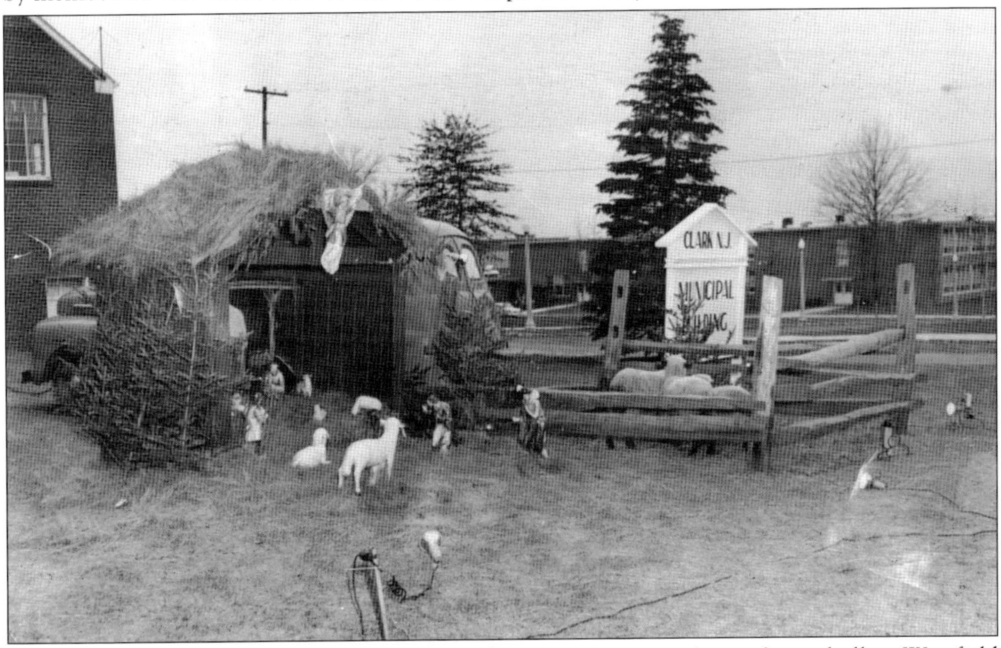

Holidays in Clark, 1957. Livestock made up the manger scene in front of town hall on Westfield Avenue in 1957. (Courtesy of the Clark History Room.)

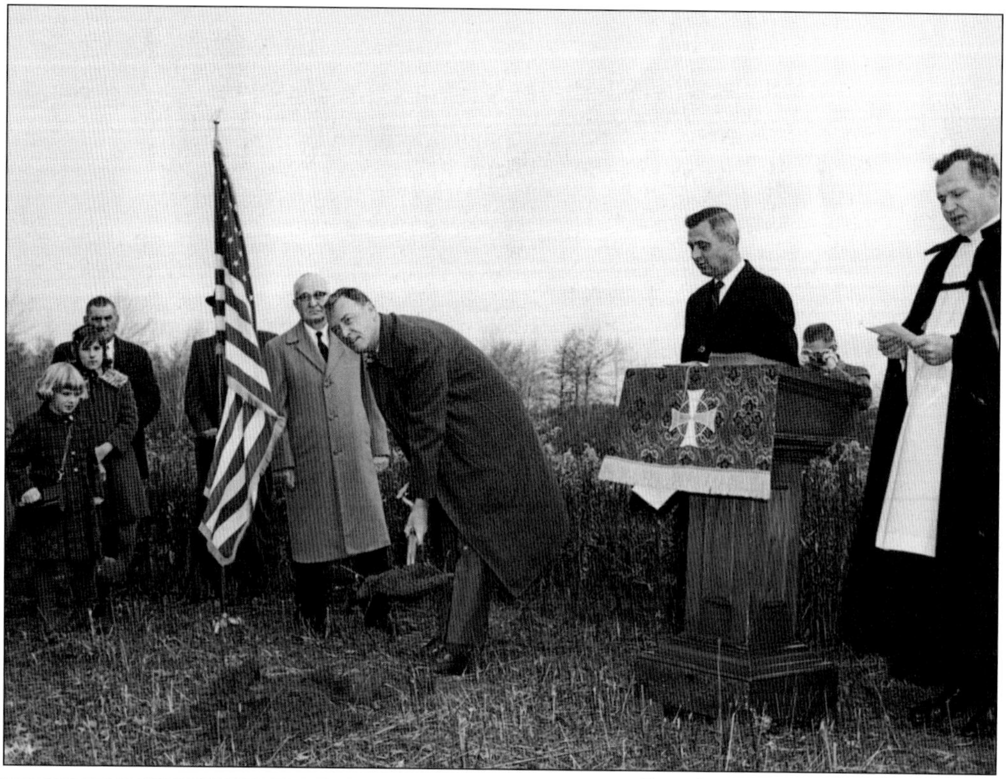

Zion Lutheran Church. Zion Lutheran Church, situated along Raritan Road, has been part of the faith community since 1967. Seen at the ground-breaking ceremony is Mayor William Maguire in 1967. (Courtesy of the Maguire family.)

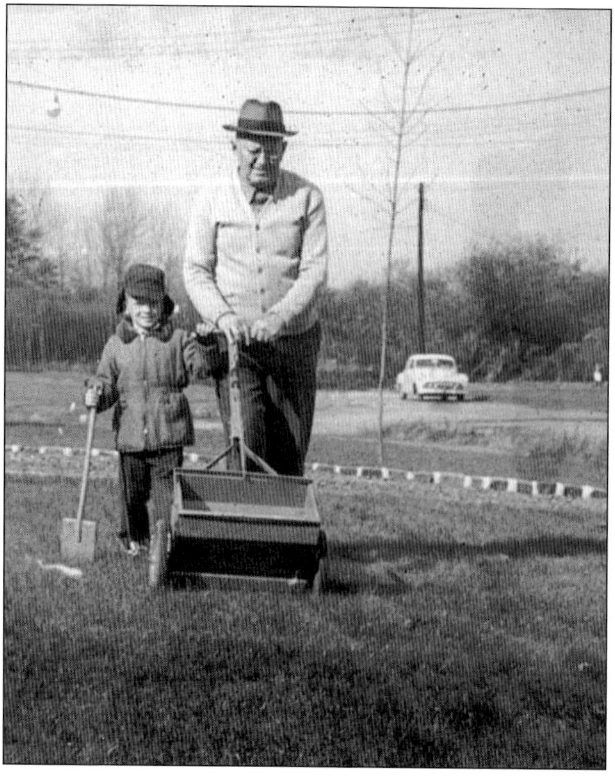

Sowing the Seeds. Nicholas Frank receives help from his grandson Kim in planting grass seed at the home the family had recently built on Wendell Place in 1954. (Courtesy of the Frank family.)

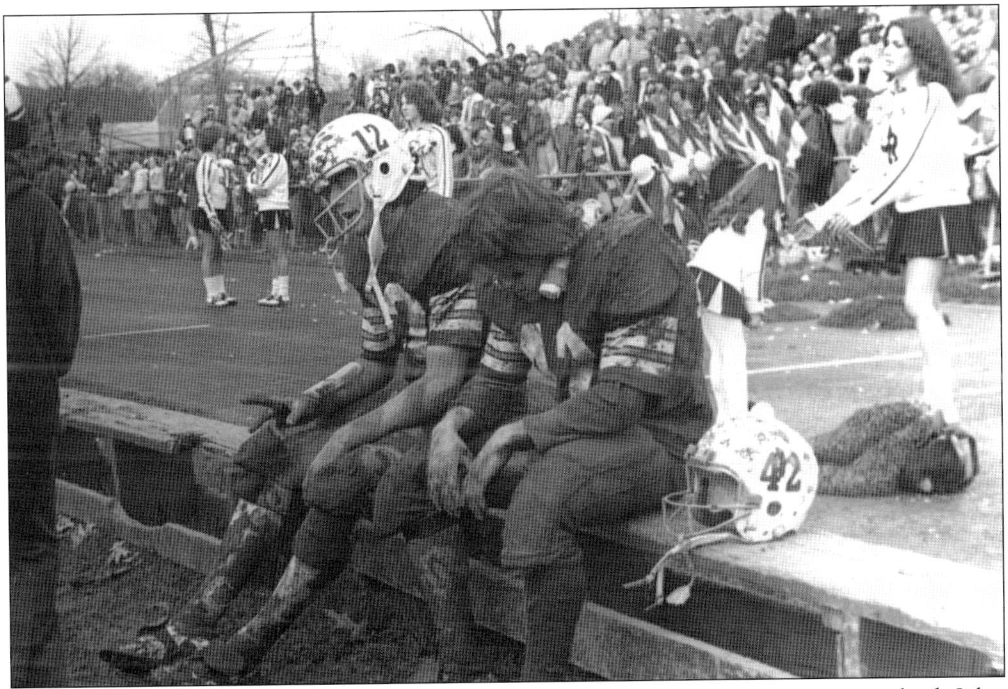

Crusaders Football, 1977. At the Crusaders football Thanksgiving game, quarterback John Metz and Wingback Thomas Roszkowski talking strategy before going back in. The three generations of the Metz and Roszkowski combination helped forge the Crusaders into winning seasons. (Courtesy of Dan Sexton.)

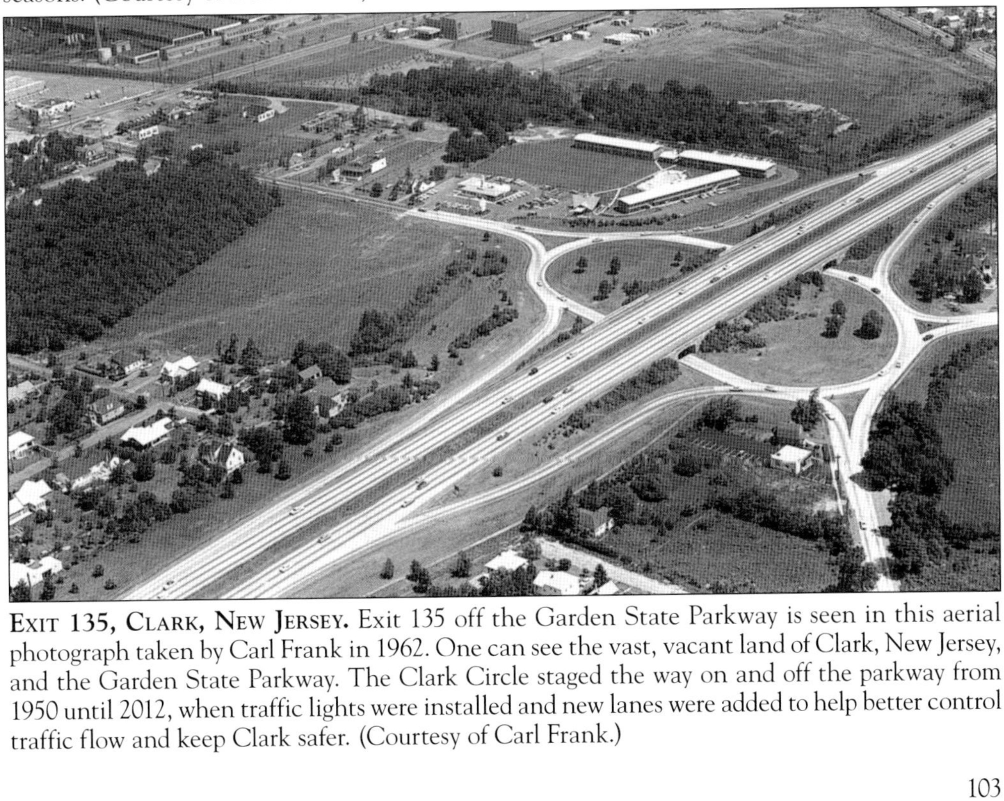

Exit 135, Clark, New Jersey. Exit 135 off the Garden State Parkway is seen in this aerial photograph taken by Carl Frank in 1962. One can see the vast, vacant land of Clark, New Jersey, and the Garden State Parkway. The Clark Circle staged the way on and off the parkway from 1950 until 2012, when traffic lights were installed and new lanes were added to help better control traffic flow and keep Clark safer. (Courtesy of Carl Frank.)

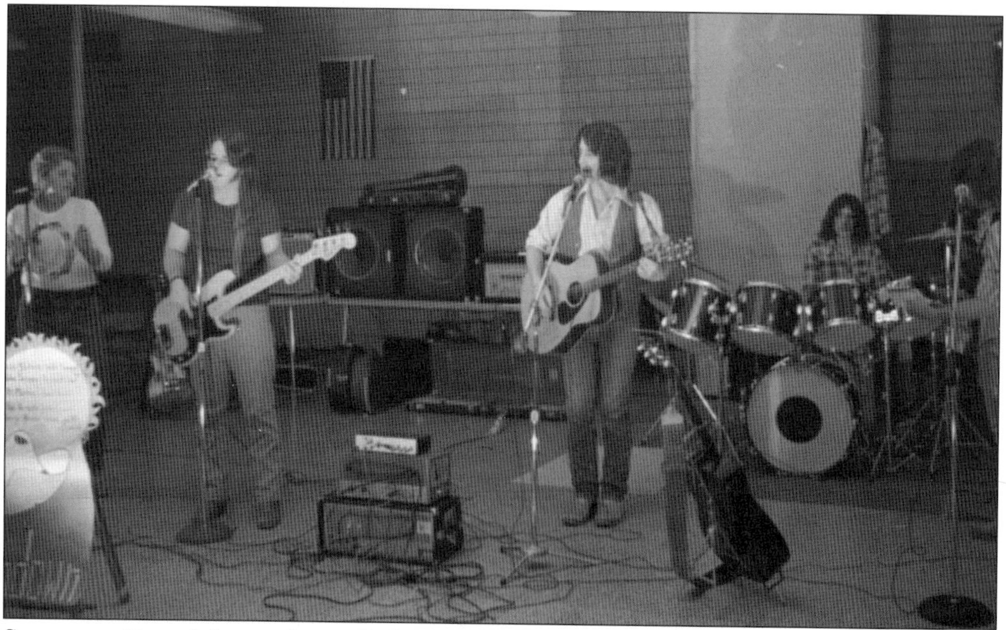

SUNDOWN. From left to right are Robert Verrastro, lead guitar and Arthur L. Johnson High School class of 1976; John Sanzone, bass guitar, lead vocals, and Arthur L. Johnson High School class of 1977; George Ambile, guitar, vocals, and Arthur L. Johnson High School class of 1977; Pat Martucci; drums, percussion, vocals, and Arthur L. Johnson High School class of 1978; and Richard Stahink, trumpet, guitar, vocals, and Arthur L. Johnson High School class of 1977. Not shown is bandmember Timothy Crystal, Arthur L. Johnson High School class of 1977. (Courtesy of Russell Frank.)

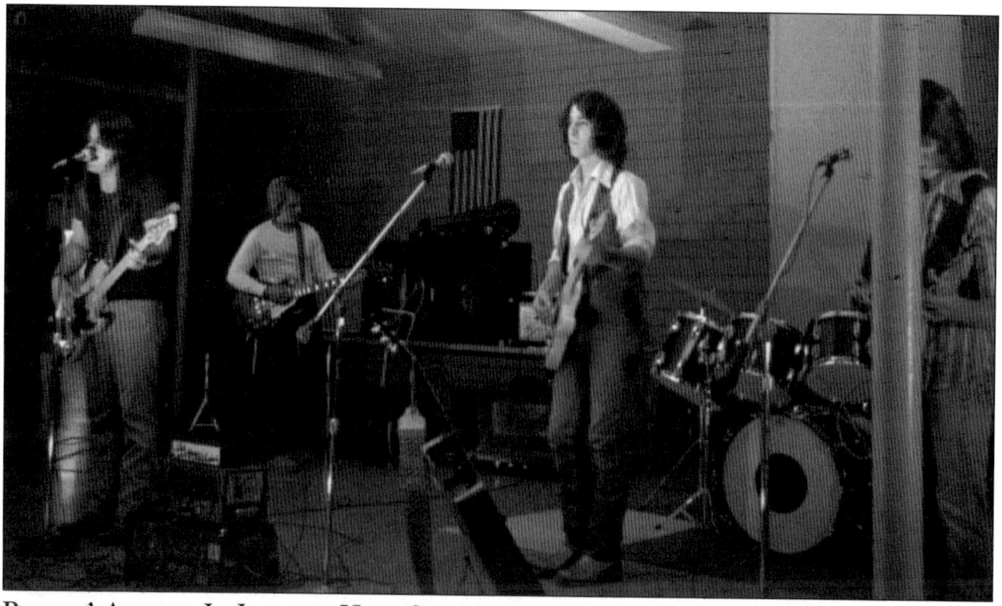

ROCKIN' ARTHUR L. JOHNSON HIGH SCHOOL. Local high school students formed the band Sundown and drew large crowds to the Arthur L. Johnson High School cafeteria, as seen in this September 1976 photograph. Seniors John Sanzone (left) and George Ambile (right) sing the Outlaws' number-one hit, "Green Grass and High Tides." (Courtesy of Pasquale Martucci Jr.)

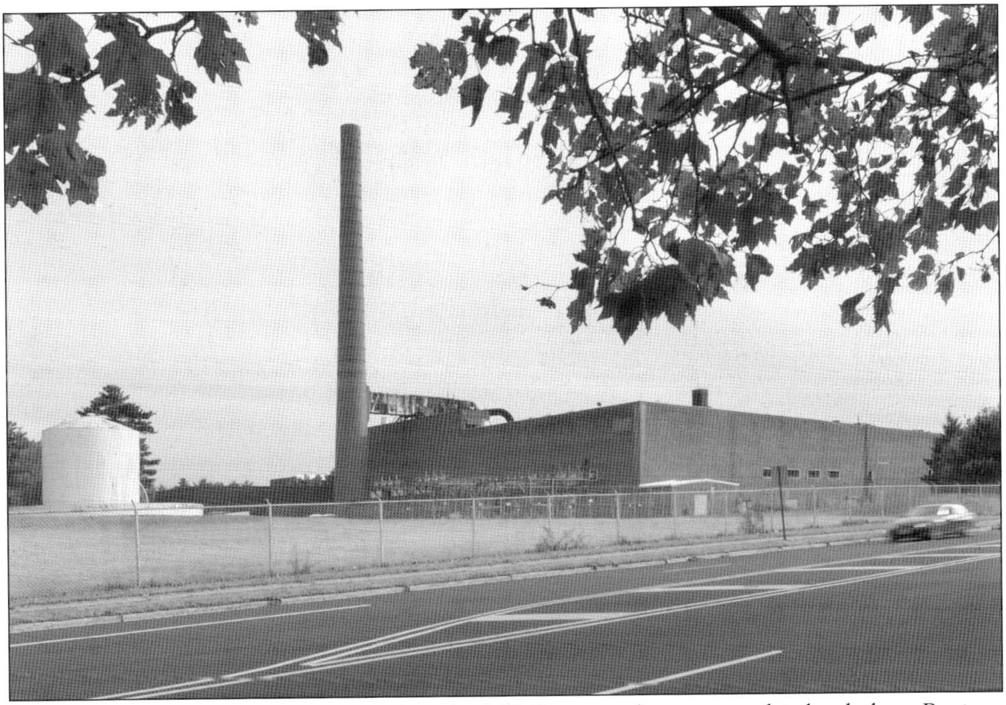

US Gypsum Plant. From 1946 to 2014, the US Gypsum plant sat on this land along Raritan Road. (Courtesy of Diane Metz.)

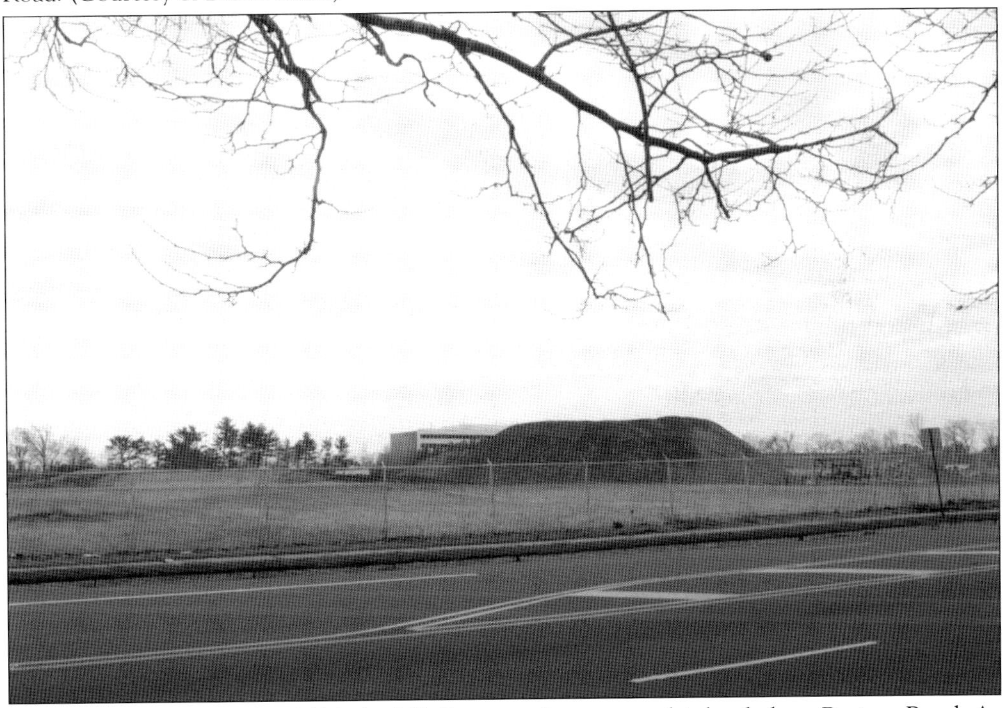

Open Space. From 1946 to 2014, the US Gypsum plant sat on this land along Raritan Road. As seen in this 2014 photograph taken by Diane Metz, the land was reverted to its original state of open space before it became the Clark Commons. (Courtesy of Diane Metz.)

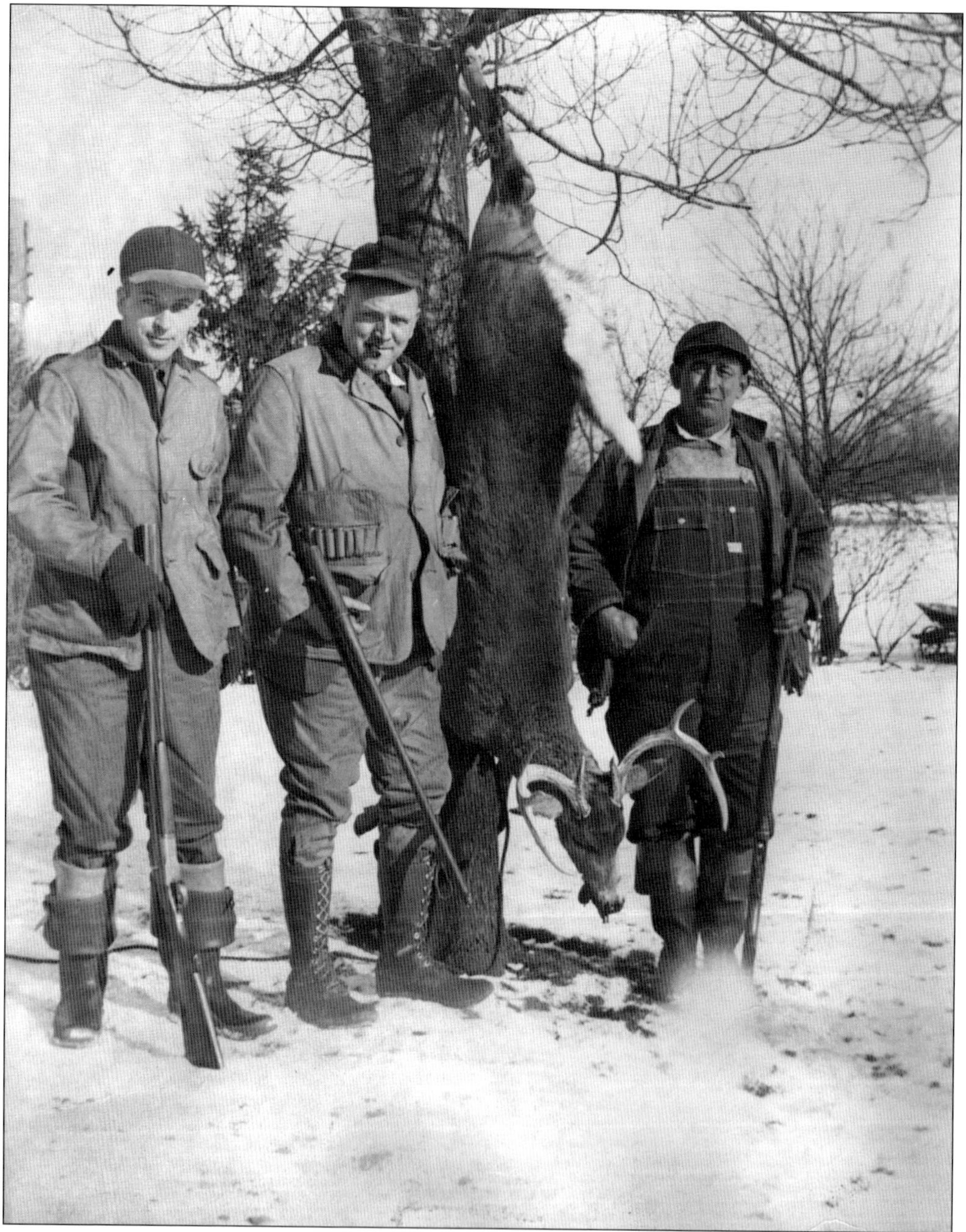

Deer Hunting in Clark. In this 1946 photograph, Clark farmers pose with a three-point buck in the woods on the Cordes Farm, along the present-day Terminal Avenue. Pictured from left to right are Clark residents August "Gus" Granrath, Fred Schieferstein, and George Cordes. (Courtesy of Schieferstein Farms.)

Nine

Portraits of Distinction

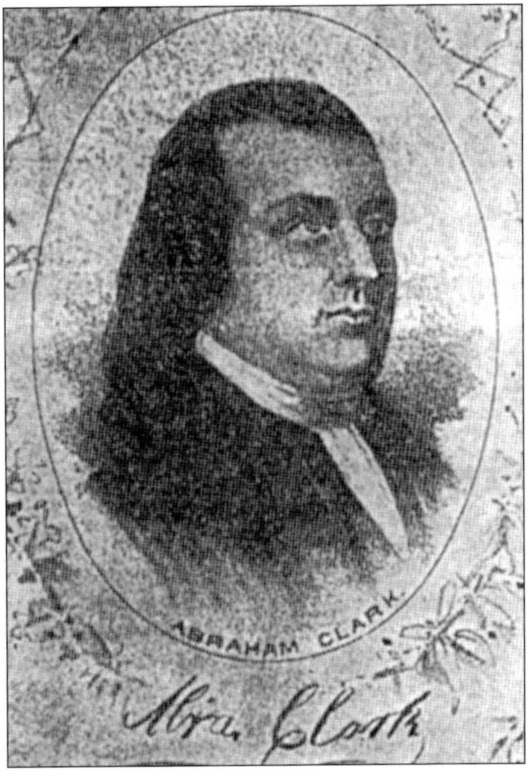

Abraham Clark. Abraham Clark (February 15, 1726–September 15, 1794) was the Township of Clark's namesake, a signer of the Declaration of Independence, and a Founding Father of the United States. He resided on a farm between Elizabeth and Rahway, New Jersey, in present-day Roselle, New Jersey. In 1864, the residents of Rahway's Fifth Ward, upon declaring their independence, created their own township and named it Clark Township. (Courtesy of the Clark History Room.)

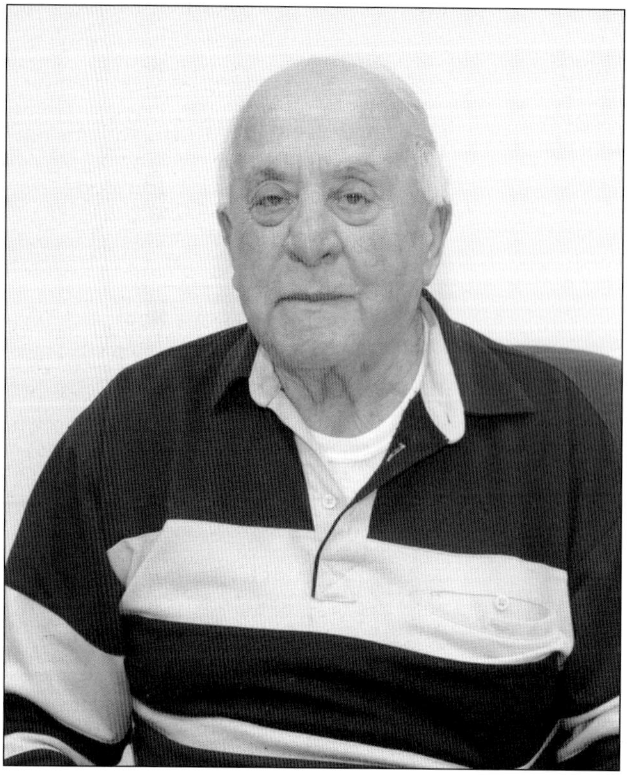

JOSEPH BONACCORSO. Joseph Bonaccorso, born November 14, 1929 in Garwood, New Jersey, has been a resident of Clark since 1967. He spent many years in Clark Little League as a coach, manager, and league president. A well-loved resident and township public works director and Shade Tree director, he also is the father of Clark mayor Salvatore Bonaccorso. (Courtesy of Diane Metz.)

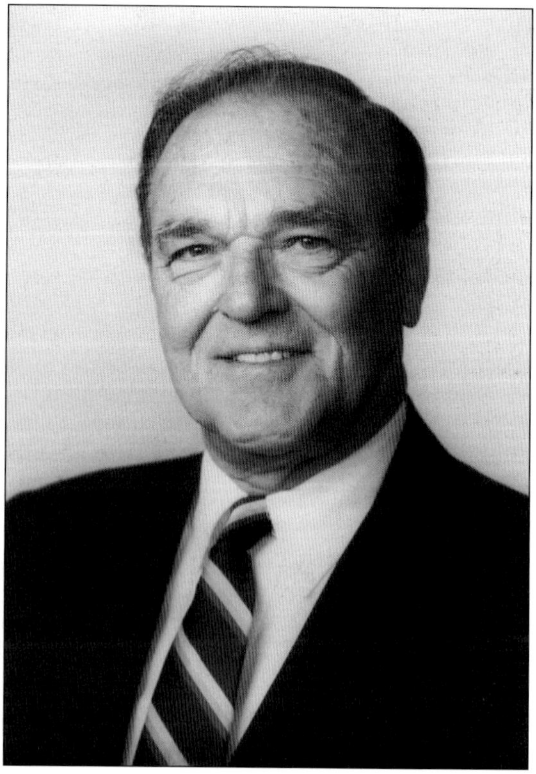

EDWARD R. MUCHMORE. Edward R. Muchmore was born July 25, 1927. He and his wife, Edith, and their four young children settled into Clark, New Jersey in 1963. He became active in Clark Little League Baseball and soon became its president. As the township grew in the 1960s, Muchmore oversaw the expansion and modernization of the league. In his honor, Muchmore Field was dedicated to him for his many years of service. He died December 8, 2011. (Courtesy of Edith Muchmore.)

Peter Nevargic. Peter Nevargic, born June 29, 1929, was a resident of Clark since the 1960s, when he, his wife, Carlene, and their sons Peter and Victor Nevargic settled into the township. A voice of reason for the community, he was elected Second Ward councilman in 1999 and was reelected in 2002. An advocate of the people, he died in office on June 3, 2004, from cancer. Nevargic Park, located in the Second Ward, is dedicated in his honor. (Courtesy of the Nevargic family.)

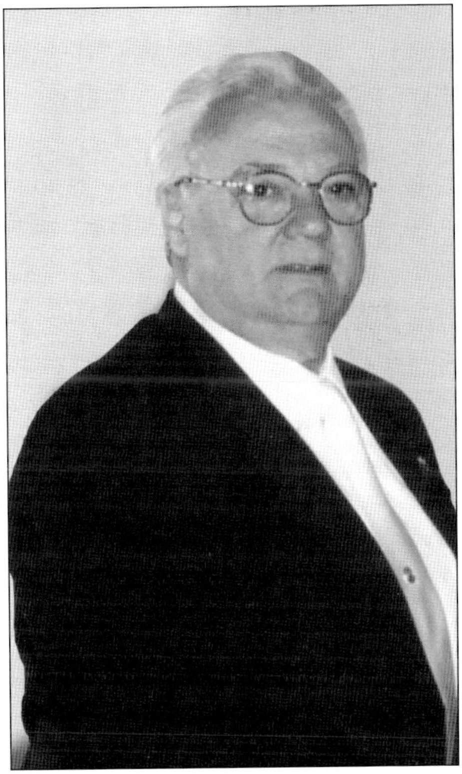

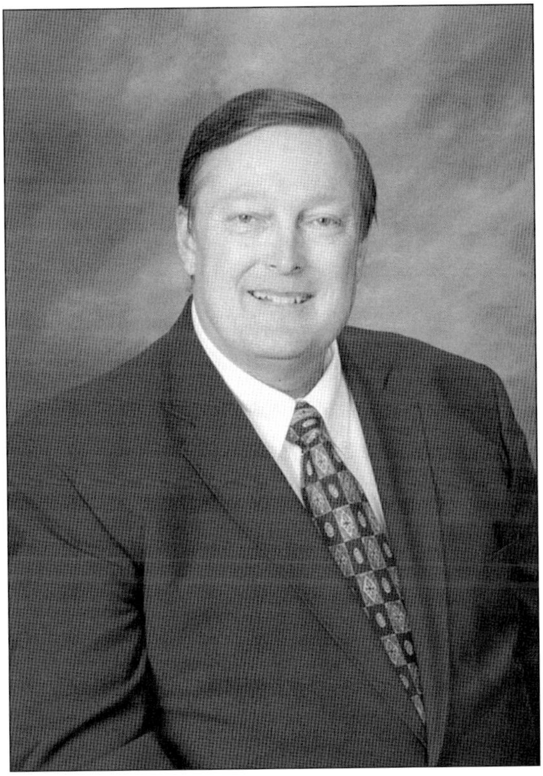

Richard Kaznowski. Richard Kaznowski, born July 5, 1952, was a beloved Third Ward councilman serving in 1993, 1994, 1999–2002, and 2007–2014. He gave countless hours to residents of Clark's Third Ward, becoming famous for his Third Ward newsletter. He died suddenly on June 3, 2014. (Courtesy of the Kaznowski family.)

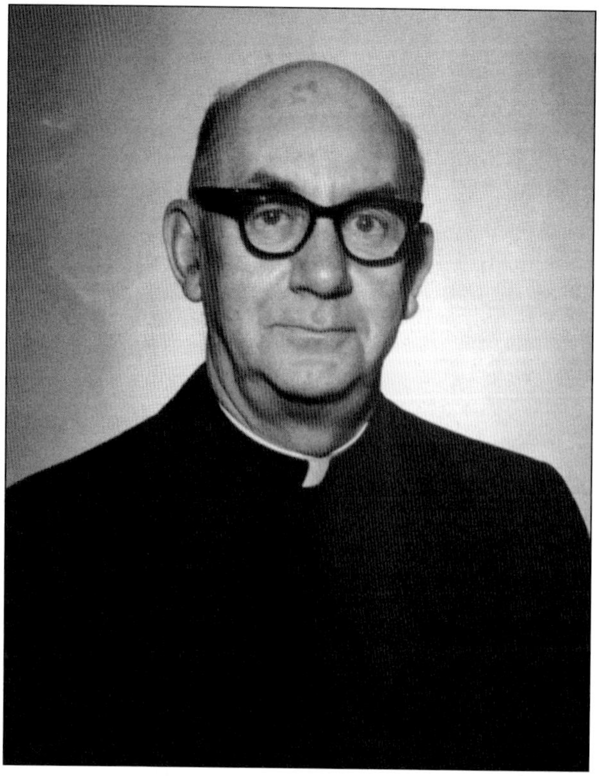

FR. DENIS J. WHALEN. Fr. Denis J. Whalen, born July 7, 1909, was the founding father of St. Agnes Roman Catholic Church on Madison Hill Road in Clark, New Jersey. In 1961, with the southerly expansion in Clark and new residents moving into housing developments, the Archdiocese of Newark, New Jersey, assigned Father Whalen to set up a new church in Clark. From 1961 until his passing on February 4, 1984, he became the township's spiritual leader and served as township chaplain for the police and fire departments. (Courtesy of St. Agnes Roman Catholic Church.)

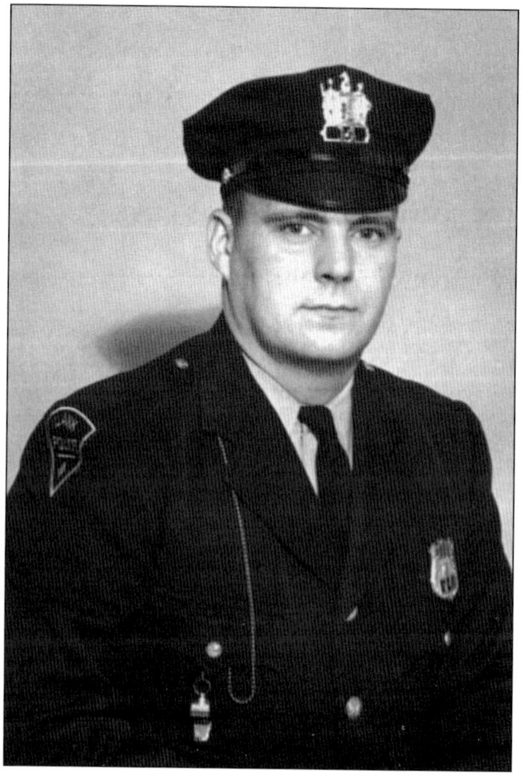

ALFRED V. YERSEVICH. Alfred V. Yersevich, born June 15, 1932, was a longtime Clark Police Department lieutenant and drill sergeant and was one of the most respected and feared men to ever wear the uniform. Known as "Big Al," he was loved and respected by the children of Clark, who knew that if they saw him coming, they behaved. He died May 2, 2007. (Courtesy of the Yersevich family.)

Joseph A. Rybak. Joseph A. Rybak, born March 16, 1924, was a longtime resident of Clark and a decorated marine in World War II. He was with the 3rd Marine Division during the Battle of Iwo Jima, which earned him the Bronze Star and a Purple Heart. He gave countless hours of service to Clark and American Legion Post 328. He was a member of the township council and was named citizen of the year in 1988. The American Legion honored him in 1999 by dedicating its new pavilion in his honor. He died October 19, 2006. (Courtesy of Dorothy Rybak.)

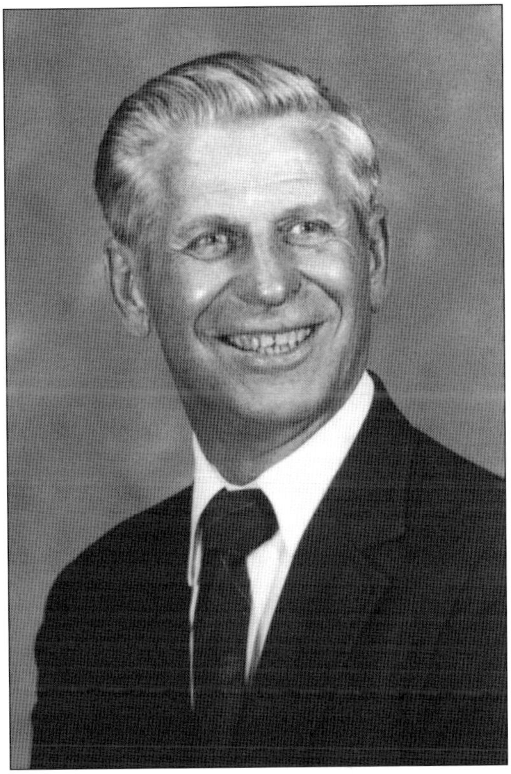

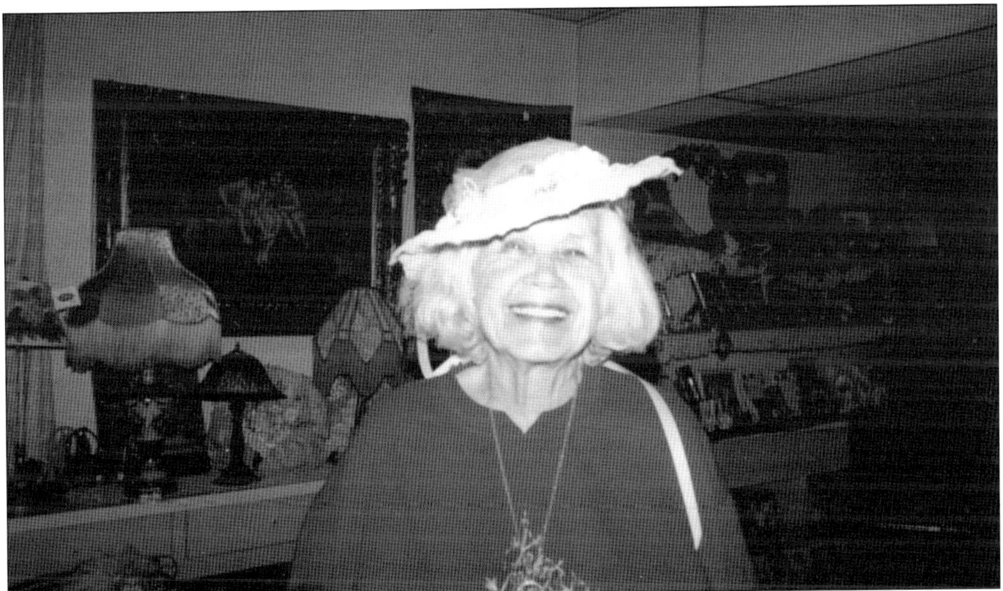

Helen C. Rokosny. Helen C. Rokosny, born on March 13, 1918, a renowned activist and voice of the people, was active in many township organizations throughout the 1960s and into the 1990s. She worked on many community projects and volunteered countless hours of her time to the township. She will always be remembered as the lady who spoke at every township council meeting, speaking on issues that she felt had to be addressed. Rokosny died March 23, 2010. (Courtesy of Delia Collins.)

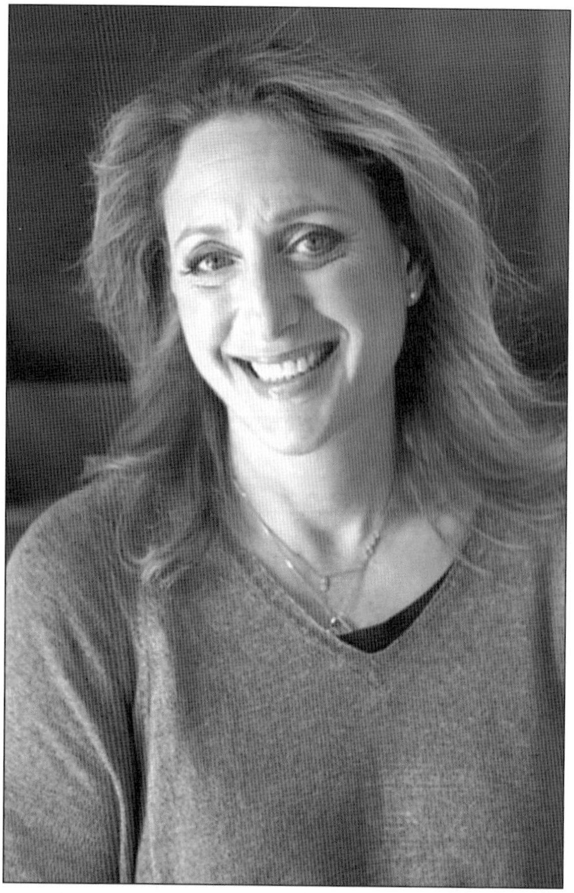

Judy Gold. Judy Gold, born November 15, 1962, is a famed comic, actress, writer, and director who grew up at 113 Mildred Terrace. She attended Carl H. Kumpf Middle School (class of 1976) and Arthur L. Johnson High School (class of 1980). She went to Rutgers University and has had incredible success following her dreams. (Courtesy of Judygold.com.)

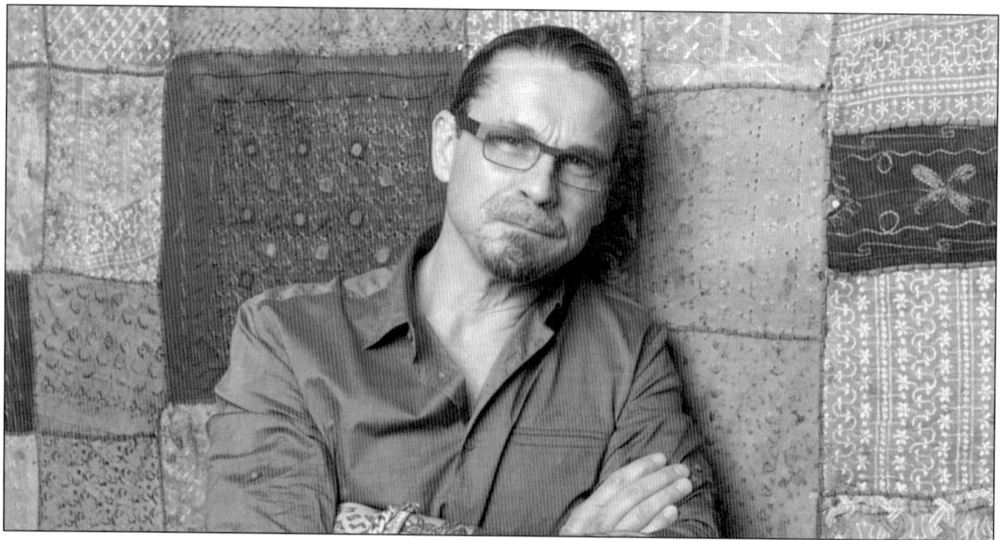

Kurt Sutter. Kurt Sutter, born May 5, 1960, was a resident of 48 Liberty Street. This young Cub Scout of Pack 45 of St. John's Roman Catholic Church on Valley Road would graduate from Union Catholic High School and Rutgers University and go onto a career in Hollywood, California, as a writer, director, producer, and actor in the show *Sons of Anarchy*. (Courtesy of Kurtsuter.com.)

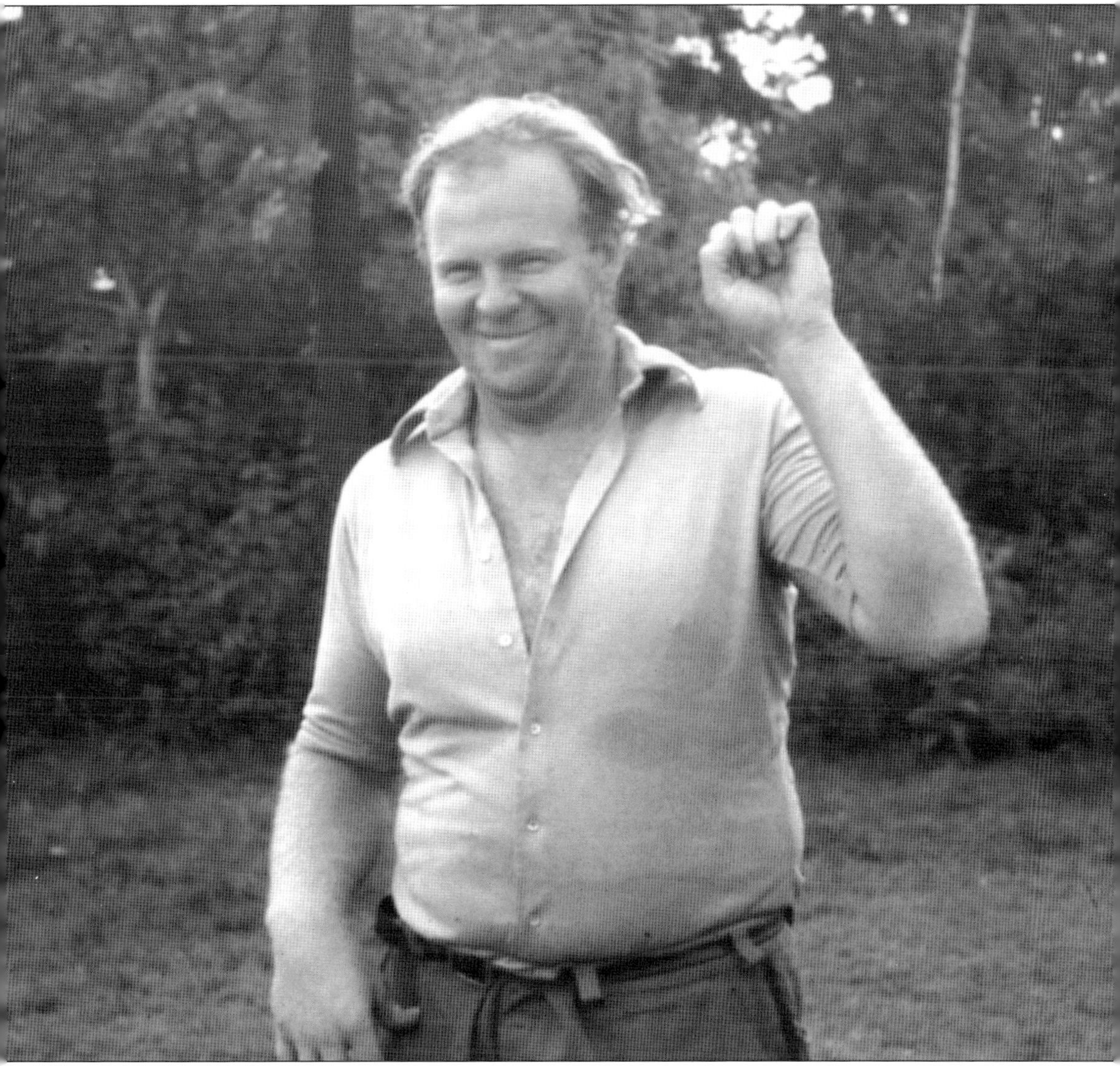

James Lake. James Lake was a legend in the township of Clark from the 1960s into the 1990s. "Laker," as he was known by many, served as a coach, umpire, referee, and friend to all. If a person grew up in Clark during this period, it is most likely he or she knew Laker. On May 9, 2006, while riding his bike across a local street, he was struck and killed by a car. (Courtesy of Jeff Barr.)

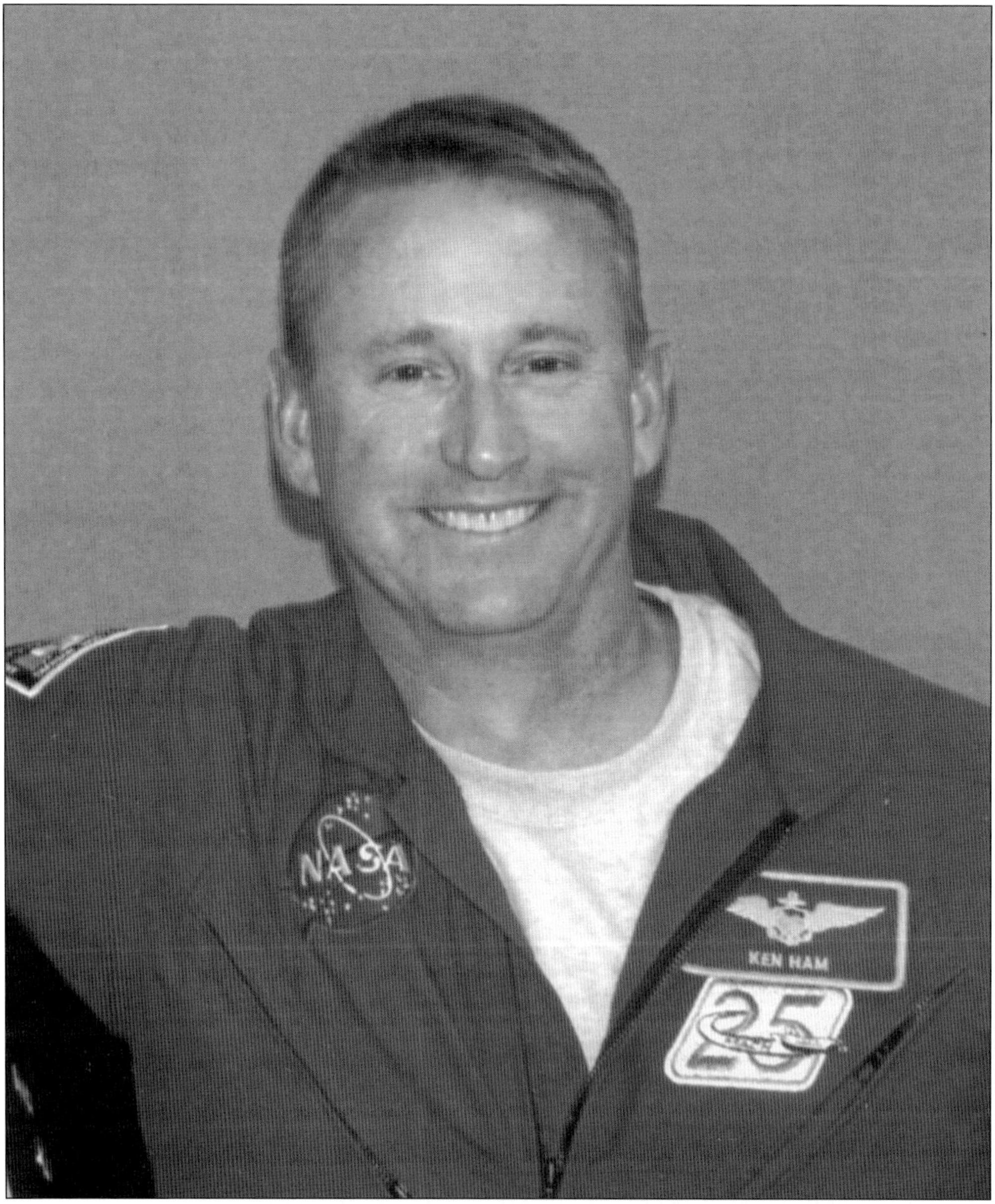

KENNETH HAM. Kenneth Ham, born December 12, 1964, is a graduate of Arthur L. Johnson High School (class of 1983) and attended the US Naval Academy and Naval Post Graduate School. An astronaut and Navy pilot, he served as commander of the Space Shuttle *Discovery*. (Courtesy of Sal Bonaccorso.)

Ten

FALLEN HEROES

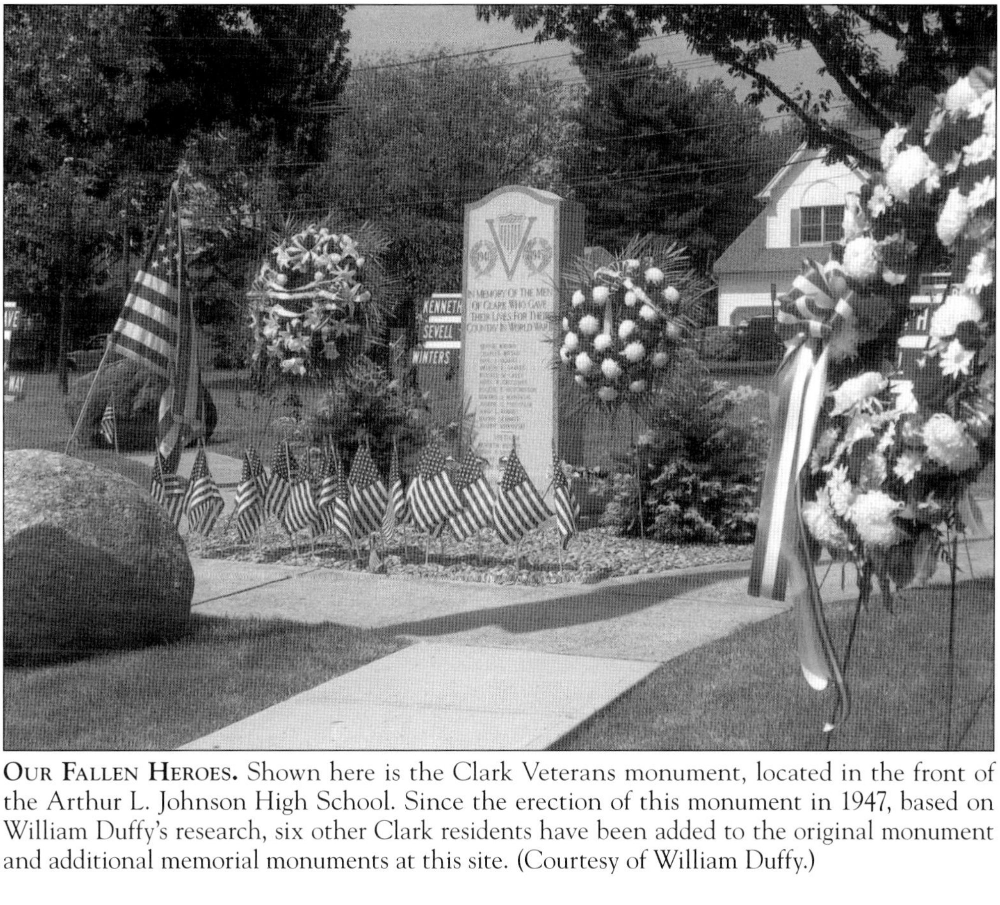

OUR FALLEN HEROES. Shown here is the Clark Veterans monument, located in the front of the Arthur L. Johnson High School. Since the erection of this monument in 1947, based on William Duffy's research, six other Clark residents have been added to the original monument and additional memorial monuments at this site. (Courtesy of William Duffy.)

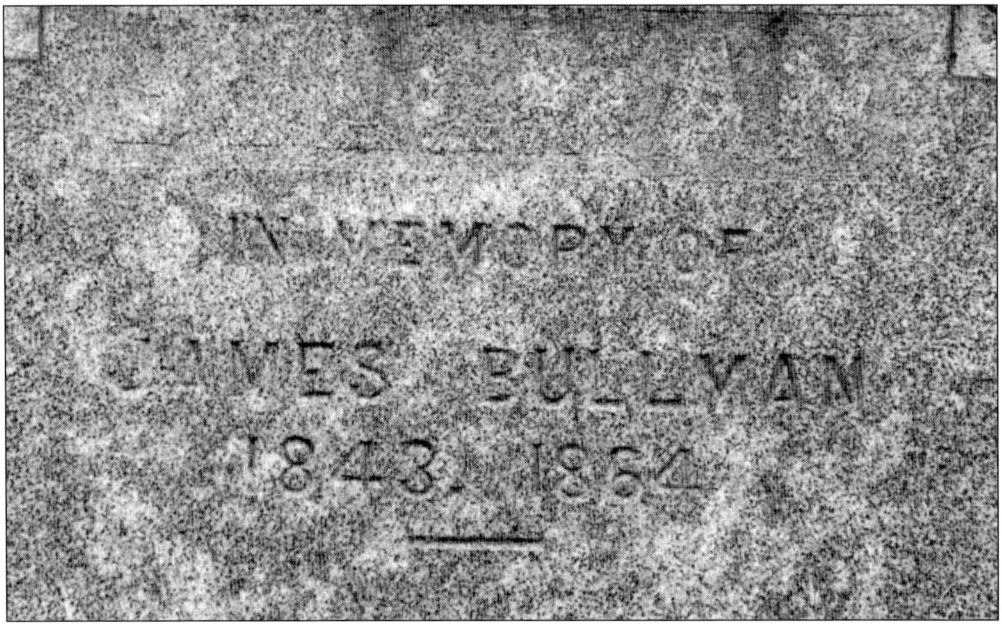

Cpl. James Bullman. Cpl. James Bullman was a member of C Company, 14th Regiment, New Jersey Volunteers. This Clark hero resided on Raritan Road, where Manny's Diner and Bank of America are presently located. He was killed in action in the Battle of Cold Harbor, Virginia, on June 1, 1864, along with 7,000 other Union soldiers. Bullman was one of the many Union County residents who answered President Lincoln's second call for volunteers in 1862. (Courtesy of William Duffy.)

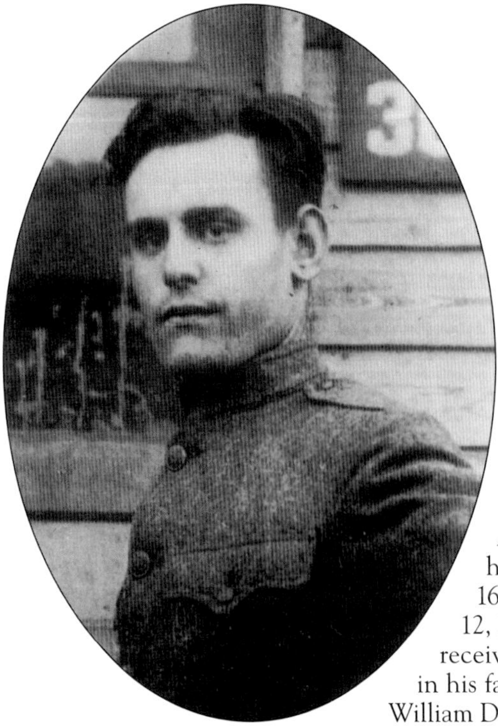

John B. Miller. John B. Miller, a member of the US Army, lived at 2 Valley Road. His father, Adam, received notice on December 9, 1918, that his son, reported as missing in action on October 16, 1918, was reported to have died on November 12, 1918, of bronchial pneumonia following wounds received in action. Miller is buried with his father in his family's plot in Queens, New York. (Courtesy of William Duffy.)

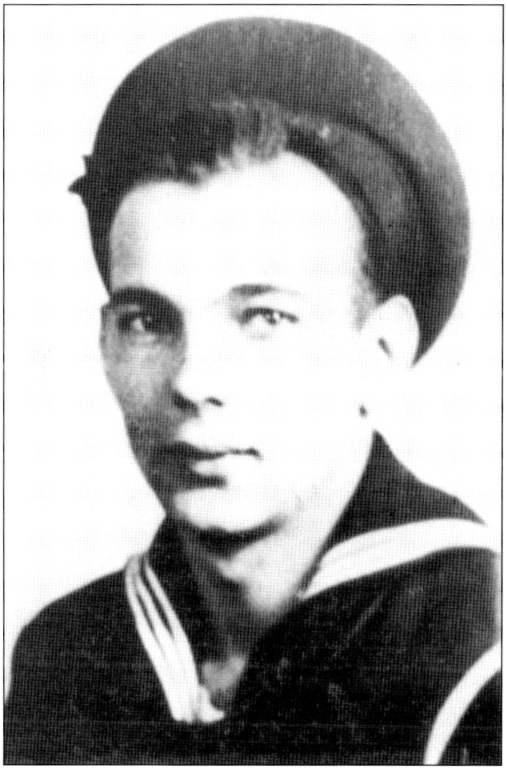

Bennie Bienko. Bennie Bienko (serial no. 02245585), a specialist first class of the US Navy, was killed in action on November 13, 1942, during the naval Battle of Guadalcanal while aboard the USS *Monssen*. Bienko fought in the battle along with fellow Clark resident John L. Ruddy Jr. He was killed at approximately 2:00 a.m. and is considered Clark's first World War II casualty. Ruddy was killed at approximately 11:00 a.m. on the same day. Prior to entry into the US Navy, the hero resided on Lincoln Boulevard. (Courtesy of William Duffy.)

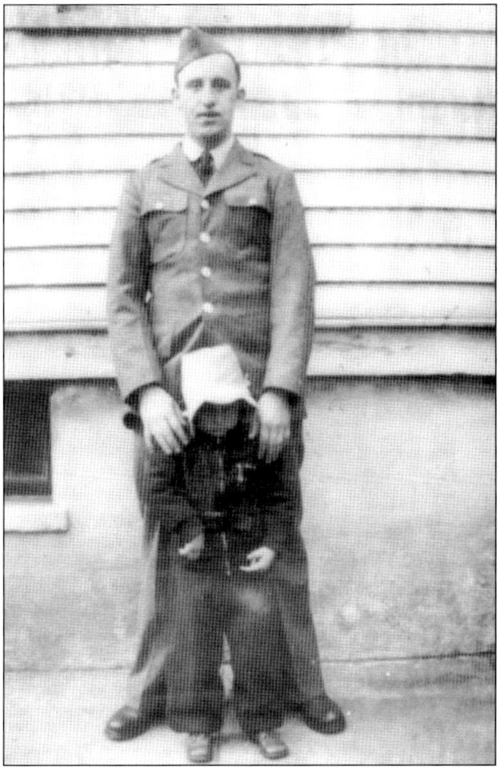

Pvt. Charles Bitsko. Pvt. Charles Bitsko (serial no. 32559648) of the US Army died in the line of duty in November 1942 while aboard a troop transport ship in the Pacific. On August 21, 1944, a new bridge was named in his honor in the vicinity of his unit's camp in the South Pacific. Both of the approaches bore a sign proclaiming its name, perpetuating the cherished memory of a good soldier. Bitsko is pictured with his niece, Gerri Johansen, prior to going overseas. Before joining the Army, this hero resided on Raritan Road with his sister. (Courtesy of William Duffy.)

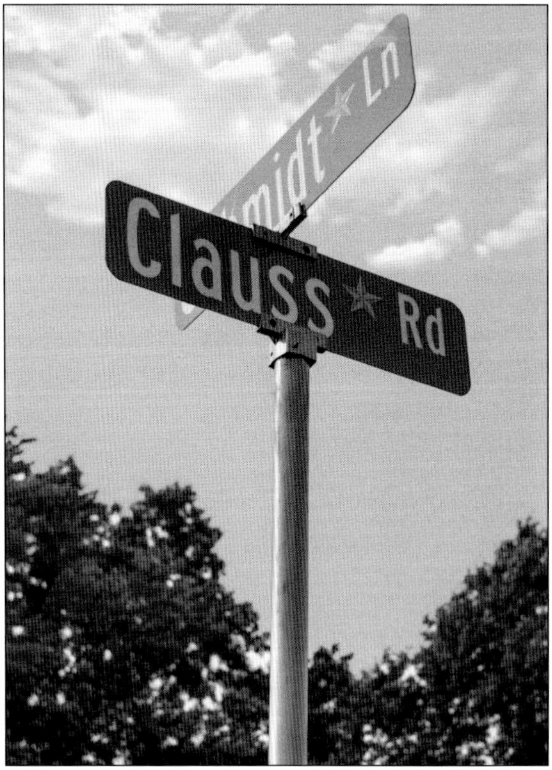

Pfc. Paul J. Clauss. Pfc. Paul J. Clauss (serial no. 3224035) of the US Army was killed in action by machine-gun fire on December 15, 1944, on Leyte Island, Philippines, while coming to the aid of a wounded soldier. After growing up in Elizabeth, he resided with his parents on Clauss Road. (Courtesy of William Duffy.)

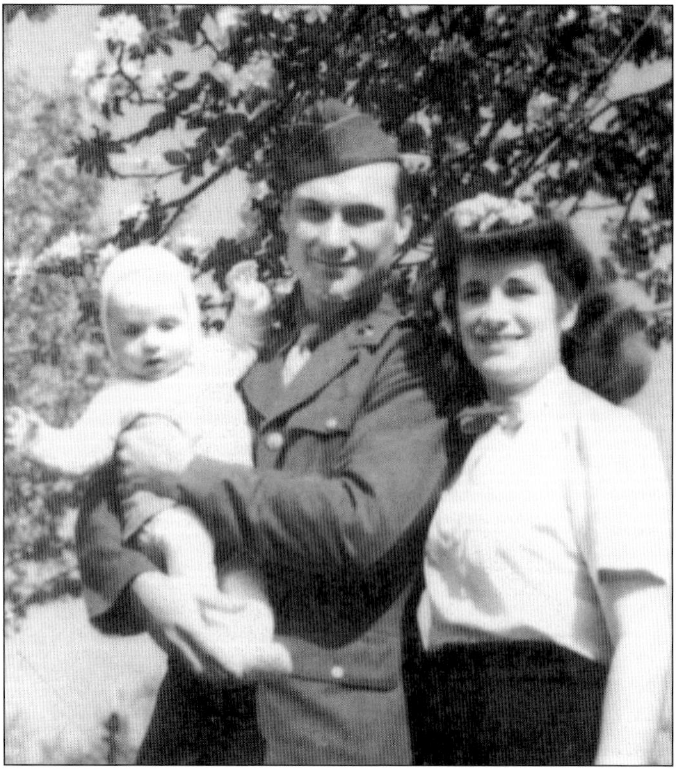

Pvt. Melvin Graves. Pvt. Melvin Graves (serial No. 42100647) of the US Army was killed in action on January 24, 1945, while serving in France. Under heavy mortar and artillery fire, he was hit in the neck by a piece of shrapnel. His father, Herman Graves, was mayor of Clark from 1927 to 1932. One month prior to his death, Melvin wrote a Christmas Eve letter to Robert telling him he would be home next Christmas, and they would all be happily together again. Prior joining into the Army, this hero resided on Valley Road. (Courtesy of William Duffy.)

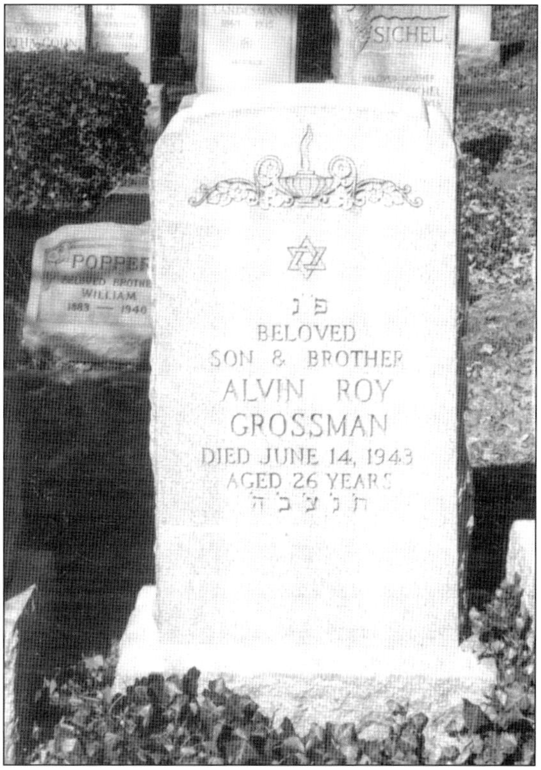

2nd Lt. Alvin R. Grossman. Second Lt. Alvin R. Grossman (serial No. 803810) of the US Army Air Corps died in the line of duty on June 14, 1943, while conducting training exercises aboard a navigation training plane. Grossman had just earned his wings as an Army pilot two weeks prior to his death. He is buried at the Oheb Sholem Cemetery on North Broad Street in Hillside. (Courtesy of William Duffy.)

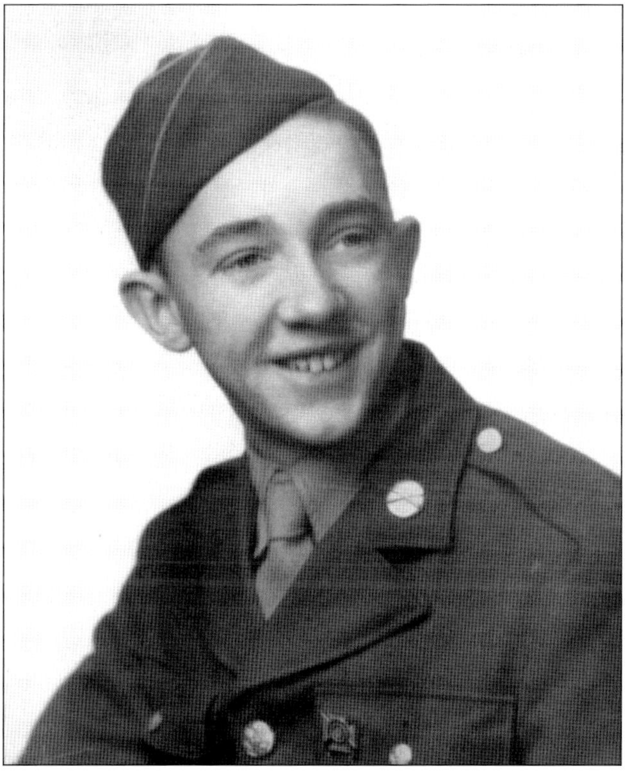

Pvt. Russell W. Green. Pvt. Russell W. Green (serial No. 42000833) of the US Army was killed in action on April 26, 1944, while serving in the Italian theater of war. He was one of the many Americans who fought and died on Anzio Beach, Italy. Russell grew up in Linden but was considered a Clark resident because his parents and sister, Lorraine, moved to a house on Raritan Road prior to his death. (Courtesy of William Duffy.)

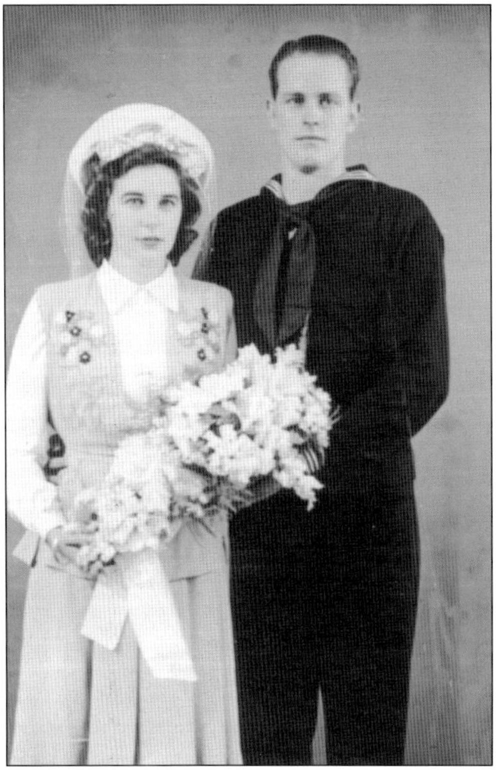

EUGENE F. HUTCHINSON. Eugene F. Hutchinson, a US Navy torpedo man's mate third class, was killed in action on November 7, 1944, while serving aboard the *Albacore* (SS-218). This submarine was sunk on its 11th patrol by mines off north Hokkaido Island, Japan. All hands were lost. Hutchinson grew up in Florida, but prior to shipping out, he married Clark resident Gertrude Amon and listed the Amon residence on Westfield Avenue as his home address. (Courtesy of William Duffy.)

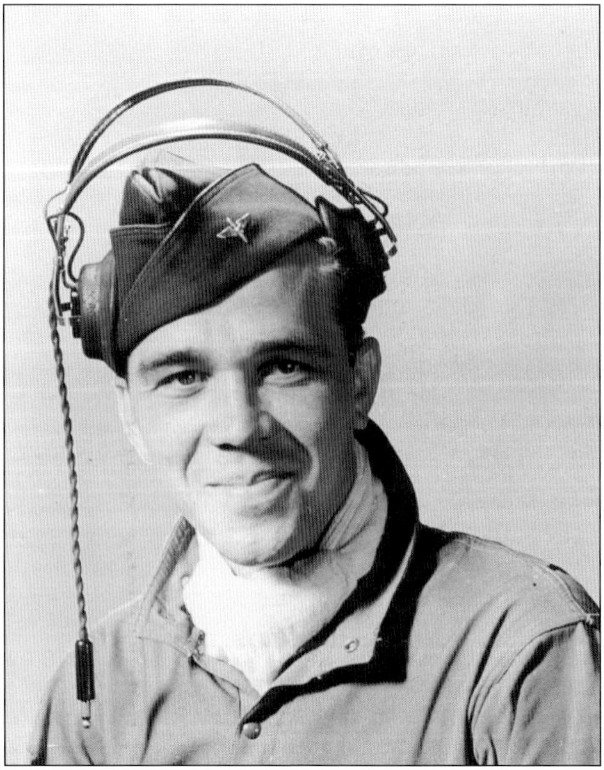

EDWARD J. MAKOWSKI. Edward J. Makowski (serial no. 0-751919) of the US Army Air Corps was killed in action on March 3, 1945, while serving as a bombardier aboard a B-24 Liberator during a combat mission over Italy. Makowski was assigned to the 14th Air Force, 450th Bomb Group, 723nd Squadron. Prior to entry into the Army Air Corps, he resided on Lake Avenue. (Courtesy of William Duffy.)

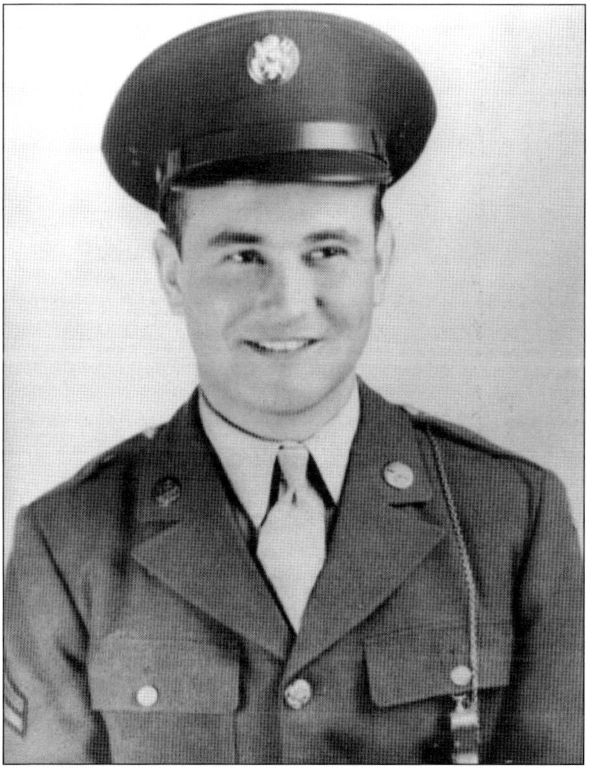

Joseph G. Padusniak. Joseph G. Padusniak (serial No. 32385995) was a US Army technician fifth grade who was killed in action on December 18, 1944, while serving with the 99th Infantry Division in the Battle of the Bulge. Padusniak was killed along with 30,000 other American troops during that battle and is buried in St. Mary's Cemetery on Madison Hill Road in Clark. Prior to joining the Army, he lived on Westfield Avenue. (Courtesy of William Duffy.)

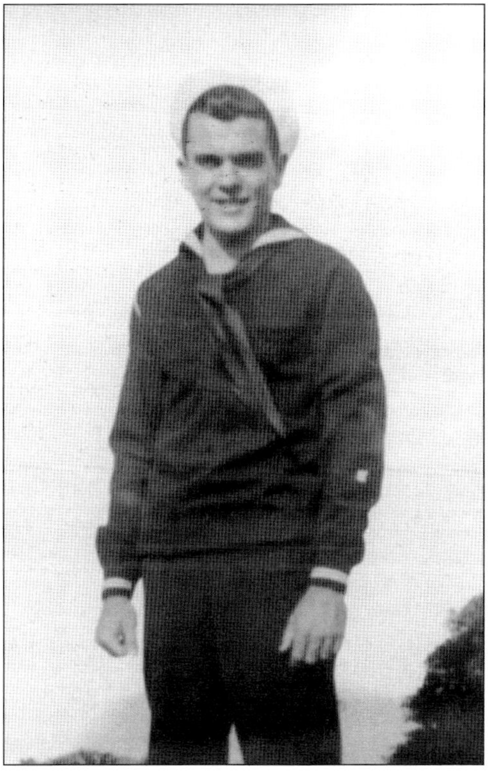

John L. Ruddy Jr. John L. Ruddy Jr. (serial No. 06464195), a US Navy specialist second class, was killed in action on November 13, 1942, at the naval Battle of Guadalcanal while aboard the USS *Juneau*. Ruddy was killed along with 900 other sailors that day, including the five Sullivan brothers from Waterloo, Iowa. Clark's Veterans of Foreign Wars post was named after Ruddy in 1950. Before he entered into the Navy, he resided on Prescott Turn. (Courtesy of William Duffy.)

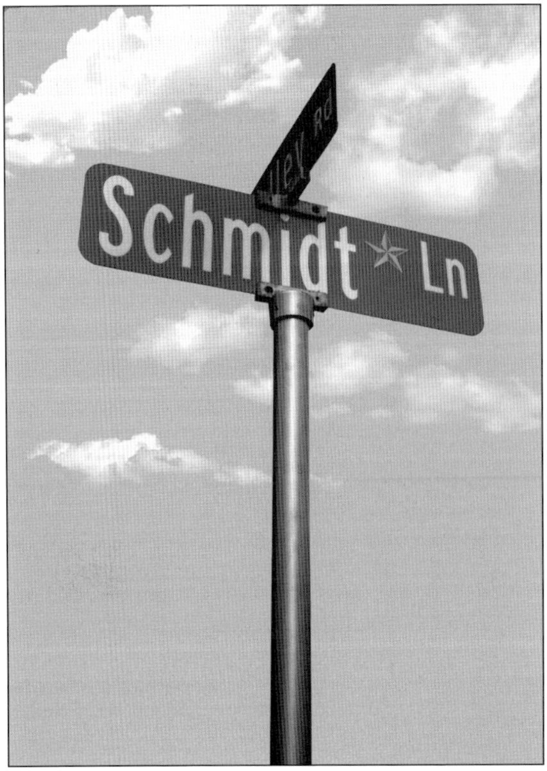

Cpl. Martin Schmitt. Cpl. Martin Schmitt (serial No. 32594212) of the US Army was killed in action on November 30, 1944, while serving with the 102nd Infantry Division near Linnoch, Germany, and was buried overseas at the American Military Cemetery in the Netherlands. Schmitt married Clark resident Margaret Carlson, who was his high school sweetheart. They were living on Westfield Avenue with her family across from the present-day American Legion building prior to his joining the service. When "Schmitt" Lane was selected for a new Clark street, whoever ordered the street sign inadvertently misspelled this hero's last name. (Courtesy of William Duffy.)

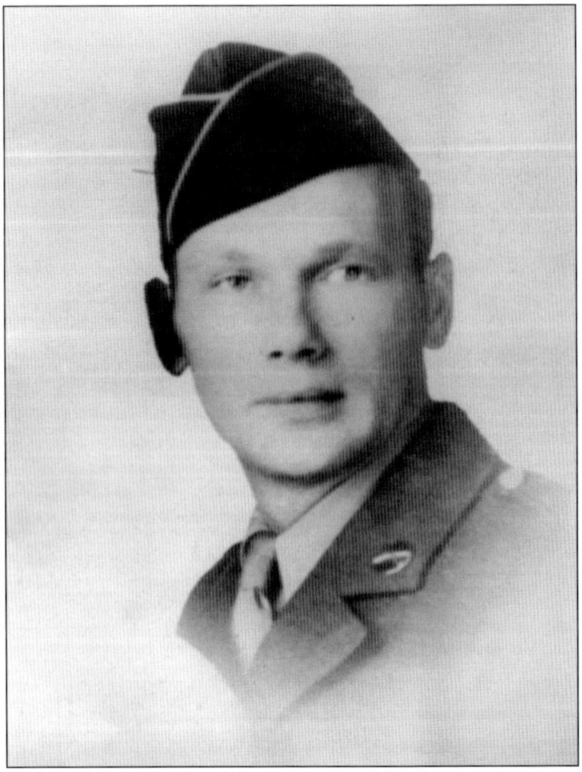

Pfc. Joseph Witkowski. Joseph Witkowski (serial No. 12203849), a private first class in the US Army, was killed in action on July 9, 1944, while serving with the 8th Infantry Division near Saint-Lô, France, during the Normandy outbreak. Prior to entry into the Army, he resided on Hart Street, which was later changed to Joseph Street in honor of him and Joseph Padusniak in 1948. (Courtesy of William Duffy.)

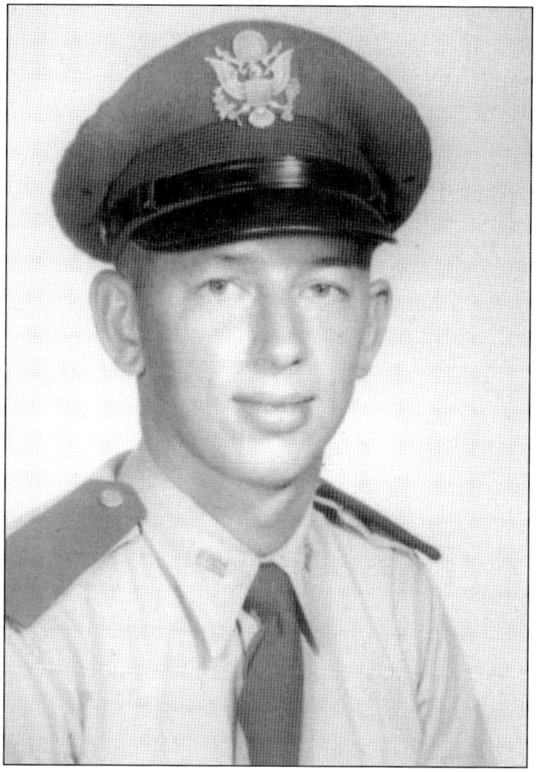

1st Lt. John Wilkes Jr. First Lt. John Wilkes Jr. of the US Air Force died in service on October 9, 1958, while piloting an F-100 Super Sabre jet. Wilkes was on a routine training flight when his jet crashed in the desert near Phoenix, Arizona. He was 28 and resided at 465 Madison Hill Road. Wilkes is considered Clark's one and only known Cold War casualty. (Courtesy of William Duffy.)

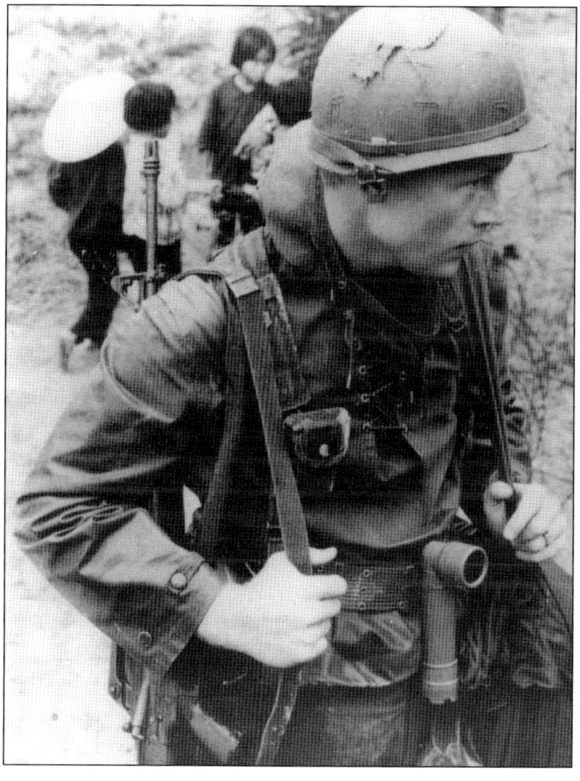

Sp4c. Kenneth Kuspiel. Kenneth Kuspiel, a specialist fourth class in the US Army, was killed in action on February 1, 1968, while serving in the infantry. He died as a result of multiple wounds from an exploding land mine in the vicinity of Chu Lai, Vietnam. Kuspiel graduated from Clark's Arthur L. Johnson High School in 1964 and attended Farleigh Dickinson University. He left school in 1966 to join the Army with his high school buddies. Prior to entry into the Army, he resided on Elm Street. (Courtesy of William Duffy.)

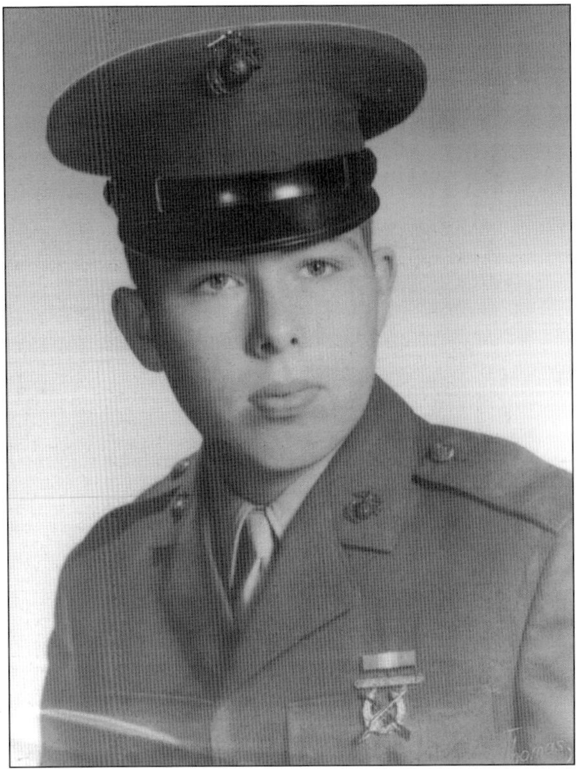

L.Cpl. John P. Winters. L.Cpl. John P. Winters, of the US Marine Corps, was killed in action on May 25, 1969, after being hit by fragments from a mortar shell near Cam Lo, Quang Tri Province, Vietnam. Winters was honored in 1998 when the residents of Clark dedicated a township street, Winters Court, in his name. Prior to his entry into the Marine Corps, this hero resided on Colonial Drive. (Courtesy of William Duffy.)

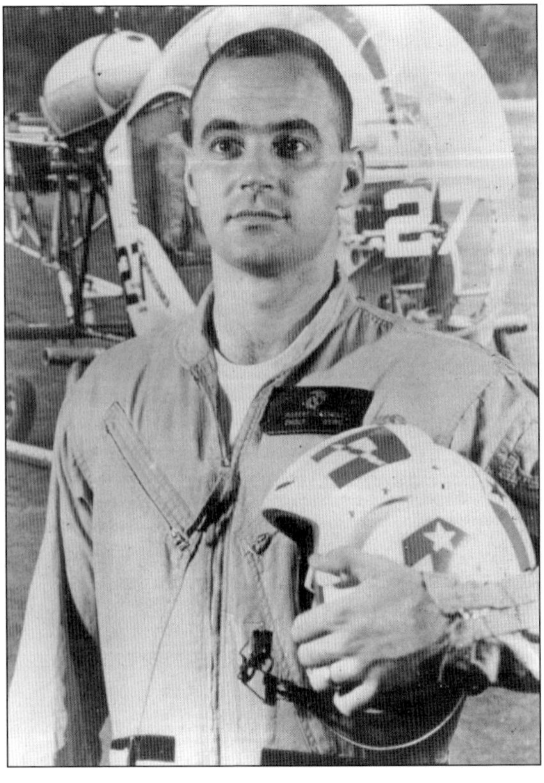

Capt. Robert L. Sevell. Capt. Robert L. Sevell (serial No. 093427) of the US Marine Corps was killed in action on February 28, 1968, while copiloting a Sea Knight helicopter on route to a downed aircraft near the beleaguered marine base at Khe Sanh, Vietnam. Sevell graduated from Clark's Arthur L. Johnson High School in 1961. He was the starting quarterback of the Crusaders football team during his junior and senior years. Prior to entering the service, Sevell and his wife, Valerie, who resided on Oakridge Road, had a son, Bobby, who was less than a year old when his father died. (Courtesy of William Duffy.)

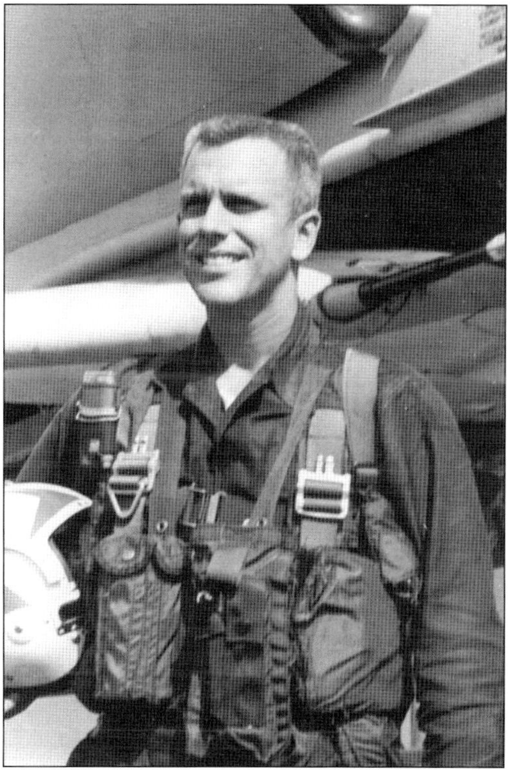

Cmdr. Richard D. Hartman. Cmdr. Richard D. Hartman (serial No. 613595) of the US Navy is pictured at age 32. On July 18, 1967, Hartman's A-4E jet airplane fell victim to anti-aircraft fire near Phu Ly, Hà Nam Province, North Vietnam. He ejected safely; however, the next day, four Navy personnel were killed during an attempted rescue of Hartman. He was eventually captured and "died in captivity," as reported by the Associated Press. His remains were repatriated on March 6, 1974, and he is buried in Arlington National Cemetery in Section 11. During his military career, he listed his home address as Gertrude Street in Clark, which was the residence of his aunt. (Courtesy of William Duffy.)

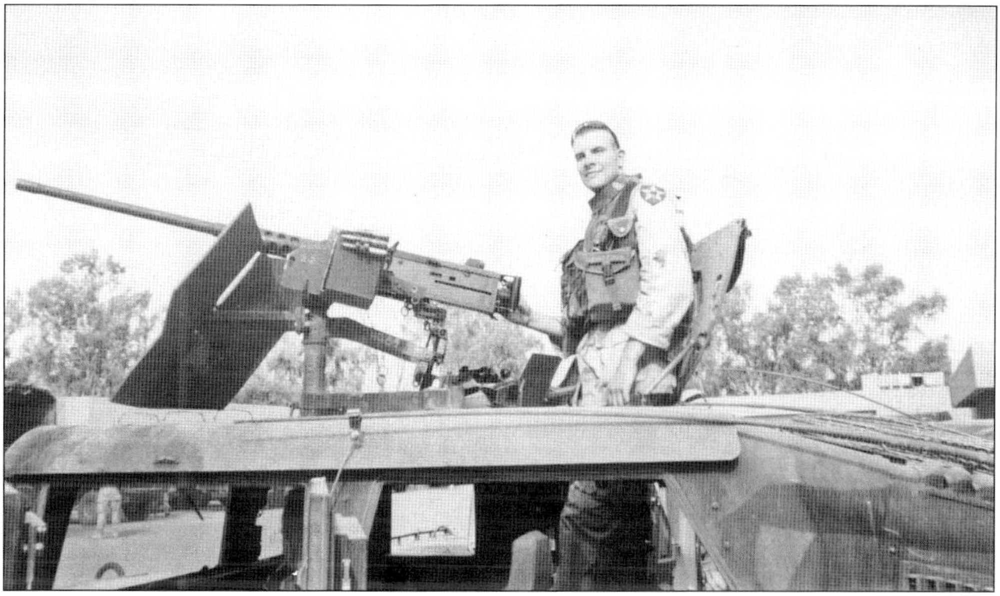

Pfc. Stephen C. Benish. Pfc. Stephen C. Benish, age 20, of the US Army, died on November 28, 2004, in Ar Ramadi, Iraq, when he received enemy fire while on a dismounted patrol. Benish was assigned to the 1st Battalion, 503rd Infantry Regiment, 2nd Brigade Combat Team, 2nd Infantry Division in Camp Howze, Korea. Prior to joining the Army, this hero resided with his family on Ivy Street. His mother, Candy, is now considered a Gold Star Mother. (Courtesy of William Duffy.)

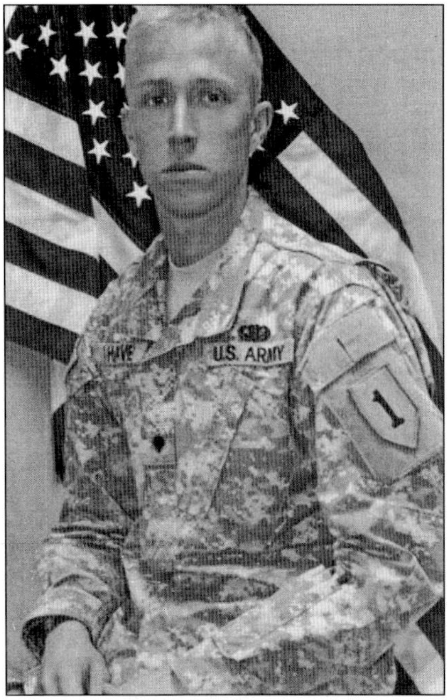

Sgt. James. W. Harvey II. Sgt. James W. Harvey II, 23 years old, of the US Army, was killed in action on June 20, 2011, in Ghazni Province, Afghanistan, of wounds suffered when insurgents attacked his unit with small-arms fire. He was assigned to the 2nd Battalion, 2nd Infantry Regiment, 3rd Brigade Combat Team, 1st Infantry Division. Harvey wrote a last letter home to his family that was only to be opened upon his death. Before joining the Army, he resided on Conger Way. His parents now reside in Toms River. His mother, Susan, is now considered a Gold Star Mother. (Courtesy of William Duffy.)

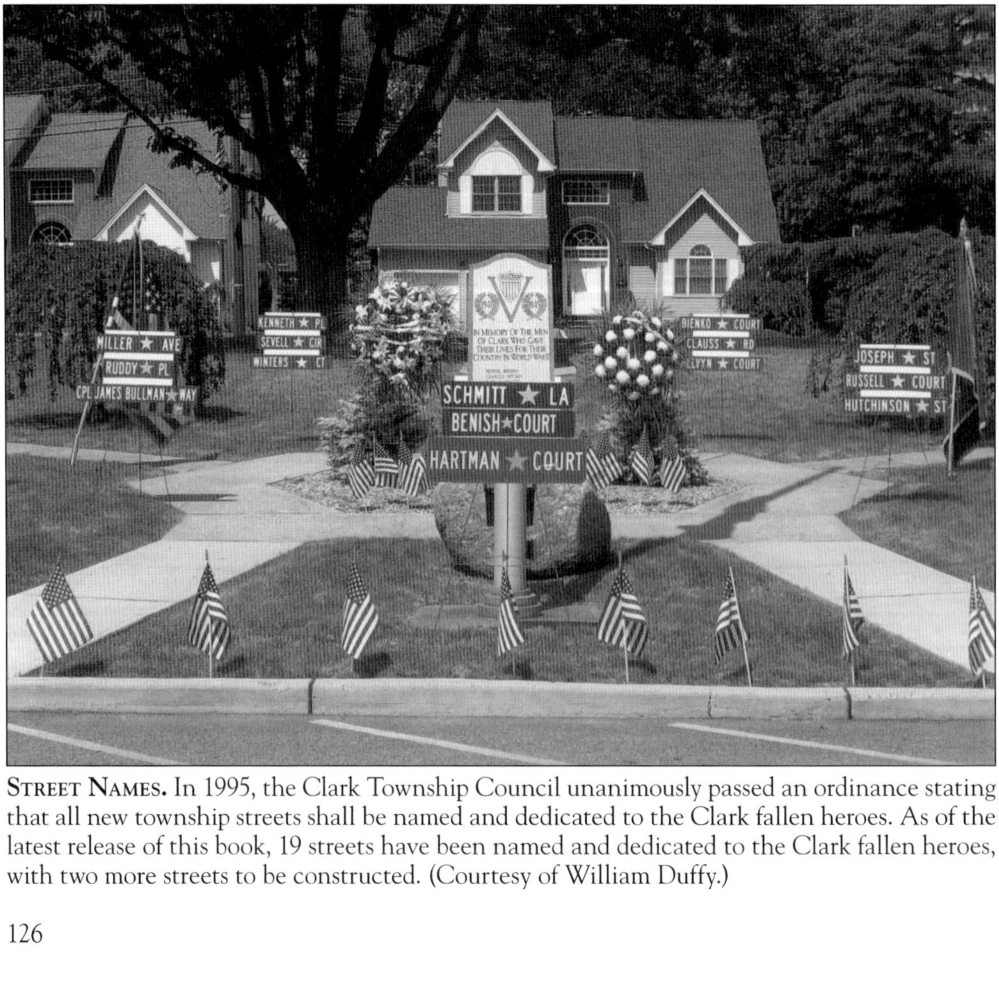

Street Names. In 1995, the Clark Township Council unanimously passed an ordinance stating that all new township streets shall be named and dedicated to the Clark fallen heroes. As of the latest release of this book, 19 streets have been named and dedicated to the Clark fallen heroes, with two more streets to be constructed. (Courtesy of William Duffy.)

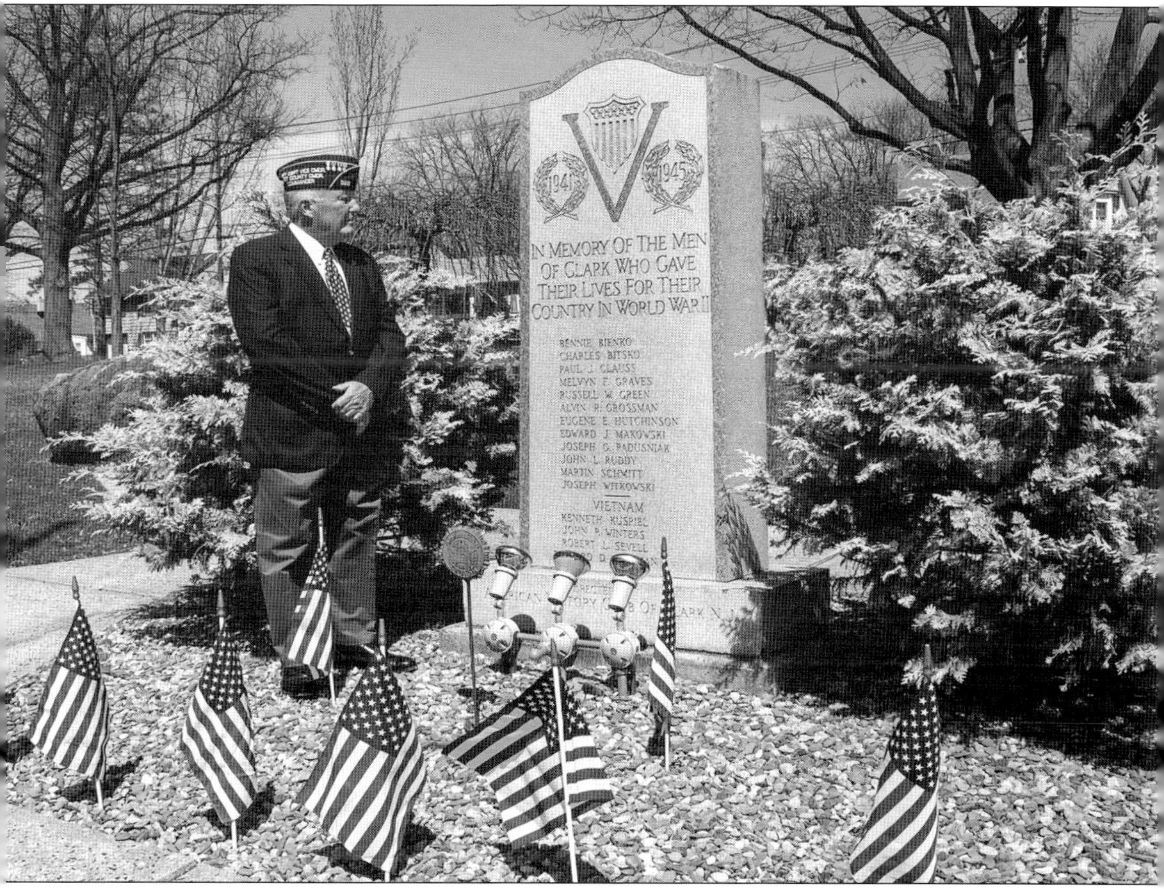

Clark Police Captain William J. "Duff" Duffy. Shown in this photograph is the retired Clark Police Department captain reviewing the Clark Memorial Honor Roll that is located in front of the Arthur L. Johnson High School along Westfield Avenue. Captain Duffy is a noted local historian on the Clark fallen heroes, who made the "supreme sacrifice" while serving in the US military. (Courtesy of William Duffy.)

Consistent with our mission to preserve history on a local level, this book was printed in South Carolina on American-made paper and manufactured entirely in the United States. Products carrying the accredited Forest Stewardship Council (FSC) label are printed on 100 percent FSC-certified paper.

MADE IN THE USA